THE HOUSEHOLD CHARTALOG

THE HOUSEHOLD CHARTALOG

100 Charts of Kitchen Tips, Equivalents, Cleaning Hints, Human, Pet and Car First Aid, Garden Care, Home Repair, and Much, Much More

EDITED BY CHERYL SOLIMINI

LAMP POST PRESS, INC.

Collier Books
Macmillan Publishing Company
New York

Collier Macmillan Publishers
London

Collier Books
Macmillan Publishing Company
866 Third Avenue, New York, NY 10022
Collier Macmillan Canada, Inc.

Book Design by Bobbi Rosenthal
Illustrations by Rose Mary Berlin

Library of Congress Cataloging-in-Publication Data

The Household chartalog: 100 charts of kitchen tips, equivalents, cleaning
    hints, human, pet and car first aid, garden care, home repair,
    and much, much more.
        p.   cm.
    Includes index.
    ISBN 0-02-038101-8
    1. Home economics.   2. Home economics — Charts, diagrams, etc.
  I. Lamp Post Press, Inc. (Firm)
  TX158.H646 1989
  640'.2 — dc19

                                                    88-38226   CIP

Macmillan books are available at special discounts for bulk purchases
for sales promotions, premiums, fund-raising, or educational use.
For details, contact:

                    Special Sales Director
                    Macmillan Publishing Company
                    866 Third Avenue
                    New York, NY 10022

10 9 8 7 6 5 4 3 2 1

Printed in the United States of America

TABLE OF CONTENTS

In The Garden

Travel

Family Almanac

INTRODUCTION

You know you filed it somewhere — the stain chart that tells you how to get ballpoint pen ink off the upholstery; or that medical listing which will let you know if your husband's chest pains are merely acid indigestion, or something more serious; or the checklist for the babysitter. How about trying to remember which cookbook gives the times and temperatures for roasting different cuts of meat. Or how often should you rotate the car's tires, or what to give your sister for her tenth wedding anniversary? Then, there's that gardening magazine: You know you put it in a safe place so you would be able to refer to it the next time those mealy bugs attacked your houseplants.

Well, if you're like most people with families, you're always on the lookout for practical, easy-to-digest advice on how to keep your kids healthy, your garden blooming, your car running smoothly, and your household organized. You've probably clipped suggestions from newspapers and magazines, marked useful passages in reference books, sent away for helpful pamphlets — and then you can never find them when you need them most.

Well, toss those clippings away. All that information — and then some — is here, in one handy and easily readable volume. Every member of your household, right down to the family pet, will benefit from this collection of basic wisdom, gathered from government agencies and professional organizations such as the Department of Agriculture, the American Academy of Pediatrics and the Red Cross. More than 100 charts list everything from cooking and housekeeping, gardening, health, travel and safety to choosing a compatible cat for your household. Homemakers will learn how long they can store fresh vegetables in the refriger- ator. Do-it-yourselfers can mix their own wood fillers. Students can use the Family Almanac section as a quick reference guide to the 50 states, the U.S. Presidents and metric conversions. And just for fun, you can chart your future and your life with guides to astrology, palm-reading and phrenology.

Whatever your how-to when-to needs, you'll find the answers on these pages — at your fingertips and at a glance.

ACKNOWLEDGMENTS

Special thanks to the many government agencies, trade organizations and private businesses that provided invaluable materials and resources; to the Science Desk staff of the Newark Public Library for their many trips to the basement; to Rose Ann Farawell for sharing her own clippings collection (a volume in itself); and to her son Martin for his 11th-hour research and 24-hour support.

IN THE KITCHEN

GROCERY CHECKLIST

Use this grocery checklist as a reminder of things you might need when you go shopping, or make copies to take along to the supermarket.

Baking Needs
- [ ] Baking powder
- [ ] Baking soda
- [ ] Cornmeal
- [ ] Flour
- [ ] Mixes
- [ ] Shortening
- [ ] Sugar
- [ ] Vanilla Extract
- [ ] _____
- [ ] _____

Beverages
- [ ] Cocoa
- [ ] Coffee
- [ ] Mineral water
- [ ] Soft drinks
- [ ] Tea
- [ ] _____
- [ ] _____

Breads/Grains/Cereals
- [ ] Beans
- [ ] Bread
- [ ] Breakfast cereal
- [ ] Crackers
- [ ] Flour
- [ ] Muffins
- [ ] Oatmeal
- [ ] Pasta
- [ ] Rice
- [ ] Rolls
- [ ] Taco shells
- [ ] Tortillas
- [ ] _____
- [ ] _____

Canned Goods
- [ ] Beans
- [ ] Broth
- [ ] Corn
- [ ] Juices
- [ ] Soups
- [ ] Tomato Sauce
- [ ] Tuna
- [ ] Vegetables
- [ ] _____
- [ ] _____

Cleaning Supplies
- [ ] Bathroom cleaner
- [ ] Bleach
- [ ] Carpet cleaner
- [ ] Dishwashing detergent
- [ ] Fabric softener
- [ ] Glass cleaner
- [ ] Laundry detergent
- [ ] Laundry prewash
- [ ] Scouring pads
- [ ] Scouring powder/liquid
- [ ] _____
- [ ] _____
- [ ] _____

Condiments/Seasoning
- [ ] Catsup
- [ ] Jam/jelly
- [ ] Mayonnaise
- [ ] Mustard
- [ ] Olives
- [ ] Peanut Butter
- [ ] Pepper
- [ ] Pickles
- [ ] Relish
- [ ] Salad dressings
- [ ] Salad oil
- [ ] Salt
- [ ] Spices/herbs
- [ ] Vinegar
- [ ] _____
- [ ] _____

Dairy Products
- [ ] Butter
- [ ] Cheese
- [ ] Cream
- [ ] Eggs
- [ ] Margarine
- [ ] Milk
- [ ] Sour cream
- [ ] Yogurt
- [ ] _____
- [ ] _____

Frozen Foods
- [ ] Breads/biscuits
- [ ] Cakes/pies
- [ ] Fish
- [ ] Frozen dinners
- [ ] Ice cream
- [ ] Juices
- [ ] Pizza
- [ ] Potatoes/French fries
- [ ] Vegetables
- [ ] _____
- [ ] _____
- [ ] _____

Meats/Poultry/Seafood
- [ ] Breakfast meats
- [ ] Beef
- [ ] Chicken
- [ ] Fish
- [ ] Ham
- [ ] Hamburger
- [ ] Hot dogs
- [ ] Lamb
- [ ] Luncheon meats
- [ ] Pork
- [ ] Turkey
- [ ] Shellfish
- [ ] Veal
- [ ] _____
- [ ] _____
- [ ] _____

Paper Products/Storage
- [ ] Aluminum foil
- [ ] Facial tissues
- [ ] Napkins
- [ ] Paper towels
- [ ] Plastic wrap
- [ ] Sandwich bags
- [ ] Toilet paper
- [ ] Trash bags
- [ ] Wax paper
- [ ] _____

Produce
- [ ] Apples
- [ ] Bananas
- [ ] Broccoli
- [ ] Cabbage
- [ ] Carrots
- [ ] Cauliflower
- [ ] Cucumbers
- [ ] Garlic
- [ ] Grapes
- [ ] Green beans
- [ ] Lemons
- [ ] Melon
- [ ] Mushrooms
- [ ] Onion
- [ ] Oranges
- [ ] Pears
- [ ] Potatoes
- [ ] Radishes
- [ ] Tomatoes
- [ ] _____

Snacks
- [ ] Candy
- [ ] Cookies
- [ ] Corn chips
- [ ] Nuts
- [ ] Popcorn
- [ ] Potato chips
- [ ] Pretzels
- [ ] _____

Toiletries
- [ ] Cotton swabs
- [ ] Deodorant
- [ ] Razor blades
- [ ] Shampoo/conditioner
- [ ] Shaving cream
- [ ] Soap
- [ ] Toothpaste
- [ ] _____

Miscellaneous
- [ ] Baby care products
- [ ] Baby food
- [ ] Batteries
- [ ] Cold remedies
- [ ] First-aid supplies
- [ ] Lightbulbs
- [ ] Pantyhose
- [ ] Pet food
- [ ] _____

CUPBOARD STORAGE GUIDE

Food	Time	Special Handling
Baking powder, soda	18 months	
Barbecue sauce, catsup, chili sauce	1 month	
Bouillon cubes, powder	1 year	
Cake mixes	1 year	
Canned foods fish	1 year	Refrigerate after opening. See Refrigerator Storage.
fruits, vegetables	1 year	
gravies, sauces	1 year	
meat, poultry	1 year	
milk (both kinds)	1 year	
soups	1 year	
Casserole mixes	18 months	
Cereals ready-to-eat	check date on package	
ready-to-cook	6 months	
Chocolate, cooking	1 year	
Coconut	1 year	Refrigerate after opening.
Coffee, vacuum pack	1 year	Refrigerate after opening vacuum pack.
Coffee, instant	6 months	Keep 2 weeks after opening.
Flour all-purpose, cake, rye, whole-wheat	1 year	Keep refrigerated.
Frosting, cans, mixes	8 months	
Fruit, dried	6 months	
Gelatin (both kinds)	18 months	
Herbs, spices whole	1 year	Keep in cool spot. Replace if aroma fades. Refrigerate red spices.
ground	6 months	
Honey	1 year	
Jam, jelly	1 year	
Macaroni, spaghetti, pasta	1 year	After opening, transfer to airtight container.
Molasses	2 years	
Nonfat dry milk	6 months	
Olive oil	1 month	For longer storage, refrigerate.

Food	Time	Special Handling
Olives, pickles	1 year	Refrigerate after opening.
Pancake mixes	6 months	
Peanut butter	6 months	Keeps 2 months once open.
Piecrust mixes	6 months	
Potato mixes, instant	18 months	
Pudding mixes	1 year	
Rice brown, wild	1 year	
white	2 years	
Salad dressings	6 months	Refrigerate after opening.
Salad Oil	3 months	Refrigerate after opening.
Sauce, gravy, soup mixes	6 months	
Shortening, solid	8 months	
Sugar brown confectioners'	4 months	
granulated	2 years	
Syrups, corn, maple-flavor, maple	1 year	Refrigerate after opening. Keep maple syrup 1 month after opening.
Tea, bags, loose	6 months	
Tea, instant	1 year	
Vegetables onions, potatoes, rutabagas, squash (hard-shelled), sweet potatoes	1 week at room temperature	For longer storage, keep at 55-60°F, but not refrigerated. Keep dry, out of sun, loosely wrapped.
Yeast, active dry	check date on pack	

PREPARED FOODS

Food	Time	Special Handling
Bread, rolls	3 days	
Bread crumbs	6 months	
Cakes	2 days	If butter-cream, whipped-cream or custard fillings, refrigerate.
Cookies, packaged	4 months	
Crackers	3 months	
Pies, pastries	3 days	Refrigerate cream, custard, chiffon fillings.

Source: U.S. Dept. of Agriculture; Rutgers University Cooperative Extension

REFRIGERATOR STORAGE GUIDE

FRESH FRUITS AND VEGETABLES

Food	Time	Special Handling
Fruit		
apples	1 month	May also store at 60-70°F.
apricots, avocados, bananas, melons, nectarines, peaches, pears	5 days	If necessary, allow to ripen at room temperature before refrigerating.
berries, cherries	3 days	
citrus fruit	2 weeks	May also store at 60-70°F.
grapes, plums	5 days	Let ripen at room temperature; then refrigerate.
pineapples	2 days	
Vegetables		
asparagus	3 days	
beets, carrots, parsnips, radishes, turnips	2 weeks	Remove any leafy tops before refrigerating.
broccoli, Brussels sprouts, green onions, soft-skinned squash	5 days	
cabbage, cauliflower, celery, cucumber, eggplant, green beans, peppers	1 week	
tomatoes		If necessary, ripen tomatoes at room temperature, away from light, before refrigerating.
corn	1 day	Leave in husk.
lettuce, spinach, all leafy greens	5 days	Rinse, drain before refrigerating.
limas, peas	5 days	Leave in shell.

DAIRY PRODUCTS

Butter	2 weeks	
Buttermilk, sour cream, yogurt	2 weeks	
Cheese		
cottage, ricotta	5 days	Cut off mold if it forms on surface of cheese.
cream, Neufchatel	2 weeks	
sliced cheese	2 weeks	
whole pieces	2 months	
Cream	1 week	
Eggs, in shell	1 month	One week for best flavor.
whites, yolks	4 days	Cover yolks with water.
Margarine	1 month	

Food	Time	Special Handling
Milk whole, skimmed	1 week	Do not return unused milk to original container: this spreads bacteria to remaining milk.

MEAT, FISH, POULTRY BEFORE COOKING

Fresh meat		Leave in plastic wrap. Or if not prepackaged in plastic, wrap loosely in waxed paper so surface can dry slightly.
beef, lamp, pork, veal chops, steaks	5 days	
roasts	5 days	
ground, stew meat	2 days	
sausage, fresh	2 days	
variety meats	2 days	
Processed meats		Times are for opened packages of sliced meat. Check date on unopened vacuum-packed meat.
bacon, frankfurters, ham	1 week	
canned (unopened)	6 months	
slices	3 days	
whole	1 week	
luncheon meats	5 days	
sausage, dry, semi-dry	3 weeks	
Fish, shellfish (all kinds)	1 day	Keep wrapped.
Poultry (all kinds) fresh, thawed frozen	2 days	If not in plastic wrap, loosely.

PACKAGED AND PREPARED FOODS — LEFTOVERS OR AFTER OPENING

Cooked or canned foods		
broths, gravy, soup	2 days	
casseroles, stews	3 days	
fruit, vegetables	3 days	
juices, drinks	6 days	
meat, fish, poultry	2 days	
stuffings	2 days	Remove stuffings from poultry and refrigerate separately.
Cakes, pies: cream, custard	2 days	
Coffee, ground	1 week	After opening
Flour: rye, whole-wheat	1 year	
Nuts (shelled)	6 months	
Pickles, olives	1 month	
Refrigerated biscuits, cookies, rolls		See expiration date on label.
Salad dressings	3 months	
Salads: potato, coleslaw	2 days	
Wine, table	3 days	
Wine, cooking	3 months	

Source: U.S. Dept. of Agriculture; Rutgers University Cooperative Extension

FREEZER STORAGE GUIDE

COMMERCIALLY FROZEN FOODS

Food	Time	Special Handling
Breads baked, dough	3 months	Pick up frozen foods immediately before going to check-out counter. Buy only foods frozen solid and with no dribbles on the package, odor or other signs of being thawed. Put all frozen foods together in one bag so they'll stay as cold as possible for trip home. Store in original wrapping. Place in home freezer as soon as possible. Cook or thaw as label directs.
Cakes angel-food layer cake, frosted pound, yellow cake	2 months 4 months 6 months	
Doughnuts, pastries	3 months	
Fish "fatty" fish — mackerel, trout, etc. "lean" fish — cod, flounder, etc.	3 months 6 months	
Fruit	1 year	
Ice cream, sherbet	1 month	
Juices, drinks	1 year	
Main dishes, pies fish, meat poultry	3 months 6 months	
Meat beef roasts, steaks ground beef lamb, veal roasts, steaks pork chops roasts	1 year 4 months 9 months 4 months 8 months	
Pancake, waffle batter	3 months	
Pies	8 months	
Poultry chicken, turkey parts chicken, turkey (whole) duckling goose turkey rolls, roasts	6 months 1 year 6 months 6 months 6 months	
Shellfish Alaska King crab breaded, cooked lobster, scallops shrimp (unbreaded)	10 months 3 months 3 months 1 year	
Vegetables	8 months	
Breads baked unbaked doughs	3 months 1 month	Use only special recipes.
Butter, margarine	9 months	

HOME-FROZEN FOODS

Food	Time	Special Handling
Cakes, baked	3 months	
Cheese dry-curd cottage cheese, ricotta natural, process	2 weeks 3 months	Cut and wrap cheese in small pieces.
Cookies, baked, dough	3 months	
Cream, heavy whipped	2 months 1 month	Thawed cream may not whip.
Egg whites, yolks	1 year	To each cup yolks, add 1 teaspoon sugar for use in sweet, or 1 teaspoon salt for non-sweet, dishes.
Fish, shellfish "fatty" fish — bluefish, trout, etc. "lean" fish — cod, flounder, etc. shellfish	3 months 6 months 3 months	All fish and shellfish: Wrap tightly in heavy-duty foil or freezer wrap.
Fruit pies	8 months	Freeze baked or unbaked.
Ice cream, sherbet	1 month	
Main dishes, cooked meat, fish poultry	3 months 6 months	Freeze in ovenproof dishes or containers.
Meat bacon frankfurters ground meat stew meat ham roast beef, lamb pork, veal roasts chops: beef, lamb, veal variety meats	1 month 2 weeks 3 months 2 months 1 year 8 months 9 months 4 months 4 months	Keep in vacuum packages. If meat is purchased fresh and wrapped in plastic wrap, check for holes. If none, freeze in this wrap up to 2 weeks. For longer storage overwrap tightly with freezer wrap or heavy-duty foil.
Nuts	3 months	
Poultry cooked, with gravy cooked, no gravy uncooked (whole) chicken, turkey duckling, goose uncooked parts	1 month 6 months 1 year 6 months 6 months	Wrap in heavy-duty foil or freezer wrap as airtight as possible. Thaw uncooked poultry in refrigerator or under cool running water. Cook within two days of thawing.
Vegetables	1 year	

Source: U.S. Dept. of Agriculture; Rutgers University Cooperative Extension

HERB GUIDE

Herb & Characteristics:	Use:
Basil Bright green leaves, up to 1½" long; mint family; sweet aroma, faint anise flavor	On pizza, in spaghetti sauce and tomato dishes, vegetable soups, meat pies, stews; with peas, zucchini, green beans, cucumbers; on broiled lamb chops
Bay Leaves Dark green leaves of the laurel tree, up to 3" long; strong flavor	1 or 2 whole leaves in stews, soups, sauces; sparingly with meats and fish
Chervil Lacy fernlike leaves; parsley family; similar to parsley but with a subtler, sweeter flavor	Small quantities in salads, stuffings, sauces, omelets, seafood dishes and cheese spreads (add to hot foods at the last minute)
Chives Tubular green leaves; onion family; more delicate onion flavor	On sour cream-topped baked potatoes; in vichyssoise, any salads or green vegetable, cheese and egg dishes, cream sauces, gravies and dips.
Coriander Stems with feathery leaves; parsley family; more delicate parsley flavor	In Latin-American, Chinese, East European dishes; with meat, chicken, rice, lentils, corn; in salads
Dill Weed Feathery, bright green leaves; parsley family; mild caraway flavor	In fish dishes, borscht, salads, sandwich fillings; sprinkle on rice, potatoes, cottage cheese
Garlic Bulb separates into many cloves; onion family; pungent flavor (available dehydrated: minced, granulated, powdered and as garlic salt)	Sparingly in meat, fowl and seafood dishes, salad dressings, soups; liberally in Mediterranean recipes — bouillabaise, scampi, spaghetti sauce, pesto
Marjoram Grayish leaves; oregano-mint family; strong, sweet aroma, cool aftertaste	With vegetables — lima beans, peas, green beans, salads — and lamb, mutton and other roasted meats; herb breads; Italian-style dishes
Mint Jagged, oval leaves; many varieties, but spearmint and peppermint most used; spicy-sweet flavor with cool aftertaste	In fruit and vegetable salads, desserts, tea and other beverages; for jelly and sauce for roast lamb; especially good cooked with peas and carrots
Onion Bulb; yellow, white and red varieties; pungent, sometimes sweet flavor (available dehydrated)	Raw in salads and sandwiches; cooked, in all dishes except desserts: meat, poultry, seafood, sauces, vegetables, soups, egg and cheese dishes
Oregano Light green leaves; mint family; like marjoram but stronger taste and aroma	On pizza and in tomato sauce and other Italian specialties; with meats, fish, cheese and egg dishes, and vegetables such as tomatoes, zucchini and green beans

Herb & Characteristics	Use
Parsley Green, curly (flat, if Italian) leaves on thin-stemmed sprigs; sold fresh or as dried flakes; mild flavor	In salad dressings, butter sauces, stuffings, sandwich spreads and dips; with fish, poultry, meats, vegetables, chowders and soups; used fresh as a garnish
Rosemary Needle-like green leaves; evergreen shrub, mint family; potent, bittersweet flavor	In sauces, salad dressings, spoon breads; with lamb, chicken, shrimp, vegetables (eggplant, turnips, cauliflower, green beans, beets, summer squash); to enhance citrus fruits
Sage Slender, silver-green leaves; mint family; pungent	In stuffings, sausages, salad dressings, chowders and cheese spreads; with pork and other meats
Savory Small, brown-green leaves; mint family; pine-like peppery aroma; sold whole or ground	With beans, meats, meat dressings, chicken, soups, salads and sauces; a pinch in scrambled eggs and omeletes
Tarragon Slender, pointed, dark green leaves; aster family; a hint of anise	In egg salad, salad dressings and bechamel or tartar sauces; with chicken and seafood
Thyme Small, grey-green leaves; mint family; penetrating aroma and flavor	In New England clam chowder, stews, Creole seafood dishes, poultry stuffing, cottage cheese, creamed chicken or chipped beef, meat loaf and cheese sauces; in thyme butter over creamed onions, squash, asparagus, green beans, eggplant and tomatoes

Source: American Spice Trade Association

SPICE GUIDE

Spice & Characteristics:	Use:
Allspice Berry from tropical evergreen tree; tastes like a blend of clove, cinnamon and nutmeg	Whole: in meat broths, gravies, pickling. Ground: in fruit cakes, pies, relishes, preserves, sweet yellow vegetables and tomatoes
Chili Powder Hot spice blend of chili pepper, cumin, oregano and garlic	In Tex-Mex dishes, chili con carne; shellfish and oyster cocktail sauces, eggs, gravy and stew, ground meat and hamburger

Spice	Description	Uses
		Ground: in baked goods, sweet vegetables (beets, sweet potatoes), boiled onions and winter squash
Anise	Gray-brown seed of parsley herb; sweet, licorice flavor	Whole: in cookies, cakes, fruit cups, compotes, and chicken, duck and veal dishes
Caraway Seed	Brown, hard seed, 3/16" long, tapered at the ends; parsley family; penetrating flavor	In rye bread and other baked goods; in cheeses; scatter lightly over pork and sauerkraut dishes, soups, meats and stews
Cardamon Seed	Dried pods or seeds from plant in ginger family; buff or green color; strong flavor; sold whole or ground; buff or green in color; strong flavor	Use sparingly in baked goods: Danish pastry and breads, apple and pumpkin pies
Celery Seed	Fruit of wild celery (smallage); tiny, brown; pungent	With fish; in oyster stews, clam juice, tomato juice, soups, potato salads, salad dressings, eggs, coleslaw and sauerkraut; good in croquettes and canape mixtures
Cinnamon	Reddish-brown, dried bark from an Asian evergreen: sweet and pungent; sold in sticks or finely ground	Ground: in baked goods — cakes, buns, breads, cookies, pies, sweet sauces, hot chocolate and chocolate desserts; Stick: in beef stews, hot apple cider or coffee
Cloves	Spiky, hard buds of tropical evergreen, dark brown; pungent, penetrating flavor	Whole: for studding ham and pork, and pickling fruits; in spicy-sweet syrups, stews and meat gravies;
Coriander Seed	Small, round, white-to-yellowish-brown seed with vertical ridges; from plant of parsley family; mild, delicate, slightly lemony flavor	Ground: buns, pastries, cookies, biscuits, gingerbread and cake; Whole: in pickling spices and poultry stuffing
Cumin	Brown, 1/8" to 1/4" seeds; similar to caraway in flavor and aroma	In chili and curry powder, Indian, Near-East and Latin-American dishes; pork and sauerkraut, cheese, deviled eggs and beans
Curry Powder	Blend of 16 to 20 spices, usually including ginger, turmeric, fenugreek, clove, cinnamon, cumin and black pepper	In Indian dishes; curried eggs, vegetables, meat and fish; just a dash in French dressing, scalloped tomatoes, clam and fish chowders and split pea soup
Dill Seed	Oval, tan, dried fruit of parsley family; caraway-like flavor, but slightly bitter	In dill pickles, meats, fish sauces, salad dressings, potato and macaroni salads, coleslaw, sauerkraut
Fennel Seed	Yellowish-brown seed, watermelon shape, to 5/16"; similar in flavor and aroma to anise	In breads, rolls, coffeecakes, apple pies, Italian-style sausage, and seafood, pork and poultry dishes
Fenugreek	Small, red-brown seeds; pea family; pleasantly-bitter flavor	In curry blends; chutney

Spice	Description	Uses
Ginger	Root (rhizome) of tuberous Southeast Asian plant; pungent, hot flavor	Ground: in gingerbread and other baked goods, puddings and fruit desserts; Whole: root sparingly rubbed or grated onto meats, poultry and fish; in sauces and in oriental and Indian dishes
Mace	Lacy, red covering of nutmeg seed; flavor similar to nutmeg, but stronger	In poundcake, cherry pie, fish sauces, puddings and beverages; on vegetables
Mustard Seed	Dark, reddish-brown seed of mustard plant; pale yellow or white when ground; potent flavor	Ground: in meat, fish and poultry sauces, salad dressings, egg and cheese dishes, Welsh rarebit; Whole: in marinades and pickling mixtures; with boiled beef and as garnish on salads, boiled cabbage and sauerkraut
Nutmeg	Tan pit (seed) of peach-like fruit of a Middle-Eastern evergreen; sweeter, more delicate flavor than mace	In cakes, cookies, pies, buns, custards, eggnog, puddings and other desserts; in chicken soup, and butters for corn, spinach, squash and candied sweet potatoes
Pepper	Black: red, slightly unripe berries from tropical vine that darken to their familiar mahogany shade as they dry; the pungent outer hull is left on, which gives it its more potent flavor	Same as black, but preferred in light-colored foods and sauces: creamed dishes, chowder, cheese and egg dishes
	White: from the same vine, except completely ripened and dehulled, which accounts for its milder flavor	
	Red (cayenne): dried pod of pepper plant, small, red; hot flavor	Ground: in meats and meat sauces, with restraint in egg, fish and vegetable dishes; Crushed: in spaghetti, pizza and other Italian dishes; in Mexican and Cajun dishes
Poppy Seed	Tiny, black seed of poppy plant; nutty flavor	As a topping for rolls, breads, cakes, cookies and pastries; crushed and mixed with sweetening as filling for pastries; in poppy seed butter on noodles, rice, broiled fish or vegetables
Saffron	Dried stigma of a crocus plant; orange-yellow; pleasant, slightly bitter taste; most expensive seasoning	As saffron tea, added to fancy rolls and biscuits; add a pinch to boiling water to flavor rice; in chicken, seafood, and soups
Sesame Seed	Small, oblong, pearly-white seed of semi-tropical plant; rich, nutty flavor	Whole: on rolls, breads and buns; in stuffings; tossed with vegetables and salads; as coating for chicken and fish; Ground: in halvah and other confections; Chopped: in place of almonds in all baked goods
Turmeric	Root of tropical plant in ginger family; bright yellow; peppery aroma and slightly bitter taste	In chicken, seafood and egg dishes; with rice, creamed potatoes and pasta

Source: American Spice Trade Association

Here are the definitions of some common terms found in recipes.

Al dente: Italian for "to the tooth"; pasta cooked until firm to the bite, but still tender.

Bake: To cook in an oven or oven-type appliance in a covered or uncovered container.

Barbecue: To roast slowly on a spit or rack over coals or under heat source, usually basting with a highly seasoned sauce. Also, foods cooked or served with barbecue sauce.

Baste: To moisten food with a liquid (such as a sauce, fruit juice, melted fat, pan drippings) as it cooks to add flavor and keep food from drying out.

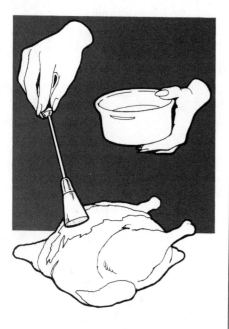

Beat: To make a mixture smooth with rapid, regular movements using a hand beater, electric mixer, wire whisk or spoon. (If using a spoon, lift mixture up and over with each stroke.)

Blanch: To cook just a few minutes in already boiling water in order to loosen the skin from some foods or to partially cook vegetables before freezing.

Blend: To thoroughly mix two or more ingredients. Also, to prepare food in a blender until pureed, chopped, etc., as desired.

Boil: To cook in water or other liquid at boiling temperature (212°F at sea level). Bubbles rise continually and break on the surface.

Bone: To remove the bones from meat, poultry or fish.

Braise: To cook meat or poultry slowly in steam from meat juices of added liquid trapped and held in a covered pan. Meat may be browned in a small amount of fat before braising.

Broil: To cook uncovered on a rack placed directly under heat or over an open fire.

Caramelize: To heat sugar or food containing sugar until it melts and a golden-brown color and characteristic flavor develop.

Chop: To cut into small pieces with a knife, blender or food processor. Compare with "mince."

Cool: To refrigerate food or let stand at room temperature until it is no longer warm to the touch.

Cream: To make mixture (such as sugar and butter) smooth and soft by beating with a spoon or mixer. Also, to cook in, or serve with, a white or cream sauce.

Cube: To cut in small (about $1/2$" square) pieces. Also, to cut through meat in a checkered pattern to increase its tenderness by breaking the fibers.

Cut in: To mix ingredients (such as butter into flour) with a cutting motion using a pastry blender or two knives scissors-fashion.

Deep-fry or French-fry: To cook in a deep kettle, in enough hot fat to completely cover or float food.

Deglaze: To dissolve meat particles stuck to the bottom of pan by adding liquid and heating.

Dice: To cut into very small (about $1/4$" square) pieces.

Dredge: To cover or coat food with flour, cornmeal, cracker crumbs, etc.

Dress: To remove scales, insides and usually head, tail and fins, from whole fish before cooking. Also, to mix salad or other food with dressing or sauce.

Flute: To make a decorative, indented edging, such as around a piecrust.

Fold: To combine two mixtures (or two ingredients such as beaten egg white and sugar) by gently cutting down through mixture, sliding under and turning over mixture and repeating until well mixed.

Fry: To cook in fat without water, uncovered.

Grease: To rub inside of pan or baking dish with a fat, such as butter or shortening, to keep food from sticking.

Grill: Same as "broil."

Julienne: To cut into long, thin strips.

Knead: To press, stretch and fold dough or other mixture to make it elastic or smooth. Bread dough becomes elastic; fondant becomes smooth and satiny.

Lukewarm: About 95°F; feels neither warm nor cold when tested on inside of wrist.

Marinate: To let foods stand in a liquid (usually a mixture of oil with vinegar or lemon juice) before cooking, to add flavor or to make more tender.

Meringue: Mixture of stiffly beaten egg whites and sugar.

Mince: To cut into tiny pieces, using a knife, blender or food processor.

Pan-broil: To cook in uncovered (ungreased or lightly greased) pan over direct, high heat, pouring off fat as it accumulates.

Pan-fry: Same as "sauté."

Parboil: To boil until partially cooked (cooking is usually then completed by another method).

Poach: To simmer gently over low heat in liquid so food retains its shape.

Pot-roast: To cook large cuts of meat by braising.

Pressure-cook: To cook in steam under pressure, using a special airtight pot.

Punch down: To deflate risen dough by pushing down on it with your fist.

Purée: To produce a smooth, thick mixture by pressing food through a food mill or fine sieve or by whirling it in a food processor or blender. Also, the thick mixture produced.

Reconstitute: To restore concentrated food — such as frozen orange juice or dry milk — to its original state, usually by adding water.

Reduce: To decrease an amount of liquid by rapid boiling it in an uncovered pan.

Rehydrate: To soak or cook dried foods to restore the water lost in drying.

Roast: To cook meats or poultry in heated air — usually in an oven — without water, uncovered.

Sauté: To cook in a frying pan or skillet over high heat in a small amount of fat.

Scald: To heat a liquid such as milk just to below the boiling point.

Score: To cut narrow slits into food surface to increase tenderness or to keep it from curling up during cooking.

Shred: To cut food into slivers with a knife or shredder.

Simmer: To cook in liquid just below the boiling point, at temperatures between 185° to 210°F. Bubbles form slowly and break below the surface.

Skim: To remove fat or scum from surface of food.

Steam: To cook food in steam, with or without pressure (see "pressure-cook"). Food is steamed in a covered container on a rack or in a perforated pan over boiling water.

Stew: To cook in liquid, just below the boiling point.

Stir-fry: To cook small pieces very quickly over high heat in a skillet or wok.

Toss: To mix foods lightly, with a lifting motion, using two utensils.

Truss: To secure poultry with string and/ or skewers so it will hold its shape while cooking.

Whip: To beat very rapidly with an electric mixer, hand beater or wire whisk to incorporate air and increase mixture's volume.

Source: U.S. Dept. of Agriculture

Emergency Food Substitutions

If you discover halfway through your special buttermilk biscuit recipe you're out of buttermilk, this recipe can be saved — and so can many others, with this list of last-minute switches.

INGREDIENT	AMOUNT	SUBSTITUTE
Baking powder, double-acting	1 tsp.	2 tsp. quick-acting baking powder OR: 1/4 tsp. baking soda + 1/2 cup sour milk or buttermilk (reduce other liquid in recipe by 1/2 cup) or 1/2 tsp. cream of tartar
Broth, beef or chicken	1 cup	1 bouillon cube OR: 1 envelope instant broth dissolved in 1 cup boiling water
Butter or margarine	1 cup	7/8 cup* vegetable or animal shortening + 1/2 tsp. salt
Buttermilk, for baking	1 cup	1 cup whole milk + 1 T. lemon juice or vinegar
Cake flour	1 cup	7/8 cup* all-purpose flour
Catsup	1 cup	8 oz. tomato sauce + 1/2 cup brown sugar + 2 T. vinegar
Chocolate, unsweetened	1 oz	3 T. cocoa + 1 T. butter or shortening
Cornstarch	1 T.	2 T. all-purpose flour
Corn syrup	1 cup	1 1/4 cups sugar + 1/4 cup water
Cream, heavy	1 cup	3/4 cup milk + 1/3 melted butter
Eggs	2 yolks	1 whole egg
Flour, for thickening	1 T.	1/2 T. cornstarch OR: 2 tsp. quick-cooking tapioca
Garlic	1 clove	1/8 tsp. garlic powder
Half-and-half	1 cup	7/8 cup* whole milk + 1 1/2 T. melted butter
Honey	1 cup	1 1/4 cups sugar + 1/4 cup water
Lemon juice	1 tsp.	1/2 tsp. vinegar
Milk, whole	1 cup	1/2 cup evaporated milk + 1/2 cup water OR: 1 cup skim milk + 2 tsp. melted butter OR 1/3 cup nonfat dry milk + 1 cup water + 2 T. melted butter
Onion, chopped	1 cup	1 T. instant minced onion, rehydrated
Sour cream, for cooking	1 cup	1 T. lemon juice + enough evaporated milk to make 1 cup
Tomato paste	1 T.	1 T. catsup
Tomato sauce	2 cups	3/4 cup tomato paste + 1 cup water
Vinegar	1 tsp.	2 tsp. lemon juice
Yogurt	1 cup	1 cup buttermilk
*7/8 cup = 1 level cup minus 2 T.		

Source: U.S. Dept. of Agriculture

WAYS TO COOK MEAT

ROASTING

1. Season, if desired.
2. Place meat, fat-side up, on rack in open roasting pan.
3. Insert meat thermometer into center of roast without tip touching fat or bone.
4. Do not add water. Do not cover.
5. Roast in slow oven (300°F. to 350°F.) to approximately 5°F. below desired doneness, as indicated on meat thermometer.
6. Allow roast to stand for 10 minutes before carving. Temperature will usually rise about 5°F. during this time.

BROILING

1. Set oven regulator for broiling (preheat, if desired); or start outdoor grill and wait until coals are covered with ash.
2. Brush meat with cooking oil on both sides.
3. Place meat 3 to 5 inches from heat or, for thinner cuts, 2 to 3 inches from heat.
4. Cook until meat is brown on one side.
5. Turn and broil second side until done.
6. Season each side after browning, if desired.

PANBROILING

1. Place meat in preheated, heavy frying pan. (With lean cuts, lightly grease pan.)
2. Do not add water. Do not cover.
3. For 5/8 to 1-inch thick cuts, cook slowly, turning occasionally. For 1/4 to 1/2 inch-thick cuts, cook over medium-high heat, turning once.
4. Pour fat from pan as it accumulates.
5. Brown meat on both sides.
6. Cook to desired doneness. Season as desired.

PANFRYING/STIRFRYING

1. Brown meat on both sides in small amount of fat.
2. Season as desired.
3. Do not cover.
4. Cook at moderate temperature for panfrying or high temperature for stirfrying.
5. Brown on both sides for panfrying; turn meat over continuously for stirfrying.
6. Remove from pan and serve at once.

BRAISING

1. Dredge meat in seasoned flour, if desired.
2. Brown meat on all sides in small amount of oil in heavy utensil. Pour off excess fat drippings.
3. Add small amount of liquid. Cover cooking vessel tightly.
4. Cook at low temperature on top of range or in oven until tender.
5. Remove meat. Thicken liquid in bottom of pot with flour or cornstarch to make a gravy or sauce, if desired.

COOKING IN LIQUID

1. Coat meat with seasoned flour, if desired.
2. Brown meat on all sides in small amount of oil, if desired. Pour off excess drippings.
3. Cover meat with liquid. Season, if desired. Cover cooking vessel tightly.
4. Simmer on top of range or in oven until tender.
5. Add vegetables just long enough to be cooked through before serving.
6. Thicken cooking liquid with flour or cornstarch, if desired.

Source: National Live Stock and Meat Board

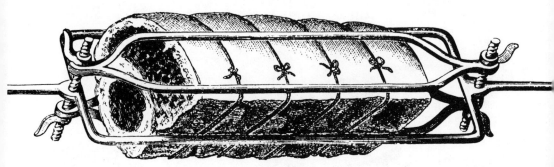

MEAT ROASTING GUIDE

Kind of Meat	Ready-to-Cook Weight	Oven Temp.	Cooking Time (Min. per Lb.)	Internal Temp. of Meat When Done
Beef				
Standing rib roast	6-8 lbs.	300-325°F	23-25	140°F. (rare)
	6-8 lbs.	300-325°F.	27-30	160°F. (med.)
	6-8 lbs.	300-325°F.	32-35	170°F. (well)
Boneless rump roast	4-6 lbs.	300-325°F	25-30	150-170°F.
Rib eye roast	4-6 lbs.	350°F.	18-20	140°F. (rare)
	4-6 lbs.	350°F.	20-22	160°F. (med.)
	4-6 lbs.	350°F.	22-24	170°F. (well)
Veal				
Loin	5 lbs.	300-325°F.	35-40	170°F.
Shoulder	6 lbs.	300-325°F.	25-30	170°F.
Lamb				
Leg	5-9 lbs.	300-325°F.	20-25	140°F. (rare)
	5-9 lbs.	300-325°F.	25-30	160°F. (med.)
	5-9 lbs.	300-325°F.	30-35	170°F. (well)
Crown roast	2¼-4 lbs.	300-325°F.	30-35	140°F. (rare)
	2¼-4 lbs.	300-325°F.	35-40	160°F. (med.)
	2¼-4 lbs.	300-325°F.	40-45	170-180°F. (well)
Shoulder				
Square cut	4-6 lbs.	300-325°F.	25-30	160°F. (med.)
	4-6 lbs.	300-325°F.	30-35	170-180°F. (well)
Boneless	3½-5 lbs.	300-325°F.	30-35	140°F. (rare
	3½-5 lbs.	300-325°F.	35-40	160"F. (med.)
	3½-5 lbs.	300-325°F.	40-45	170-180°F. (well)
Pork, fresh				
Loin roast				
Center	3-5 lbs.	325-350°F.	30-35	170°F.
Half	5-7 lbs.	325-350°F.	35-40	170°F.
Crown roast	6-10 lbs.	325-350°F.	25-30	170°F.
Arm picnic shoulder				
Bone-in	5-8 lbs.	325-350°F.	30-35	170°F.
Boneless	3-5 lbs.	325-350°F.	35-40	170°F.
Country-style ribs, Spareribs, back-ribs	—	325-350°F.	1½-2 hrs.	—
Pork, smoked				
Ham (fully cooked)				
Whole (boneless)	8-12 lbs.	300-325°F.	15-18	130-140°F.
Whole (bone-in)	14-16 lbs.	300-325°F.	15-18	130-140°F.
Half (boneless)	4-6 lbs.	300-325°F.	18-25	130-140°F.
Half (bone-in)	7-8 lbs.	300-325°F.	18-25	130-140°F.
Portion (boneless)	3-4 lbs.	300-325°F.	27-33	130-140°F.
Ham (cook-before-eating)				
Whole (boneless)	8-12 lbs.	300-325°F.	17-21	160°F.
Whole (bone-in)	14-16 lbs.	300-325°F.	18-20	160°F.
Half (bone-in)	7-8 lbs.	300-325°F.	22-25	160°F.
Portion (bone-in)	3-5 lbs.	300-325°F.	35-40	160°F.

Sources: U.S Dept. of Agriculture, National Live Stock and Meat Board.

ROASTING POULTRY

Kind of Poultry	Ready-to-Cook Weight	Roasting Time (at 325°F.)
Chicken		
Broilers, fryers	1½-2½ lbs.	1-2 hrs.
Roaster, stuffed	2½-4½ lbs.	2-3½ hrs.*
Duck	4-6 lbs.	2-3 hrs.
Goose	6-8 lbs.	3-3½ hrs.
	8-12 lbs.	3½-4½ hrs.
Turkey		
Roasters, stuffed	6-8 lbs.	3-3½ hrs.*
	8-12 lbs.	3½-4¼ hrs.*
	12-16 lbs.	4½-5½ hrs.*
	16-20 lbs.	5½-6½ hrs.*
	20-24 lbs.	6½-7 hrs.*
Halves, quarters and half breasts	3-8 lbs.	2-3 hrs.
	8-12 lbs.	3-4 hrs.
Boneless roasts	2-10 lbs.	2-4 hrs.

*Unstuffed poultry may take slightly less time.
Source: U.S. Dept. of Agriculture

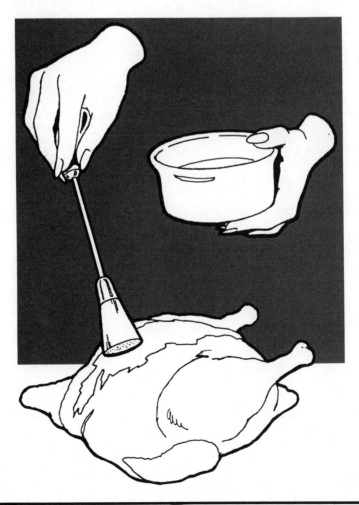

Beef Cuts

Cooking Method

Chuck Arm Pot-Roast

Contains round arm bone and sometimes cross sections of rib bones. Includes several muscles that vary in size, separated by connective tissue.

Braise

Chuck Arm Steak

Same muscle and bone structure as Arm Pot-Roast. Cut thinner, usually less than 1/2 inch thick.

Braise

Chuck Shoulder Pot-Roast Boneless

Part of arm portion of chuck. Boneless with very little fat cover.

Braise

Chuck Shoulder Steak Boneless

Same muscle structure as Beef Chuck Shoulder Pot-Roast. Boneless, cut thinner.

Braise

Chuck Cross Rib Pot-Roast

Cut from the arm half of beef chuck. Square cut, thicker at one end, containing two or three rib bones and alternating layers of lean and fat. May be tied.

Braise

Chuck Short Ribs

Rectangular-shaped, alternating layers of lean and fat. Contain rib bones, cross sections of which are exposed.

Braise, Cook in Liquid

Chuck Flanken-Style Ribs

Cut lengthwise, rather than between ribs as short ribs. Contain rib bones and alternating streaks of lean and fat.

Braise, Cook in Liquid

Beef for Stew

May be cut from chuck, brisket, rib, or plate. Meaty pieces contain varying amounts of fat, cut into 1- to 2-inch squares.

Braise, Cook in Liquid

Chuck Blade Roast

Contains blade bone, backbone, rib bone, and a variety of muscles. Usually cut about 2 inches thick.

Braise, Roast

Chuck Blade Steak

Same as Beef Chuck Blade Roast, cut thinner.

Braise, Broil or Panbroil

Chuck 7-Bone Pot-Roast

Cut from center of the blade portion of chuck. Identified by 7-shaped blade bone. Contains backbone, rib bone, and a variety of muscles.

Braise

Chuck 7-Bone Steak

Same muscle and bone structure as Beef Chuck 7-Bone Pot-Roast. Cut thinner, usually less than 1 1/2 inches thick.

Braise

Chuck Top Blade Pot-Roast

Contains short 7-shaped blade bone and two or three muscles from top portion of blade roast. Fat covering on one side.

Braise

Chuck Under Blade Pot-Roast

Contains bones and muscles of bottom portion of blade roast, including chuck eye muscles and rib bone.

Braise, Roast

Chuck Under Blade Steak

Same muscle and bone structure as Beef Under Blade Pot-Roast. Cut thinner, usually less than 1 1/2 inches thick.

Braise, Broil, Panbroil, Panfry

Chuck Under Blade Pot-Roast Boneless

Bones removed from Beef Chuck Under Blade Pot-Roast, leaving chuck eye, several other muscles and narrow streaks of fat.

Braise, Broil, Panbroil, Panfry

Chuck Under Blade Steak Boneless

Same muscle structure as Beef Chuck Under Blade Pot-Roast Boneless. Cut thinner, usually less than 1 1/2 inches thick.

Braise, Broil, Panbroil, Panfry

Chuck Mock Tender

Cut from above blade bone. Naturally boneless, consisting of a single tapering muscle with minimal fat covering.

Braise

Chuck Top Blade Roast Boneless

Triangular-shaped cut taken from above blade bone. Naturally boneless, with large amount of connective tissue.

Braise

Chuck Top Blade Steaks Boneless

Same muscle structure as Beef Chuck Top Blade Roast. Boneless, cut into thin slices. Steaks are oval shaped with minimal fat covering.

Braise, Panfry

Chuck Eye Roast Boneless

Contains meaty inside muscle of blade chuck, some seam fat, and thin fat cover, if any.

Braise, Roast

Chuck Eye Steak Boneless

Same muscle structure as Beef Chuck Eye Roast boneless, sliced.

Braise, Broil, Panbroil, Panfry

Shank Cross Cuts

Cut from hindshank or foreshank, perpendicular to bone, 1 to 2 1/2 inches thick.

Braise, Cook in Liquid

Brisket Point Half Boneless

Brisket (breast) section, between foreshank and plate. Contains layer of fat and lean but no bones. May be cured in salt brine (pickling) to make Corned Beef Brisket.

Braise, Cook in Liquid

Brisket Flat Half Boneless

Brisket (breast) section. Cut from rear portion of lean and fat closest to plate layers. Breast and rib bones removed. May be cured in salt brine (pickling) to make Corned Beef Brisket.

Braise, Cook in Liquid

Plate Skirt Steak Boneless

"Skirt" is inner diaphragm muscle.

Braise, Broil, Panbroil, Panfry

Plate Skirt Steak Rolls Boneless

"Skirt" is inner diaphragm muscle with elongated muscle. Usually sliced 3/4 to 1 inch thick, rolled to form pinwheels and either tied or skewered.

Braise, Broil, Panbroil, Panfry

Flank Steak

Boneless flat-oval cut containing elongated muscle fibers and very little fat. Surface may be scored.

Broil. Braise

Flank Steak Rolls

Flank Steak, rolled and secured with ties or skewers, cut crosswise into 3/4 to 1-inch slices.

Braise, Broil, Panbroil, Panfry

Rib Roast Large End

Cut from large end of rib primal, ribs six to nine, or any combination of two or three ribs. Contains large eye muscle with elongated muscling, streaked with strips of fat that surround rib eye. Good fat covering.

Roast

Rib Roast Small End

Cut from small end of primal rib. Contains large rib eye muscle and two or more ribs.

Roast

Rib Steak Small End

Same as Rib Roast Small End, usually cut 1 inch thick or less.

Broil, Panbroil, Panfry

Rib Steak Small End Boneless

Same as Rib Steak Small End, rib bone removed.

Broil, Panbroil, Panfry

Rib Eye Roast

Large center muscle of rib (rib eye). All other muscles, bones, and seam fat removed.

Roast

Rib Eye Steak

Cut across grain from Beef Rib Eye Roast. Little or no fat cover.

Broil, Panbroil, Panfry

Loin Top Loin Steak*

Contains top loin muscle and backbone running length of cut. Tenderloin removed. Outside fat covering

Broil, Panbroil, Panfry

*May be referred to as Beef Loin Strip Steak

Loin Top Loin Steak Boneless

Same as Beef Loin Top Loin Steak, backbone removed.

Broil, Panbroil, Panfry

Loin T-Bone Steak

Derives name from T-shape of finger bone and backbone. Contains top loin and tenderloin muscles. Tenderloin is smaller in Beef Loin T-Bone Steak than in Beef Loin Porterhouse Steak. (Diameter of tenderloin no less than 1/2 inch when measured across center.)

Broil, Panbroil, Panfry

Loin Porterhouse Steak

Contains top loin, tenderloin muscles, backbone, and finger bone. Similar to Beef Loin T-Bone Steak, but tenderloin is larger. (Diameter of tenderloin no less than 1 1/4 inches when measured across center.)

Broil, Panbroil, Panfry

Loin Wedge Bone Sirloin Steak*

Contains portion of backbone and hip bone. Varies in bone and muscle structure depending on location in sirloin section of loin. Shape of hip bone resembles wedge.

Broil, Panbroil, Panfry

*May be referred to as Beef Loin Sirloin Steak.

Loin Round Bone Sirloin Steak*

Contains portion of backbone and muscle structure. Largest muscles include top sirloin and tenderloin, interspersed with fat. Shape of hip bone resembles round bone.

Broil, Panbroil, Panfry

Loin Flat Bone Sirloin Steak*

Contains top sirloin and tenderloin muscles. Hip bone shape is long and flat.

Broil, Panbroil, Panfry

*May be referred to as Beef Loin Sirloin Steak

Loin Pin Bone Sirloin Steak*

Contains top sirloin and tenderloin muscles. Also includes a backbone and portion of hip bone, which vary in size.

Broil, Panbroil, Panfry

*May be referred to as Beef Loin Sirloin Steak

Loin Shell Sirloin Steak

Similar to other Beef Loin Sirloin Steaks, tenderloin muscle is removed.

Broil, Panbroil, Panfry

Loin Sirloin Steak Boneless

Same as Beef Loin Sirloin Steak, bones removed. Muscle structure varies.

Broil, Panbroil, Panfry

Loin Top Sirloin Steak Boneless

Beef Loin Sirloin Steak, bones and tenderloin removed.

Broil, Panbroil, Panfry

Loin Tenderloin Roast

Cut from tenderloin muscle. Elongated with rounded large end, gradually tapered to thin, flat end. Boneless with little if any fat covering. Very tender.

Roast, Broil

Loin Tenderloin Steaks*

Cut across grain from Beef Loin Tenderloin Roast. Probably most tender steak in carcass.

Roast, Broil

*May be referred to as Beef Loin, Filet Mignon.

Round Steak

Lean, oval-shaped cut containing round bone and three major muscles; top, bottom, and eye of round. Thin fat covering on outer edges.

Braise, Panfry

Round Rump Roast

Contains aitchbone and three major round muscles: top round, eye of round, and bottom round. Fat covering on outer surface.

Braise, Roast

Round Rump Roast Boneless

Same as Beef Round Rump Roast, bone removed. Usually tied.

Braise, Roast

Round Heel of Round

Boneless, wedge-shaped cut, containing top, bottom, and eye of round muscles. Least tender cut of round. Has considerable connective tissue.

Braise, Cook in Liquid

Round Top Round Roast

Contains inside top muscle of round. Boneless, with small amount of fat on outer surface.

Roast

Round Top Round Steak

Same muscle structure as Beef Round Top Round Roast, cut thinner.

Broil, Panbroil, Panfry

Round Bottom Rump Round Roast

Irregular-shaped, thick cut, from outside (or bottom) of round. Comes from sirloin end of bottom round. Slight fat covering.

Braise, Roast

Round Bottom Round Roast

Thick cut from outside of round. Irregular shape, elongated muscling, slight fat covering.

Braise, Roast

Round Eye Round Roast

Cut from eye round muscle, which has been removed from bottom round. Elongated naturally boneless, slight fat covering.

Braise, Roast

Round Eye Round Steaks

"Eye" is smallest muscle and is round, elognated and naturally boneless. Steaks cut crosswise from "eye" muscle have slight fat covering.

Braise, Panbroil, Panfry

Round Tip Roast

Wedge-shaped cut from thin side of round. Contains cap muscle of sirloin.

Braise, Roast

Round Tip Roast Cap Off

Same as Beef Round Tip Roast, bone, cap muscle, and thin layer of outer fat removed. Compact and easy to carve.

Braise, Roast

Round Tip Steak Cap Off

Boneless cut with only slight amount of outer fat. Cap muscle removed. Usually very lean.

Broil, Panbroil, Pantry

Round Cubes for Kabobs

Lean pieces of round cut into cubes. Usually taken from meatiest muscles, such as tip.

Braise, Broil

Cubed Steak

Square-or rectangular-shaped. Cubed effect made by machine that tenderizes mechanically. May be made from muscles of several primal cuts.

Braise, Panfry

Ground Beef

Ground beef made generally from lean meat and trimmings from round, chuck, loin, flank, neck or shank, ground mechanically. Usually sold according to percentage of lean in relation to fat.

Broil, Panbroil, Panfry, Roast, Bake

Lamb Cuts

Cooking Method

Shoulder Square Cut Whole
Square-shaped cut containing arm, blade, and rib bones. Thin, paperlike outside covering is called "fell."

Roast

Shoulder Blade Chops
Chops cut from blade portion of shoulder. Contain part of blade bone and backbone.

Braise, Broil, Panbroil, Panfry

Shoulder Arm Chops
Cut from arm portion of shoulder. Contain cross section of round arm bone and rib bones.

Braise, Broil, Panbroil

Shoulder Neck Slices
Cross cuts of neck portion containing small round bone. Lean interspersed with connective tissue.

Braise

Breast
Part of forequarter, containing ribs. Oblong in shape with layers of fat within lean. Generally fat covering on one side.

Braise, Roast

Breast Riblets
Cuts from breast, containing ribs with meat and fat in layers. Cuts are long and narrow.

Braise, Cook in Liquid

Shank
Cut from arm of shoulder. Contains leg bone and part of round shoulder bone. Covered by thin layer of fat and fell.

Braise, Cook in Liquid

Rib Roast
Contains rib bones, backbone, and thick, meaty rib eye muscle. Fell usually removed.

Roast

Rib Chops
Contains backbone and depending on thickness, a rib bone. Meaty area is rib eye muscle. Outer surface covered by fat with fell removed.

Broil, Panbroil, Panfry, Roast, Bake

Leg Shank Half
Sirloin half removed. Lower half of leg and round leg bone included. Heavily muscled with fat and fell covering.

Roast

Leg Frenched-Style Roast
Sirloin section of whole leg removed. Small amount of meat trimmed to expose 1 inch or more of shank bone.

Roast

Leg American-Style Roast
Sirloin section of whole leg removed. Contains same muscles and bones as Lamb Leg Frenched Style, shank bone removed, meat folded back into pocket on inside of leg, and fastened with skewers.

Roast

Lamb for Stew
Meaty pieces containing small amount of fat, cut into 1- to 2-inch squares.

Braise, Cook in Liquid

Ground Lamb
Lean meat and trimmings from leg, loin, rib, shoulder, flank, neck, breast, or shank. Mechanically ground. Sold in bulk or patties.

Braise, Broil, Panbroil, Panfry, Roast, Bake

Rib Crown Roast
Cut from half of rib. Rib bone trimmed 1 to 2 inches from end. Ribs curved and secured to resemble crown when roasts sits on backbone.

Roast

Loin Chops
Contains part of backbone. Muscles include the eye of the loin (separated from the tenderloin by T-shaped finger bones) and the flank. Kidney fat on top of tenderloin and outer surface covered with fat; fell removed.

Broil, Panbroil, Panfry

Loin Double Chops
Flank removed from cut. Contains top loin (larger muscle) and tenderloin (smaller muscle). Cut is "double" because it is a cross cut of loin containing both sides of carcass.

Broil, Panbroil, Panfry

Loin Double Chops Boneless
Bone removed from loin double chop and cut, rolled pinwheel fashion, and secured to make compact, boneless chop.

Broil, Panbroil, Panfry

Leg Sirloin Chops
Cut from sirloin section of leg. Contains backbone and part of hip bone, which vary in shape with each chop. Muscles include top sirloin, tenderloin, and flank. Fat on outside, fell removed.

Broil, Panbroil, Panfry

Leg, Whole
Contains sirloin section with hip bone, and shank portion with round bone. Outside covered with fell.

Roast

Pork Cuts

Cooking Method

Shoulder Arm Picnic

Contains arm bone, shank bone, and portion of blade bone. Shoulder muscles interspersed with fat. Shank and part of lower area covered with skin.

Roast

Shoulder Arm Roast

Cut from Arm Picnic. Shank removed, leaving round arm bone and meaty part of Arm Picnic. Outside covered with thin layer of fat.

Roast

Shoulder Arm Steak

Same muscle and bone structure as Pork Shoulder Arm Picnic, cut thinner.

Braise, Panfry

Shoulder Blade (Boston) Roast

Top portion of whole shoulder. Contains blade bone, exposed on two sides. Some intermuscular fat.

Roast

Shoulder Blade Steak

Cut from Pork Shoulder Blade Boston Roast. Contains blade bone and several muscles.

Braise, Broil, Panbroil, Panfry

Cubed Steaks

Square or rectangular. Cubed effect made by machine that tenderizes mechanically. May be made from muscles of several primal cuts.

Braise, Broil, Panbroil

Cubes for Kabobs

Boneless and lean. Cut into cubes.

Broil, Braise, Panfry, Roast

Hocks

Cut from Picnic Shoulder. Similar to Pork Shank Cross Cuts. Contains two round shank bones exposed at both ends.

Braise, Cook in Liquid

Smoked Hocks

Contains two round shank bones exposed at both ends. Oval shaped, 2 to 3 inches thick. Cured and smoked.

Braise, Cook in Liquid

Smoked Loin Canadian Style Bacon

Made from boneless loin. Cured and smoked. Single elongated muscle with little fat.

Roast, Bake if sliced, Broil, Panbroil, Panfry

Smoked Loin Rib Chops

Same muscle and bone structure as fresh Pork Loin Rib Chops. Cured and smoked.

Roast, Bake, Broil, Panbroil, Panfry

Smoked Loin Chops

Same muscle and bone structure as fresh Pork Loin Chops. Cured and smoked.

Roast, Bake, Broil, Panbroil, Panfry

Smoked Ham Whole

Same muscle and bone structure as Pork Leg (Fresh Ham) Whole. Cured and smoked.

Roast, Bake

Smoked Ham Shank Portion

Same muscle and bone structure as Pork Leg (Fresh Ham) Shank Portion. Cured and smoked.

Roast, Bake

Smoked Ham Rump Portion

Portion of cured and smoked ham that contains aitchbone and part of leg bone. Thin fat cover on outer surface.

Roast, Bake

Smoked Ham Center Slice

Cut from center portion of cured, smoked ham. Contains top, bottom, tip muscles, and round bone.

Broil, Panbroil, Panfry, Roast Bake

Slab Bacon

Cured and smoked side. Contains streaks of lean and fat on one side. Other side maybe covered with skin.

Broil if sliced, Panbroil, Panfry, Roast, Bake

Sliced Bacon

Sliced from Slab Bacon. May be shingled. Outer skin removed.

Broil, Panbroil, Panfry, Roast, Bake

Sausage Links

Made from ground, fresh meat and seasonings such as salt, pepper, and sage. Stuffed in casings and shaped into links.

Braise, Panfry, Roast, Bake

Loin Sirloin Roast

Contains hip bone and backbone. Largest muscle is eye of loin, separated from smaller tenderloin muscles by finger bones.

Roast

Loin Sirloin Chops

Cut from sirloin end of loin. Same muscle and bone structure as Pork Loin Sirloin Roast.

Braise, Broil, Panbroil, Panfry

Loin Sirloin Cutlets

Boneless slices cut from sirloin end of loin after tenderloin, hip bone, and backbone are removed.

Braise, Broil, Panbroil, Panfry

Loin Tenderloin Whole

Boneless cut taken from inside of loin. Largest end is round in shape and gradually tapers to the thin flat end. Very tender.

Roast, Bake, Braise, Broil

Spareribs

Cut from side. Contain long rib bones with thin covering of meat on outside and between ribs. May contain rib cartilage.

Roast, Bake, Broil, Cook in Liquid

Fresh Side Pork

Same cut as Slab Bacon but fresh, from section of side that remains after loin and spareribs are removed. Layered lean from fat generally used as seasoning.

Cook in Liquid

Leg (Fresh Ham) Whole

Hind Leg bone-in. Usually covered with skin and fat about halfway up leg.

Roast

Leg (Fresh Ham) Shank Portion

Lower portion of leg. Contains shank bone and part of femur bone. Skin covers shank and small portion of outside muscle.

Roast, Cook in Liquid

Ground

Unseasoned, ground, from wholesale cuts which are generally in limited demand. Also made from lean trimmings. Sold in bulk form.

Broil, Panbroil, Panfry, Roast, Bake

Smoked Shoulder Picnic Whole

Same muscle and bone structure as fresh Pork Shoulder Arm Picnic. Cured and smoked.

Roast, Bake, Cook in Liquid

Smoked Shoulder Roll

Cured and smoked, meaty, boneless eye of Pork Shoulder Blade Boston Roast.

Roast, Bake, Cook in Liquid

Loin Blade Roast

Contains part of blade bone, rib bones, and backbone. Large loin eye muscle surrounded by several smaller muscles.

Roast

Loin Blade Chops

Cut from blade end of loin. Contains same muscle and bone structure as Pork Loin Blade Roast.

Braise, Broil, Panbroil, Panfry

Loin Country Style Ribs

Made by slitting blade end of loin into halves lengthwise. Contains part of loin eye muscle and either rib bones or backbones.

Roast, Bake, Braise, Broil, Cook in Liquid

Loin Back Ribs

Cut from blade and center section of loin. Contain rib bones. Meat between ribs called finger meat. Layer of meat covering ribs comes from loin eye muscle.

Roast, Bake, Braise Broil, Cook in Liquid

Loin Center Rib Roast

Cut from center rib area of loin. Contains loin eye muscle and rib bones.

Roast

Loin Rib Chops*

Contains loin eye muscle and backbone. Rib bone may be present, depending on thickness. Fat covering on outside edge.

Braise, Broil, Panbroil, Panfry
*May be called Center Cut Chops

Loin Center Loin Roast

Cut from center of loin. Contains rib eye, tenderloin muscles, rib bones, T-shaped bones. Thin fat covering.

Roast

Loin Top Loin Chops

Contain top loin muscles and backbone running length of cut. Tenderloin removed. Outside fat covering.

Braise, Broil, Panbroil, Panfry

Loin Butterfly Chops

Double chop, about 2 inches thick, from boneless loin eye muscle. Sliced almost in half to form two sides resembling butterfly.

Braise, Broil, Panbroil, Panfry

Loin Top Loin Roast Boneless (Double)

Two boneless loins reversed and tied together with fat side out to make boneless roast.

Roast

Loin Chops

Cut from sirloin end of loin. Eye muscle and tenderloin divided by T-shaped bone. Also contains backbone.

Braise, Broil, Panbroil, Panfry

Veal Cuts

Cooking Method

Shoulder Arm Roast
Shoulder cut containing arm bone, rib bones from underside, and cross sections of bones exposed on face side. Muscles include shoulder, forearm, and thin layer of lean meat from brisket.

Braise, Roast

Shoulder Arm Steak
Same structure as Veal Shoulder Arm Roast, cut thinner. Cross sections of arm and rib bones exposed. Muscles include shoulder, forearm, and thin layer of lean brisket.

Braise, Panfry

Shoulder Blade Roast
Contains blade bone exposed on cut surface, ribs and backbone from underside. Muscles include chuck, top blade, and chuck tender.

Braise, Roast

Shoulder Blade Steak
Same structure as Veal Shoulder Blade Roast, except for thickness. Contains blade bone, backbone, and depending on thickness, a rib bone.

Braise, Panfry

Breast
Rear portion of foresaddle. Contains lower ribs. Quite lean with some fat layered within lean. Elongated muscling. Scant fat covering

Braise, Roast

Breast Riblets
Long narrow cuts containing rib bones and slight fat covering. Some connective tissue layered within lean.

Braise, Cook in Liquid

Rib Crown Roast
Cut from half of primal rib. Contains ribs six to twelve which have rib bones trimmed 1 to 2 inches from end. Ribs curved and tied to resemble crown when roast rests on backbone.

Roast

Veal for Stew
Meaty pieces cut into 1- to 2-inch squares. May be cut from shoulder, shank, or round.

Braise, Cook in Liquid

Rib Roast
Contains ribs six to twelve, rib eye muscle, featherbones, and part of chine bone. Does not contain tenderloin.

Roast

Rib Chops
Contain featherbone, part of chine bone, and, depending on thickness, rib bone. Largest muscle is rib eye.

Braise, Panfry

Loin Roast
Contains to loin and tenderloin muscles, backbone, and T-shaped fingerbone.

Roast

Loin Chops
Contains backbone and fingerbone. Muscles include top loin and tenderloin. Tenderloin differentiates this chop from rib chop. Size of chops gets smaller as chops near rib.

Braise, Panfry

Loin Kidney Chops
Contains backbone and featherbones. Muscles contained are loin and tenderloin. Side includes kidneys. Cut contains cross-sectional cut of kidney attached by kidney fat.

Braise, Panfry

Loin Top Loin Chops
Same as Veal Loin Chops, tenderloin removed.

Braise, Panfry

Leg Sirloin Steak
Contains portion of backbone and hip bone. Size and shape of muscles and bones vary with each steak.

Braise, Panfry

Leg Round Roast
Cone-shaped with round leg bone exposed. Contains top, bottom, and eye muscles.

Braise, Roast

Leg Round Steak
Cut from center of leg. Contains top, bottom, eye muscles, and cross section of leg bones. Has thin outer covering of fat and skin.

Braise, Panfry

Leg Rump Roast
Contains three major round muscles: top round, eye round, and bottom round, separated by connective tissue. Also contains aitchbone and fat covering on outer muscle. Irregularly shaped roast.

Braise, Roast

Leg Sirloin Roast
Contains portion of hip bone, backbone, and variety of muscles.

Roast

Cubed Steaks
Can be made from any boneless lean cut of leg. Identified by square or rectangular appearance. Cubed effect made by a machine that tenderizes mechanically. Steaks made from several pieces of meat. All cuts have appearance of a single piece.

Braise, Panfry

Cutlets
Thin, boneless slices from leg. Very lean.

Braise, Panfry

Ground
Lean meat and trimmings mechanically ground. Sold in bulk or patty form.

Braise, Panfry, Roast

Source: National Live Stock and Meat Board

Pasta Guide

Cooking Perfect Pasta

1. In a large pot, bring to a rolling boil 1 quart water for every 4 ounces pasta; if desired, add 2 tablespoons salt to the water per pound of pasta. (You can also add a tablespoon of olive oil to the water.)

2. Add pasta to pot slowly, to keep rolling boil.

3. Stir frequently to prevent sticking. Do not cover.

4. Test for doneness after about 5 minutes. (Note: Homemade pastas cook more quickly than commercial varieties.) Pasta should be al dente ("to the tooth") — tender, yet firm. DO NOT OVERCOOK.

5. Pour pasta slowly into a colander, drain briefly, add sauce and serve at once. (For cold pasta salads, rinse with cold water.)

PASTA	DESCRIPTION	USE
Anelli (rings)	Small, ring shapes	In soup and salads
Bucati (pierced)	Spaghetti with a small hole down center	With thick (marinara or meat) sauces
Capellini (also called *Capelli d'Angelo* — angel hair)	Delicate, long, thin strands	In soups; with thin sauces — seafood or olive oil based
Cannelloni (big pipes)	Large tubes, like rolled crepes	Fill with cheese, seafood or vegetable mixtures
Capelletti (little hats)	Shaped dumplings usually filled with minced chicken or meat	With thick tomato or cream sauces
Cavatelli (also called *gnocci*, "dumpling," if made of potato flour)	Curled in, short shells with grooved surface	With chicken livers or meat or vegetable sauces; or bake with butter and cheese
Conchiglie (shells)	Conch shape	Small sizes, in soup and salads; large ones, stuff with cheese, meat or vegetable fillings
Ditalini (little thimbles)	Small, short tubes	In soups
Elbow macaroni (Such as *creste di galli* — "cockscombs" — and *capelli di prete* — priests' hats")	Short, slightly curved tubes (some have ruffled edges)	In soups, macaroni salads, casseroles
Farfalle (butterflies)	Bowtie or butterfly shape (jagged-edged rectangles, pinched together in the middle)	Small: in soups, salads Large: with light sauces, butter and cheese, vegetables as in primavera
Fettuccine (small ribbons)	1/4-inch-wide ribbon	With cream or butter and cheese sauce
Fusilli (thin spindles)	Corkscrew-curled strands of spaghetti	With tomato or cream sauce
Gemelli (twins)	Two short strands, twisted together	With thick tomato sauces

Name	Description	Usage
Lasagne (pot)	Flat, broad ribbon with ruffled edges	Baked, layered with cheese or rolled up with filling tomato or cream sauce
Linguine (small tongues)	Narrow, flat strands	With olive oil or seafood-based sauce
Manicotti (small muffs)	Large, long tubes with diagonally cut ends	Stuffed with cheese; rich tomato or cream sauce
Mostaccioli (small mustaches)	Medium-size tubes, ridged or plain surface, diagonally cut ends	With thick sauces, with meat or chopped vegetables
Orzo (barley)	Tiny, rice-shaped	In soups, or use as rice substitute
Pastina (little pasta)	Tiny, round	In soups, with butter sauce
Penne (quill)	Diagonally cut, medium-size tubes	With thick sauces
Perciatelli (small and pierced)	Strands thicker than spaghetti, with hole down center	With marinara, or meat and tomato sauce
Ravioli	Squares stuffed with meat or cheese, "pinked" edges	With rich tomato or cream sauce
Rigatoni (large striped)	Large, curved, grooved tube	With flavorful thick tomato sauces
Rotelle, rotini (spirals)	Corkscrew shapes about 1 1/2 inches long	In soups, salads; with thick tomato sauces
Ruote (wagon wheels)	Die-cut, cartwheel shapes	With thick meat or seafood sauces
Spaghetti (from spago, length of string)	Long solid strands in a variety of thicknesses	With meat or seafood-base tomato sauces
Spaghettini (narrow spaghetti)	Long strands, thinner than spaghetti	More delicate olive oil seafood or vegetable sauces
Stellini (little stars)	Tiny star shapes	In soups; with butter sauce
Tagliatelle (to cut)	3/4-inch-wide ribbon	With cream or cheese sauce
Tortellini, tortelloni (fritters)	Semicircles stuffed with meat or cheese and formed into ring	In soups, salads; with cream or cheese sauces
Tripolini	Tiny, pinched bows	In soups, salads
Tubetti (little tubes)	Short, tiny tubes	In soups, salads
Vermicelli (little worms)	Very thin strands, sometimes sold in clusters	Thin olive oil or seafood-based sauces
Ziti (bridegrooms)	Medium-size tubes	With robust tomato sauces; baked with cheese in casserole

Source: National Pasta Association

SEAFOOD COOKING GUIDE

Below are the eight basic methods for preparing fish. Check the chart that follows for cooking times and temperatures for each method.

BAKING
1. Place clean, dressed fish in a greased baking dish.
2. Brush with oil or melted butter or top with sauce to keep fish moist.
3. Bake until fish flakes easily when tested with a fork.

BROILING
1. Arrange fish (pieces should be at least 1″ thick) in a single layer on a greased broiler rack set about 3″ to 4″ from source of heat.
2. Before and during broiling, baste well with oil or melted butter or a sauce.
3. About halfway through cooking time, turn over thicker servings (such as whole fish or steaks) and baste again.

CHARCOAL BROILING
1. Use a barbecue with closely spaced grill or, for smaller pieces, use a specially designed fish grill or basket. Grease grill well.
2. Set grill with fish 4″ above hot coals.
3. Before and during cooking, baste with barbecue sauce or marinade.
4. Broil until fish flakes easily with a fork.

DEEP-FAT FRYING
1. Using only very small fish or fillets, dip fish into seasoned milk or beaten egg, and then into bread or cracker crumbs, cornmeal, flour or other batter.
2. Set fish on a single layer in a wire frying basket.
3. In a deep kettle, place enough oil or fat to float fish. (Do not fill kettle more than halfway.) Heat fat to 350°F.
4. To prevent excess bubbling, gently lower basket with fish into kettle.
5. Cook until lightly browned and pieces flake easily when tested with a fork.

6. Drain on absorbent paper.
7. Be sure to let fat return to 350°F before frying remaining batches of fish.

OVEN-FRYING
1. Dip fish portions into seasoned milk or beaten egg, and then into bread or cracker crumbs, cornmeal, flour or other batter.
2. Bake in preheated oven until fish flakes easily when tested with a fork.

PAN-FRYING
1. Dip clean, dressed small fish into seasoned milk or beaten egg, and then into bread or cracker crumbs, cornmeal, flour or other batter.
2. Heat about ⅛″ of fat or oil in the bottom of a heavy frying pan or skillet.
3. Arrange coated fish in a single layer in the hot fat.
4. Fry until lightly browned and fish flakes easily when tested with a fork.

POACHING
1. Arrange fish in a single layer in a wide, shallow pan.
2. Barely cover fish with liquid, such as lightly salted water or milk.
3. Bring liquid to boiling, reduce heat and simmer until fish flakes easily when tested with a fork.

STEAMING
1. Use a steam cooker or deep pot with tight-fitting lid. (The pot should be deep enough to hold a wire rack or basket and keep fish above the liquid.)
2. Pour about 2″ of plain or seasoned water into pot.
3. Set rack or basket with fish in pot above water.
4. Cover pot tightly and steam until fish flakes easily when tested with a fork.

TIMETABLE FOR COOKING FISH

Cooking method and market form	Approximate ready-to-cook weight or thickness	Cooking temperature	Approximate cooking time in minutes
BAKING			
Dressed	3 pounds	350°F.	45 to 60
Pan-dressed	3 pounds	350°F.	25 to 30
Fillets or steaks	2 pounds	350°F.	20 to 25
Portions	2 pounds	400°F.	15 to 20
Sticks	2¼ pounds	400°F.	15 to 20
BROILING			
Pan-dressed	3 pounds		10 to 16
Fillets or steaks	½ to 1 inch		10 to 15
Portions	³/₈ to ½ inch		10 to 15
Sticks	³/₈ to ½ inch		10 to 15
CHARCOAL BROILING			
Pan-dressed	3 pounds	Moderate	10 to 16
Fillets or steaks	½ to 1 inch	Moderate	10 to 16
Portions	³/₈ to ½ inch	Moderate	8 to 10
Sticks	³/₈ to ½ inch	Moderate	8 to 10
DEEP-FAT FRYING			
Pan-dressed	3 pounds	350°F.	3 to 5
Fillets or steaks	½ to 1 inch	350°F.	3 to 5
Portions	³/₈ to ½ inch	350°F.	3 to 5
Sticks	³/₈ to ½ inch	350°F.	3 to 5
OVEN-FRYING			
Pan-dressed	3 pounds	500°F.	15 to 20
Fillets or steaks	½ to 1 inch	500°F.	10 to 15
PAN-FRYING			
Pan-dressed	3 pounds	Moderate	8 to 10
Fillets or steaks	½ to 1 inch	Moderate	8 to 10
Portions	³/₈ to ½ inch	Moderate	8 to 10
Sticks	³/₈ to ½ inch	Moderate	8 to 10
POACHING			
Fillets or steaks	2 pounds	Simmer	5 to 10
STEAMING			
Fillets or steaks	2 pounds	Boiling	5 to 10
Clams		Boiling	5-10 (just until they open)
Lobster		Boiling	12-15 (until shell is red)

SHELLFISH	Broiling time in minutes	Baking time and temperature
Clams		
Live	4 to 5	10 to 15/450°F.
Shucked	4 to 5	8 to 10/350°F.
Crabs	—	8 to 10/350°F.
Lobsters	12 to 15	20 to 25/400°F.
Oysters		
Live	4 to 5	10 to 15/450°F.
Shucked	4 to 5	8 to 10/350°F.
Scallops	6 to 8	20 to 25/350°F.
Shrimp	8 to 10	20 to 25/350°F.

Sources: U.S. Dept. of Agriculture; National Marine Fisheries Service

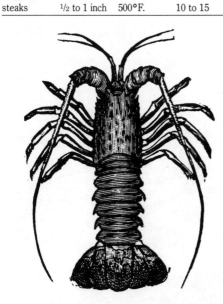

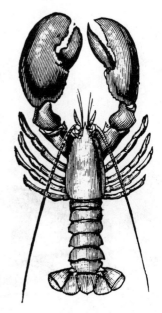

COOKING FRESH VEGETABLES

Vegetables will retain more of their nutrients when not overcooked. Here are recommended times for steaming (the most nutritious cooking method) or boiling.

Vegetable	Steam (Min.)	Boil (Min.)
Artichokes		
French or globe	30-45	30-45
Jerusalem, slices	—	15-30
Asparagus		
Spears	12-16	10-15
Tips	7-10	5-10
Beans		
Lima	25-35	12-20
Green (whole)	20-35	15-30
(French-cut)	12-25	10-20
Beets (whole)	40-60	30-45
Broccoli (split stalks)	15-20	10-15
Brussels sprouts (whole)	15-20	10-20
Cabbage		
Green (quartered)	15	10-15
(shredded)	8-12	3-10
Red (shredded)	10-15	8-12
Carrots		
Whole	20-30	15-20
Sliced, diced	15-25	10-20
Cauliflower		
Whole	25-30	15-25
Flowerets	10-20	8-15
Celery (sliced)	25-30	15-18
Collards	—	10-20
Corn		
On cob	10-15	6-12
Kernels	10-12	6-8

Vegetable	Steam (Min.)	Boil (Min.)
Eggplant (sliced)	15-20	10-20
Kale	15	10-15
Okra (sliced)	20	10-15
Onions		
Small (whole)	25-35	15-30
Large (whole)	35-40	20-40
Parsnips		
Whole	30-45	20-40
Quartered	30-40	8-15
Peas	10-20	12-16
Potatoes		
Whole	30-45	25-40
Quartered	20-30	20-25
Rutabaga (diced)	35-40	20-30
Spinach	5-12	3-10
Squash		
Acorn (quartered)	25-40	18-20
Butternut (cubed)	20-35	16-18
Summer (sliced)	15-20	8-15
Sweet potatoes		
Whole	30-35	35-55
Quartered	25-30	15-25
Turnips		
Whole	—	20-30
Sliced	20-35	15-20

Source: U.S. Dept. of Agriculture.

SEASONAL GUIDE TO FRUITS

Below is a month-by-month chart showing the availability of the year's fruit crop. Buying fresh fruits during their peak seasons ensures that they're at their most flavorful — and most inexpensive.

	Jan	Feb	Mar	Apr	May	Jun	Jul	Aug	Sep	Oct	Nov	Dec
Apples	2	2	2	2	2	1	1	1	3	3	3	3
Apricots	1	1	1	1	1	3	3	1	1	1	1	1
Bananas	3	3	3	3	3	3	3	2	2	3	3	3
Blueberries	1	1	1	1	1	3	3	3	1	1	1	1
Cantaloupes	1	1	1	1	2	3	3	3	3	1	1	1
Cherries	1	1	1	1	2	3	3	2	1	1	1	1
Cranberries	1	1	1	1	1	1	1	1	2	3	3	3
Grapefruit	3	3	3	3	2	2	1	1	1	2	3	3
Grapes	1	1	1	1	1	2	3	3	3	3	3	2
Lemons	2	2	2	2	3	3	3	3	2	2	2	2
Limes	1	1	1	1	2	3	3	3	2	2	2	2
Nectarines	1	1	1	1	1	3	3	3	3	1	1	1
Oranges	3	3	3	3	3	2	1	1	1	1	2	3
Peaches	1	1	1	1	1	3	3	3	3	1	1	1
Pears	2	2	2	2	1	1	1	3	3	3	3	2
Pineapples	2	2	3	3	3	3	3	3	1	1	2	2
Plums	1	1	1	1	1	3	3	3	3	1	1	1
Strawberries	1	1	2	3	3	3	2	1	1	1	1	1
Watermelons	1	1	1	1	3	3	3	3	2	1	1	1

1 Low supply or not available 2 Fair supply 3 Peak to good supply

Sources: U.S. Dept of Agriculture; United Fresh Fruit and Vegetable Association

SEASONAL GUIDE TO VEGETABLES

This month-by-month chart indicates the market availability of fresh vegetables. Shop for them during their peak seasons for the best flavor — and price.

	Jan	Feb	Mar	Apr	May	Jun	Jul	Aug	Sep	Oct	Nov	Dec
Artichokes	1	1	2	3	3	3	2	2	2	2	1	1
Asparagus	1	1	3	3	3	2	1	1	1	1	1	1
Beans, snap	2	2	2	2	3	3	3	3	2	2	2	2
Beets	1	1	2	2	2	3	3	3	3	3	2	1
Broccoli	3	3	3	3	2	2	1	1	2	2	3	3
Brussels sprouts	3	3	2	2	1	1	1	1	2	3	3	3
Cabbage	3	3	3	3	3	3	3	2	3	3	3	3
Cauliflower	2	2	2	2	1	1	1	1	3	3	3	2
Celery	3	3	3	3	3	3	3	2	2	3	3	3
Corn	1	1	1	2	3	3	3	3	3	1	1	1
Cucumbers	1	1	1	2	3	3	3	3	2	2	2	2
Lettuce	3	3	3	3	3	3	3	3	3	3	2	3
Mushrooms	3	3	3	3	3	3	2	2	2	3	3	3
Onions	3	2	3	3	3	3	3	3	3	3	3	3
Peas	2	3	3	3	3	3	3	2	2	1	1	1
Peppers	2	2	2	2	2	3	3	3	3	2	2	2
Potatoes	3	3	3	3	3	3	3	3	3	3	3	3
Pumpkins	1	1	1	1	1	1	1	1	1	3	1	1
Radishes	2	2	3	3	3	3	3	2	2	2	2	2
Spinach	3	3	3	3	2	2	2	1	2	2	2	2
Squash	2	2	2	2	2	3	3	3	3	3	3	2
Sweet potatoes	2	2	2	2	1	1	1	1	3	3	3	3
Tomatoes	2	2	2	2	3	3	3	3	2	1	1	1

1 Low supply or not available   2 Fair supply   3 Peak to good supply

Sources: U.S. Dept of Agriculture; United Fresh Fruit and Vegetable Association

EQUIVALENT AMOUNTS

EQUIVALENT MEASURES

Dash	2 to 3 drops or less than 1/8 teaspoon
1 tablespoon	3 teaspoons
1/4 cup	4 tablespoons
1/3 cup	5 tablespoons plus 1 teaspoon
1/2 cup	8 tablespoons
1 cup	16 tablespoons
1 pint	2 cups
1 quart	4 cups
1 gallon	4 quarts
1 peck	8 quarts
1 bushel	4 pecks
1 pound	16 ounces

FOOD EQUIVALENTS

Apples *1 pound*	3 medium (3 cups sliced)
Bananas *1 pound*	3 medium (1 1/3 cups mashed)
Berries *1 pint*	1 3/4 cups
Bread *1 1-pound loaf*	14 to 20 slices
Bread crumbs, fresh *1 slice bread with crust*	1/2 cup bread crumbs
Broth, chicken or beef *1 cup*	1 bouillon cube or 1 envelope bouillon or 1 teaspoon instant bouillon dissolved in 1 cup boiling water
Butter or margarine *1/4-pound stick*	1/2 cup
Cheese *1/4 pound*	1 cup shredded
Cheese, cottage *8 ounces*	1 cup
Cheese, cream *3 ounces*	6 tablespoons
Chocolate, unsweetened *1 ounce*	1 square
Chocolate, semisweet pieces *1 6-ounce package*	1 cup
Coconut *flaked, 3 1/2-ounce can* *shredded, 4-ounce can*	1 1/3 cups 1 1/3 cups
Cream, heavy or whipping *1 cup*	2 cups whipped cream
Cream, sour *8 ounces*	1 cup

FOOD EQUIVALENTS (*continued*)

Egg whites, large, *1 cup*	8 to 10 whites
Egg yolks, large *1 cup*	12 to 14 yolks
Flour *1 pound* *all-purpose* *cake*	about 3 1/2 cups about 4 cups
Gelatin, unflavored *1 envelope*	1 tablespoon
Lemon *1 medium*	3 tablespoons juice, about 1 tablespoon grated peel
Lime *1 medium*	2 tablespoons juice
Milk, evaporated *5 1/3- or 6-ounce can* *13- or 14 1/2-ounce can*	2/3 cup 1 2/3 cups
Milk, sweetened condensed *14-ounce can*	1 1/4 cups
Nuts, 1 pound **Almonds,** *in shell* *shelled*	1 to 1 1/4 cups nutmeats 3 cups
Brazil nuts, *in shell* *shelled*	1 1/2 cups nutmeats 3 1/4 cups
Filberts, *in shell* *shelled*	1 1/2 cups nutmeats 3 1/2 cups
Peanuts, *in shell* *shelled*	2 to 2 1/2 cups nutmeats 3 cups
Pecans, *in shell* *shelled*	2 1/4 cups nutmeats 4 cups
Walnuts, *in shell* *shelled*	2 cups nutmeats 4 cups
Onion *1 large*	3/4 to 1 cup chopped
Orange *1 medium*	1/3 to 1/2 cup juice 2 tablespoons grated peel
Potatoes *1 pound* *white* *sweet*	3 medium (2 1/4 cups diced) 3 medium
Raisins *1 pound*	3 cups, loosely packed
Rice, regular long-grain *1 cup*	3 cups cooked
Salad oil *16 ounces*	2 cups
Sugar *1 pound* *granulated* *brown* *confectioners'*	2 1/4 to 2 1/2 cups 2 1/4 cups packed 4 to 4 1/2 cups
Syrup *corn 16 ounces* *maple 12 ounces*	2 cups 1 1/2 cups
Tomatoes *1 pound*	3 medium

Source: U.S. Dept. of Agriculture

ENTERTAINING

SETTING THE TABLE

These are very general guidelines for table settings; make adjustments according to what will be served and the order of your courses. Traditionally, flatware is arranged by order of use, from the outside working in toward the plate. The knives' cutting edges should be facing the plate. The napkin can be to the left of the forks or placed directly on the plate.

INFORMAL DINNER

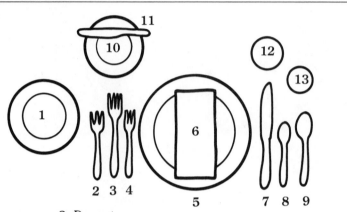

1. Salad plate
2. Salad fork
3. Dinner fork
4. Dessert fork
5. Dinner plate
6. Napkin
7. Dinner knife
8. Dessert spoon
9. Soup spoon
10. Butter plate
11. Butter knife
12. Water goblet
13. Wine or other beverage glass

FORMAL DINNER

1. Napkin
2. Salad fork
3. Fish fork
4. Meat fork
5. Dinner plate
6. Soup plate with liner plate
7. Meat knife
8. Fish knife
9. Soup spoon and/or fruit spoon
10. Shellfish fork
11. Butter knife
12. Butter plate
13. Dessert spoon
14. Dessert fork
15. Water goblet
16. Champagne glass
17. Red and/or white wine glasses
18. Sherry glass

Arrange glasses according to size, in a row that slants diagonally down from water goblet at upper left

BUFFET

Everything should be arranged to allow traffic to move easily, whether the table sits in the center of the room or against a wall. If you have many guests and a large table, you could set up the same service on opposite sides of the table, to accommodate two serving lines.

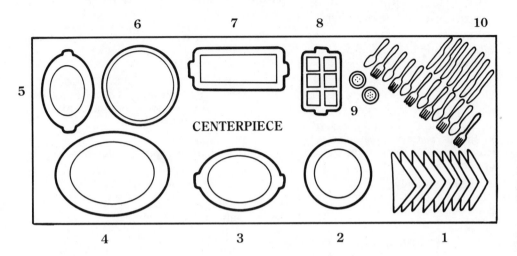

1. Napkins (or roll up with utensils, at end)
2. Dinner plates
3. Side dish (noodles, rice, potatoes)
4. Main dish
5. Vegetables
6. Salad
7. Bread
8. Condiments/relishes
9. Salt and pepper
10. Forks, spoons, knives

On separate table: Cold beverages, coffee, tea, dessert, with appropriate plates, silverware, cups and glassware.

GUIDE TO LIQUEURS

These sweetened, flavored spirits, also called cordials, can be offered before a meal (aperitif) or, more usually, after (as a digestif). Serve chilled or over cracked or shaved ice. Liqueurs can also be used to flavor coffee, fruit, ice cream and other desserts.

Amaretto
Bitter almond flavor, from apricot pits and spices.

Anisette
Licorice taste; aniseed; very sweet.

Bénédictine
27 herbs and dried plants, including juniper berry, Ceylon tea, balm, angelica, cloves, cinnamon, nutmeg, vanilla; brandy base.

Blackberry Brandy
Fairly sweet blackberry flavor. Also good on ice cream or fruit.

Campari
Quinine and gentian, slightly bitter aperitif.

Chartreuse, green
Peppery-minty-herbal taste; made from secret recipe containing 130 herbs.

Chartreuse, yellow
Honey flavored; lower proof than green.

Cherry Brandy
Cherry and almond flavor, from cherry pulp and kernels.

Cointreau
Orange, made with peels of both bitter and sweet oranges. Use in Crêpes Suzette.

Cordial Médoc
Lightly sweet; raspberry and other fruits, brandy base.

Crème de Cacao
Rich, sweet chocolate flavor from cacao beans and vanilla. Use in Grasshopper or Brandy Alexander. Pour over vanilla ice cream.

Crème de Cassis
Black currant, very sweet; + dry white wine = Kir.

Crème de Menthe
Peppermint and other mints; sweet.

Crème de Moka
Coffee flavor; less sweet.

Crème de Noisettes
Hazelnut flavor, with mace, lemon peel, allspice.

Crème de Noyaux
Light almond flavor; from apricot or peach pits.

Curacao
Orange flavor from peel of West Indian green oranges, sweet oranges, spices (sweeter than *Triple Sec*).

Drambuie
Herbal, honey, spicy; Scotch base.

Fraise
Strawberry base, very sweet.

Framboise
Light, dry raspberry taste.

Galliano
Anise-vanilla-herbal, moderately sweet.

Goldwasser
Coriander, orange and lemon peels, mace — with flakes of gold leaf floating in bottle.

Grand Marnier
Bitter orange with cognac.

Irish Cream
Irish whiskey and chocolate.

Kahlùa
Strong Mexican coffee; + vodka = Black Russian.

Metaxa
Citrus-apricot; brandy base.

Midori
Honeydew melon flavor.

Peach Brandy
Delicate peach flavor.

Pernod
Herbal flavor from anise, parsley, coriander, chamomile.

Sabra
Orange and chocolate flavor.

Sambuca
Lighter licorice flavor than anisette; from fruit of the elder bush. Serve with three roasted coffee beans

Triple Sec
Orange base, drier than curaçao.

Vandermint
Chocolate and mint; sweet, heavy.

MIXED DRINK GUIDE

Key:
1 jigger = 1½ oz.
2/3 jigger = 1 oz.
1/3 jigger = 1/2 oz.

Alexander

1 part fresh cream
1 part crème de cacao
1 part brandy
Shake thoroughly with cracked ice. Strain into cocktail glass.

Bloody Mary

2 jiggers tomato juice
1/3 jigger fresh lemon juice
Dash of Worcestershire sauce
1 jigger vodka
Salt and pepper to taste.
Shake with cracked ice.
Strain into 6 oz. glass.

Daiquiri

Juice of 1/2 lime or 1/4 lemon
1 tsp. sugar
1 jigger light rum
Shake with cracked ice until shaker frosts. Strain into cocktail glass.

Gimlet

4 parts gin or vodka
1 part Rose's sweetened lime juice
Shake with cracked ice and strain into a cocktail glass. Garnish with slice of fresh lime.

Gin and Tonic

Juice and rind of 1/4 lime
1 jigger gin
Quinine (tonic) water
Squeeze lime over ice cubes in tall glass and add rind. Pour in gin; fill with tonic water and stir.

Grasshopper

1/2 jigger fresh cream
2/3 jigger white crème de cacao
2/3 jigger green crème de menthe
Shake with cracked ice or mix in electric blender. Strain into cocktail glass.

Manhattan

1 jigger bourbon or rye
1/3 jigger sweet vermouth
Dash of bitters (optional)
Stir with cracked ice and strain into glass.
Add a cherry.

Margarita

1 jigger tequila
1/3 jigger triple sec
2/3 jigger fresh lime or lemon juice
Shake ingredients with cracked ice. Moisten rim of cocktail glass with fruit rind and spin rim in salt. Strain drink into salt-dipped glass.

Martini

4 parts gin or vodka
1 part dry vermouth
Stir with cracked ice and strain into chilled cocktail glass. Or serve on ice. Garnish with green olive or twist of lemon peel.

Old-Fashioned

1/2 tsp. sugar
1 tsp. water
Dash of bitters
1 jigger of whiskey
Mix sugar, water and bitters in old-fashioned glass. Add ice, pour whiskey over and stir.

Pina Colada

1 jigger rum
2/3 jigger cream of coconut
1⅓ jigger unsweetened pineapple juice
Shake with 1/2 cup crushed ice. Pour into tall glass filled with ice cubes. Add a cherry.

Screwdriver

1 jigger vodka
Orange juice
Put ice cubes into 6 oz. glass. Add vodka; fill with orange juice and stir.

Sour

1 jigger bourbon or rye
1/2 jigger fresh lemon juice
1 tsp. sugar
Shake with cracked ice and strain into glass. Add an orange slice and a cherry.

Stinger

1 jigger brandy
2/3 jigger white crème de menthe
Shake with cracked ice. Strain into glass.

Tom Collins

1/2 jigger fresh lemon juice
1 jigger gin
1 tsp. sugar
Sparkling water
In a tall glass, dissolve the sugar in the lemon juice; add ice cubes and gin. Fill with sparkling water. Stir.

Source: Distilled Spirits Council of the United States, Inc.

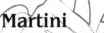

WINE GUIDE

This chart gives suggested wines and vintages to serve with various types of food. But use it only as a suggestion — your final choice is a matter of personal taste.

WHITE WINES

NAME	CHARACTERISTICS	FAVORED VINTAGES	SERVE WITH	STAY AWAY FROM
Sauturne (Bordeaux)	sweet, smooth, delicate	'82, '80, '79, '75	meat, pate, fois grois, dessert, fruits, pastries	'77, '75, '74
Graves (Bordeaux)	dry, light, fragrant	'82, '81, '79, '78	shellfish, cakes, oysters, dessert mousses, fruits, flan, veal in cream sauces	'76, '74, 72
Pouilly-Fuissé (Burgundy)	dry, vigorous, distinctive	'82, '81, '79, '78	shellfish, poached or grilled fish, egg dishes, kidneys, pork	'80, '77, '75, '74
Chablis (Burgundy)	dry, fruity, very fine	'82, '81, '80, '79	shellfish, broiled fish, cold meats, clams, oysters, egg dishes	'80, '77, '75, '74
Mâcon (Burgundy)	dry, fruity, agreeable	'82, '81, '80, '79	shellfish, cold meats, fish	'77, '76, 74
Soave (Italian)	dry, delicate	'82, '80, '79	cold chicken, broiled fish, light meats	'81, '78
Pinot Chardonnay (Calif)	dry, crisp, highly acid	'82, '80, '79, '78	oysters, shellfish, seafood ragout	
Chenin Blanc (Calif)	medium dry, much finesse	'82, '81, '79, '78	broiled fish, cold poultry, light meats	
Johannesberg Riesling (Calif)	medium dry, excellent	'81, '80, '79	broiled fish, poached fish, light meats, cold turkey or chicken	
Grey Riesling (Calif)	dry, pleasantly mild	'81, '80, '79, '78	quiche Lorraine, shellfish	
Pinot Blanc (Calif)	dry, refreshing	'80, '79, '78	cold meats, broiled fish, poached fish, cold poultry, shellfish	
Sauvignon Blanc (Calif)	dry, sweet, smokey grey	'80, '78, '77	desserts, light meats, fruits	
Semillon	sweet, fruity	'82, '81, '79, '78	good with all foods, and light meats, shellfish, broiled fish	

RED WINES

NAME	CHARACTERISTICS	SERVE WITH	FAVORED VINTAGES
Saint-Émilion (Bordeaux)	dry, light-bodied, warm	light meats, chicken, turkey,	'82, '81, '79, '76
Médoc (Bordeaux)	dry, delicate	lamb, veal, filet of beef,	'82, '81, '79, '76
Pomerol (Bordeaux)	dry, distinctive flavor	liver, fois gras, beef or lamb	'82, '81, '79, '76
Graves (Bordeaux)	dry, full-bodied	stew, hamburgers, steaks, pâtés,	'82, '81, '79, '76
Merlot (Bordeaux)	dry, delicate	soft fermented cheese, light game, pasta	'82, '81, '79, '76
Côte de Nuits (Burgundy)	dry, robust, full-bodied	rich red meats, such as prime	'82, '79, '78, '75
Côte de Beaune (Burgundy)	dry, less hearty	rib, duck, goose	'82, '79, '78, '75
Côte Chalonnaise (Burgundy)	dry, strong, very hearty	game, meats marinated in red wine, fish in heavy sauce, strong-flavored food, ripe cheese	'82, '79, '78, '75
Beaujolais	dry, refreshing, gay	turkey, roast chicken, pâtés	'82, '79, '78, '75
Bardolino (Italian)	dry, acidic, full-bodied	cheese, game, red meat	'82, '79, '77
Valpolicello (Italian)	dry, robust	cheese, game, red meat	'82, '80, '79
Cabernet Sauvignon (Calif)	dry, full-bodied, excellent	lamb, strong cheese, red meat	'79, '78, '77, '75
Petite Sirah (Calif)	dry, mellow	cheese, game, red meat, turkey	'80, '79, '78, '77
Pinot Noir (Calif)	dry, full-bodied, robust	heavier stews, red meat, cheese	'79, '77, '76
Zinfandel (Calif)	dry, rich, unique	eggs, stuffed omelets, light stews	'82, '79, '76, '77
Charbano (Calif)	dry, brash	cheese, game, red meat	'81, '80, '79
Gamay Beaujolais (Calif)	dry, fresh, fruity	ideal with picnics & barbeques	'79, '78, '77
Barbera (Calif)	dry, full-bodied	cheese, game, red meat	'82, '81, '80, '79

NAME	STAY AWAY FROM
Bardolino (Italian)	'80, '78, '75
Beaujolais	'81, '80, '78, '74
Côte de Beaune (Burgundy)	'81, '80, '78, '74
Côte Chalonnaise (Burgundy)	'81, '80, '78, '74
Côte de Nuits (Burgundy)	'81, '80, '77, '74
Graves (Bordeaux)	'80, '78, '77, '73
Médoc (Bordeaux)	'80, '78, '77, '73
Merlot (Bordeaux)	'80, '78, '77, '73
Pomerol (Bordeaux)	'80, '78, '77, '73
Saint-Émilion (Bordeaux)	'80, '78, '77, '73
Valpolicello (Italian)	'81, '78, '74

CHEESE AND WINE/FRUIT GUIDE

CHEESE	COLOR, SHAPE, FLAVOR	WINE	FRUIT
Blue, Gorgonzola	White, marbled with blue-green mold; wheel; piquant, spicy	Claret, burgundy, port, brandy, chianti, champagne	Pears, apples, oranges, peaches
Brie	Edible white crust; creamy yellow-white interior; small wheels; mellow	Dry port, cognac, calvados, burgundy	Pears, apples, peaches, nectarines, strawberries
Brick	Light yellow to orange; brick-shaped; mild	Rosés, white wine, cream sherry	Apples, cantaloupe, apricots, cherries, grapes
Camembert	Edible white crust, creamy yellow interior; small wheels; mild to pungent	All ports, red wine, pink champagne, cognac	Apples, plums, pineapple, grapes
Cheddar	White to orange; varied shapes and styles, with or without rind; mild to sharp	Ports, sherry, madeira, claret, burgundy	Apples, cherries, melon, pears, grapes
Colby	Light yellow to orange; cylindrical; mild	Ports, sherry, claret, burgundy	Apples, cherries, melon, pears
Cream	White; foil wrapped in rectangular portions; mild, slightly acid	Sparkling wines, rosés, sweet wine	Oranges, tangerines, preserved kumquats, strawberries
Edam	Creamy yellow with red wax coat; cannonball shape; mild, nutlike	Tokay, cold duck, claret, muscatel	Apples, grapes, oranges, pineapple
Gouda	Creamy yellow with or without red wax; round and flat; mild, nutlike	Tokay, cold duck, rosés	Apples, grapes, oranges, pineapple, honeydew
Liederkranz	Creamy-white, soft with edible white crust; small rectangular shape; full, delicately piquant flavor, aromatic	Dry red wines	Apples, Tokay grapes, pears
Limburger	Creamy white; rectangular; robust, highly aromatic	Dry red wines	Apples, Tokay grapes, pears
Monterey Jack	Creamy white wheels; mild	Rosés, white wines, cream sherry	Apples, cantaloupe, honeydew, apricots, pears
Muenster	Yellow, tan or white surface, creamy white interior, small wheels or blocks, mild to mellow	Rosés, white wines, cream sherry	Apples, cantaloupe, apricots, cherries, grapes, pears
Neufchatel	White; foil wrapped in rectangular portions; mild	Sparkling wines, rosés, white wines	Oranges, tangerines
Port du Salut	Creamy yellow color; firm resistant rind and soft interior; full-flavored	Red, white or rosés, light, dry and fruity	Apples, pears
Provolone	Light golden yellow to golden brown, shiny surface, bound with cord, yellowish-white interior, pear, sausage and salami shapes; mild to sharp and piquant, usually smoked	Dry red, dry white	Green grapes, apples, pears
Stilton	Blue veined, smooth	Fruit wines, port, burgundy, cognac, sherry	Oranges, tangerines
Swiss	Rindless blocks and large wheels with rind; rather sweet, nutlike	Sauterne, brut (dry) champagne, dry or sweet white wine, sparkling burgundy	Oranges, tangerines, pineapple

Source: American Dairy Association

Health & Nutrition

VITAMIN REQUIREMENTS

NAME	DEFICIENCY SYMPTOMS	BENEFITS	FOOD SOURCES	MINIMUM DAILY REQUIREMENT *
A	Night blindness; scaly eyelids; rough itchy skin; acne; adrenal gland dysfunction.	Growth & repair of cell membranes; healthy eyes, skin, reproductive system.	Milk, egg yolks, liver, kidney, heart, butter, fish, carrots, spinach, melon, fresh green vegetables.	5,000 to no more than 10,000 IU.
B$_1$ (thiamin)	Heart dysfunction; mental confusion; muscle cramps or weakness; lack of appetite, weight loss, fatigue.	Promotes proper body growth and repair.	Yeast, whole grain products, whole cereals, liver, lean pork, fresh green vegetables, steak, swordfish, orange juice.	1.5 mg.
B$_2$ (riboflavin)	Mouth lesions, anemia, tongue inflammation; low resistance to infection; intolerance to light.	Helps convert protein to energy; maintains mucuous membranes.	Dairy products, fresh green vegetables, eggs, liver, lean meat, whole grain cereals.	1.7 mg.
B$_3$ (niacin)	Dermatitis; diarrhea; dementia; inflammation of the tongue; dry scaly skin; sleeplessness.	Promotes proper body growth; may reduce blood cholesterol.	Dairy products, eggs, lean beef, liver, whole grain cereals, tuna, salmon, peanuts, lima beans, yeast.	20 mg.
B$_6$ (pyridoxine)	Convulsions; eczema; fatigue; lethargy; conjunctivitis.	Controls function of red blood cells; helps prevent cavities and dental infection; aids hormone function and production of bile salts.	Beef liver, kidneys, pork loin, ham, leg of veal, all fresh fish, bananas, cabbage, avocados.	2 mg.

As recommended by the Food and Drug Administration for adults and children over four years of age.

VITAMIN REQUIREMENTS

NAME	DEFICIENCY SYMPTOMS	BENEFITS	FOOD SOURCES	MINIMUM DAILY REQUIREMENT
Pantothenic Acid (B₅)	Fatigue; lethargy; headache; general malaise; sleeplessness; nausea; vomiting.	Required for the synthesis of hormones; promotes intake of amino acids.	Beef, lamb, pork, liver, kidney, lima beans, cashews, walnuts, egg yolks, yeast, broccoli, kale, avocado, split peas, lentils.	10 mg.
Biotin	Lethargy; sleeplessness; muscle pain; numbness; eczema; loss of appetite; nausea.	Maintains sweat glands, nerve tissue, bone marrow, male sex glands, blood cells, skin tone & hair quality.	Liver, kidney, egg yolks, fresh vegetables.	0.3 mg.
Folic Acid	Anemia; behavioral difficulties; irritability; convulsion; birth defects.	Regulates fetal development of nerve cells; maintains sex organs; intestinal tract, white blood cells, nervous system.	Liver, kidney, wheat germ, yeast, spinach, broccoli, endive, swiss chard.	04 mg.
B₁₂ (cobalamin)	Pernicious anemia.	Helps regulate function of red blood cells; essential to liver, neural, kidney, heart, muscle & bone metabolism.	Liver, kidney, round beef, shellfish, camembert cheese, milk, eggs.	6 mcg.
C (ascorbic acid)	Adrenal gland dysfunction; scurvy; slow-healing wounds.	Assists in formation of bones & teeth; stimulates white blood cell growth.	Lemons, oranges, limes, liver, mangos, broccoli, spinach, apples, lettuce.	60 mg.
D	Rickets.	Regulates growth & repair of bones.	Milk, cod liver oil.	400 IU
E (tocopherol)	Reproductive failure; heart degeneration; eye and other organ disturbances.	Essential for proper digestion of polyunsaturated fats; may slow aging process; ensures proper function of circulatory, nervous, digestive, excretory & respiratory systems.	Fresh beef liver, wheat germ, fruits, green leafy vegetables, margarine, mayonnaise, nuts, vegetable oils.	30 IU
K	Hemorrhages, liver damage.	Helps blood clotting and improves liver function.	Spinach, lettuce, kale, kelp, alfalfa, cabbage, cauliflower, liver, fish oils, egg yolk, blackstrap molasses.	No RDA

A GUIDE TO MINERALS

MACROMINERALS

These nutrients are needed in relatively large amounts for your body's normal processes.

CALCIUM
RDA*: 1,000 mg (800 mg)

Importance
Essential for strong bones and teeth; needed for normal response of muscles and nerves; controls blood clotting

Sources
Milk and other dairy products, dark green leafy vegetables (broccoli, spinach, kale, turnip and mustard greens), molasses, almonds, dried peas and beans, citrus fruits, sardines

Deficiency/Excess
Too little: Rickets and low growth rate in children, osteoporosis (fragile, thinning bones) in older women
Too much: Drowsiness, calcium deposits, kidney stones

MAGNESIUM
RDA: 400 mg (200 mg)

Importance
Essential for healthy nerves and muscles and for releasing energy; builds strong bones and teeth; helps body adjust to cold temperatures

Sources
Green leafy vegetables, almonds and cashews, wheat germ, soybeans, seeds, apples, corn, figs

Deficiency/Excess
Too little: Weakness, sleeplessness, muscle cramps, tremors, irregular heartbeat
Too much: Calcium imbalance

PHOSPHORUS
RDA: 1,000 mg (800 mg)

Importance
Essential for strong bones and teeth; needed for growth, cell maintenance and energy

Sources
Milk, cheese, egg yolk, whole grains, wheat germ, dried peas and beans, mustard, nuts, turkey, cod

Deficiency/Excess
Too little: Weight lost, anemia, abnormal growth
Too much: A calcium imbalance or deficiency

POTASSIUM
No RDA

Importance
Maintains fluid and electrolyte balance in the cells; helps to control nerves and muscles and to release energy from food

Sources
Bananas, raisins, sunflower and sesame seeds, nuts, dried peas and beans, potatoes, oranges, meats, mint leaves

Deficiency/Excess
Too little: An electrolyte imbalance; weakness, abnormal heart rhythms (arrhythmia), kidney and lung failure
Too much: Abnormal heart rhythms

SODIUM
No RDA (but see "High-Sodium Foods," page 53)

Importance
Attracts water into the blood vessels and maintains normal blood pressure and volume; needed for proper functioning of nerves and muscles

Sources
Table salt, most processed foods, sauerkraut, pickles, celery, soy sauce, beet greens, chard

Deficiency/Excess
Too little: An electrolyte imbalance
Too much: Water retention and swelling, high blood pressure (hypertension), heart and kidney diseases, stroke

SULFUR
No RDA

Importance
Keeps skin, hair and nails healthy

Sources
Wheat germ, peanuts, dried peas and beans, beets, clams

Deficiency/Excess
Too little: Effect not known
Too much: Effect not known

TRACE MINERALS

These microminerals are used in relatively small amounts by the body, so you need only tiny doses in your daily diet.

COPPER
RDA: 2 mg (1 mg)

Importance
Helps in utilizing and storing iron for development of hemoglobin in red blood cells, and for bones, nerves and connective tissues

Sources
Abundant in most unprocessed foods, particularly shellfish, dried peas and beans, nuts, organ meats, egg yolk

Deficiency/Excess
Too little : Anemia, poor growth, respiratory ailments — but deficiency is uncommon
Too much: Diarrhea, vomiting

IODINE
RDA: 150 mcg (70 mcg)

Importance
Regulates metabolism and helps thyroid gland function properly

Sources
Seafood, iodized salt

Deficiency/Excess
Too little: Goiter (overgrown thyroid)
Too much: No effect known

IRON
RDA: 18 mg (10 mg)

Importance
Manufactures hemoglobin (the oxygen-carrying compound in red blood cells); helps cells release energy; increases resistance to stress and disease

Sources
Liver and other organ meats, shellfish, lean meats, egg yolk, green leafy vegetables, dried beans, peas, dried fruits, molasses, whole-grain cereals

Deficiency/Excess
Too little: Anemia
Too much: Toxic levels in the body

MANGANESE
No RDA

Importance
Activates enzymes in the body; forms and maintains bones and tendons

Sources
Found in many foods, particularly bran, wheat germ, tea, coffee, nuts, peas, beans

Deficiency/Excess
Too little: Effect not known — deficiency uncommon
Too much: Blurred speech, tremors

ZINC
RDA: 15 mg (8 mg)

Importance
Essential for general growth and the development of reproductive organs; helps move carbon dioxide to the lungs to be exhaled; helps healing

Sources
Lean meats, eggs, liver, seafood, green leafy vegetables, nuts, milk, whole-grain cereals

Deficiency/Excess
Too little: Decrease in sense of taste and smell, slowed growth and healing, delayed sexual maturity
Too much: Nausea, vomiting, stomach pain, anemia

---

*These U.S. Recommended Daily Allowances (RDAs) were adapted by the Food and Drug Administration from recommendations published by the Food and Nutrition Board of the National Acadamy of Sciences National Research Council. The figures given here are for adults and children 4 years and older; the numbers in parentheses are RDAs for children under 4 years old.

Sources: U.S. Dept. of Agriculture; Food and Drug Administration

HIGH-FIBER FOODS

	Serving	Calories	Grams of Fiber
Breads and Cereals			
All Bran-Extra Fiber†™	1/2 cup	60	13.0
Fiber-One™	1/2 cup	60	12.0
All-Bran, Fruit & Almonds™	2/3 cup	100	10.0
100% Bran™	1/2 cup	75	8.4
All Bran™	1/3 cup	70	8.5
Bran Buds™	1/3 cup	75	7.9
Bran Chex™	2/3 cup	90	4.6
Corn bran™	2/3 cup	100	5.4
Cracklin' Oat Bran™	1/3 cup	110	4.3
Bran Flakes	3/4 cup	90	4.0
Grapenuts™	1/4 cup	100	1.4
Air-popped popcorn	1 cup	25	2.5
Whole-wheat bread	1 slice	60	1.4
Whole-wheat spaghetti	1 cup	120	3.9
Legumes, cooked			
Kidney beans	1/2 cup	110	7.3
Lima beans	1/2 cup	130	4.5
Navy beans	1/2 cup	110	6.0
Vegetables, cooked			
Beans, green	1/2 cup	15	1.6
Broccoli	1/2 cup	20	2.2
Brussels sprouts	1/2 cup	30	2.3
Cabbage, red and white	1/2 cup	15	1.4
Carrots	1/2 cup	25	2.3
Cauliflower	1/2 cup	15	1.1
Corn	1/2 cup	70	2.9
Green peas	1/2 cup	55	3.6
Kale	1/2 cup	20	1.4
Parsnip	1/2 cup	50	2.7
Potato, with skin	1 medium	95	2.5
Fruits			
Apple	1 medium	80	3.5
Apricot, fresh	3 medium	50	1.8
Apricot, dried	5 halves	40	1.4
Banana	1 medium	105	2.4
Blueberries	1/2 cup	40	2.0
Cantaloupe	1/4 melon	50	1.0
Cherries	10	50	1.2
Dates, dried	3	70	1.9
Dried prunes	3	60	3.0
Grapefruit	1/2	40	1.6
Orange	1 medium	60	2.6
Peach	1 medium	35	1.9
Pineapple	1/2 cup	40	1.1
Raisins	1/4 cup	110	3.1
Strawberries	1 cup	45	3.0

† The use of trademark names is for identification purposes only.

Source: National Cancer Institute

GUIDE TO HIGH-SODIUM CONTENT FOODS

Though your body does need sodium to function properly, most Americans consume much more than the 1,100 to 3,300 mg recommended by the National Academy of Sciences. Too much of this mineral in your diet may contribute to high blood pressure or hypertension. The following foods and products contain high amounts of sodium per average serving and would best be avoided if you are concerned about hypertension.

BEVERAGES
- Condensed milk
- Chocolate milk
- Fruit-flavored powdered drink mixes
- Instant cocoa mixes
- Instant coffee treated with a sodium compound such as sodium hydroxide
- Malted milk, milk shakes, and all other kinds of fountain drinks
- Mineral waters (check label)
- Salted buttermilk
- Soft drinks, regular and low-calorie

DAIRY PRODUCTS
(Also see Beverages)
- Cheeses, unless low-sodium dietetic
- Ice cream
- Sherbet
- Salted cottage cheese

EGGS, MEAT, POULTRY, SEAFOOD
- Brains or kidneys
- Canned, salted or smoked meats (bacon, bologna, chipped or corned beef, ham, hotdogs, meats koshered by salting, luncheon meats, salt pork, sausage, smoked tongue)
- Canned, salted or smoked fish (anchovies, caviar, salted cod, herring, sardines, etc.)
- Canned tuna or salmon, unless low-sodium
- Egg substitutes
- Frozen fish fillets
- Shellfish (clams, crabs, lobsters, oysters, scallops, shrimp, etc.)
- Smoked turkey or chicken

FATS
- Bacon and bacon fat
- Butter or margarine, regular
- Commercial salad dressings or mayonnaise, unless low-sodium dietetic
- Party spreads and dips
- Salt pork

FRUITS
- Canned fruits (check label for sodium content)
- Cranberry sauce
- Dried or sulfured fruits

GRAIN PRODUCTS
- Breads, crackers, etc. (regular)
- Commercial mixes
- Cooked cereal containing a sodium compound (read label)
- Dry cereals with more than 6 mg sodium per 100 g cereal
- Self-rising cornmeal or self-rising flour
- Stuffing mixes

SNACKS AND SWEETS
- Commercial candies

- Commercial gelatin and pudding mixes
- Corn chips
- Peanut brittle
- Peanut butter
- Pretzels
- Popcorn, salted
- Potato chips
- Salted nuts

SOUPS
- All canned or dehydrated varieties, unless low-sodium dietetic or homemade

VEGETABLES AND SALADS
- Any canned vegetables or vegetable juices, unless low-sodium dietetic
- Any frozen vegetables if processed with salt
- Commercial salads (macaroni, pasta, bean)
- Fermented soybeans (miso)
- Frozen peas and lima beans (check label for sodium content)
- Artichokes
- Beet greens
- Beets
- Carrots
- Celery
- Chard
- Dandelion greens
- Whole hominy
- Kale
- Mustard greens
- Sauerkraut
- Spinach
- White turnips

CONDIMENTS AND SEASONINGS
- Barbecue sauces
- Bouillon in any form (if not homemade)
- Catsup
- Celery leaves or flakes
- Celery salt
- Celery seed
- Chili sauce
- Cooking wine
- Garlic salt
- Horseradish (if made with salt)
- Meat and vegetable extracts (if not homemade)
- Meat sauces
- Meat tenderizers
- Molasses
- Olives
- Onion salt
- Pickles
- Prepared mustard
- Relishes
- Salt substitutes (unless recommended by your doctor)
- Sodium cyclamate
- Sodium saccharin
- Soy sauce
- Worcestershire sauce

NONPRESCRIPTION MEDICINES
- Alkalizers or antacids
- Antibiotics
- Cough medicines
- Headaches remedies (other than plain aspirin)
- Laxatives
- Sedatives

READ THE LABEL: SODIUM COMPOUNDS TO LOOK OUT FOR
- Baking soda (bicarbonate of soda, sodium bicarbonate)
- Baking powder
- Brine (salt and water)
- Di-sodium phosphate
- Monosodium glutamate (MSG)
- Salt (sodium chloride)
- Sodium alginate
- Sodium benzoate
- Sodium cyclamate
- Sodium hydroxide
- Sodium propionate
- Sodium saccharin
- Sodium sulfite

Sources: American Heart Association; U.S. Dept. of Agriculture

DRUG INTERACTIONS

Combining certain food or beverages or other drugs with some prescription and nonprescription medications can cause dangerous side effects, or at least limit the medication's effectiveness. Here's a list of some common interactions, but be sure to check with your physician about possible consequences when taking any medication.

DRUG	COMBINED WITH	MAY CAUSE
ANTIHISTAMINES* e.g. — brompheniramine (Dimetane, Bromphen), chlorpheniramine (Chlor-Trimeton, Teldrin), diphenhydramine (Benadryl, Benaphen)	Alcohol	Drowsiness, slowed reactions
BRONCHODILATORS e.g. — aminophylline (Phyllocontin, Somophyllin), theophylline (Slo-Phyllin, Theo-Dur)	Foods or beverages containing caffeine (chocolate, cocoa, coffee, tea, colas)	Rapid heartbeat, jitteriness, insomnia
ANTICOAGULANTS e.g. — warfarin (Coumadin, Panwarfin), heparin (Liquaemin)	1. Vitamin K-rich foods (spinach, brussels sprouts, etc.) 2. Acetaminophen, aspirin, ibuprofen, penicillin, tricyclic antidepressants	1. Reduced effectiveness of drug, resulting in blood clots 2. Internal bleeding because they increase blood-thinning effect of drug
ANTIHYPERTENSIVES atenol (Tenormin), capotpril (Capoten), hydralazine (Apresoline), methyldopa (aldomet), metoprolol (Lopressor)	Sodium (salt) or natural licorice (which also causes water retention)	Elevated blood pressure
DIURETICS e.g. — furosemide (Lasix), hydrochlorothiazide (HCTZ; Esidrix, Hydrodiuril), triameterene (Dyrenium)	1. Other heart drugs — such as digitalis, metaprolol, propanolol — and blood pressure drugs, such as reserpine 2. Lithium	1. Extremely low blood pressure, irregular heartbeat 2. Lithium to have toxic effect
VASODILATORS e.g. — nitroglycerine (Nitrogard, Nitrostat)	Sodium (salt)	Elevated blood pressure
BIRTH-CONTROL PILLS Norethindrone and ethinyl (Loestrin), norethinodrone and mestranol (Ortho-Novum)	1. Barbituates, penicillins 2. Smoking	1. Decreased effectiveness and result in unplanned pregnancy 2. Blood clotting or heart attack
ERYTHROMYCIN e.g. — erythromycin (E-Mycin), erythromycin estolate (Ilosone), erythromycin ethysuccinate (E.E.S., E-Mycin E)	1. Acidic beverages (soft drinks, fruit juices) 2. Penicillins	1. A delay in recovery from infection 2. Reduced effectiveness of penicillins
METRONIDAZOLE e.g. — Flagyl	Alcohol	Stomach pain, nausea, vomiting, headache, flushed face
PENICILLINS e.g. — amoxicillin, ampicillin, bacampicillin, penicillin G and penicillin V	Any food (except when taken with amoxicillin, bacampicillin); citrus fruits and juices; erythromycins, tetracyclines	Reduced effectiveness of drug
SULFA DRUGS co-trimoxazole (Bactrim, Septra), sulisoxazole (Gantrisin)	Alcohol	Nausea

*Many over-the-counter antihistamines contain aspirin in combination with other active ingredients, so also check ASPIRIN interactions.

DRUG	COMBINED WITH	MAY CAUSE
TETRACYCLINES e.g. — tetracycline hydrochloride (Acrhromycin, Symycin, Panmycin)	Dairy products (milk, yogurt, cheese) or calcium or iron supplements, within two hours of taking drug	Delayed recovery from infection
MAO INHIBITORS isocarboxazid (Marplan), phenelzine (Nardil), tranycypromine (Parnate)	Foods high in tyramine: alcoholic beverages such as beer, sherry, wine (especially chianti); avocados, bananas; caffeine; cheeses, especially strong, aged varieties, chocolate; fava beans; canned figs; beef or chicken livers, meat prepared with tenderizers; aged meats (salami, pepperoni, bologna); pickled herring; pineapple; raisins; sauerkraut; sour cream; soy sauce; yeast extract; yogurt	Sudden, severe high blood pressure — potentially fatal
ACETAMINOPHEN e.g. — Anacin 3 with Codeine, Datril, Liquiprin, Pavadon, Tempra, Tylenol	1. Alcoholic beverages 2. Crackers, bread, carbohydrates 3. Blood-thinning drugs	1. Liver damage 2. Delay in relief of pain and fever 3. Increase blood-thinning effect
ASPIRIN e.g. — Anacin, Bayer, Bufferin, Empirin, etc.	Alcohol, fruit juices; blood-thinning drugs	Increased risk of stomach ulcers, internal bleeding (Don't take aspirin on an empty stomach)
CODEINE e.g. — aspirin with codeine, Tylenol with Codeine	1. Alcohol 2. An empty stomach	1. Increased sedation 2. Stomach irritation (Take with meals, small snacks or milk)
CORTICOSTEROIDS e.g. — betamethasone, dexamethasone, hydrocortisone, methylprednisolone, prednisone, triamcinolone	1. Alcohol 2. Sodium (salt)	1. Increased stomach irritation 2. Water retension, swelling
OTHER NARCOTIC ANALGESICS e.g. — meperidine, morphine, oxycodone, pentazocine, propoxyphene	Alcohol	Blood pressure to drop too low and depressed nervous system and breathing (Take with food to reduce stomach irritation)
IBUPROFEN AND OTHER ANTI-INFLAMMATORY AGENTS ibuprofen (Advil, Haltran, Medipren, Motrin, Nuprin), naproxen (Naprosyn)	1. Alcohol, anticoagulant drugs 2. Aspirin, acidic foods	1. Internal bleeding or ulcers 2. Stomach upset (Take with food or milk)
BARBITURATES e.g. — pentobarbital (Nembutal), phenobarbital (Barbita, Luminal), secobarbital (Seconal, Secobarbital and amobarbital (Tuinal)	1. Alcohol 2. Anticoagulants	1. Increased drowsiness, breathing failure, drop in blood pressure 2. Decreased blood-thinning effect of drugs
ANTACIDS Alumna and magnesia (Maalox), dihydroxaluminum sodium carbonate Rolaids), magnesia (Milk of Magnesia)	Some blood-pressure and blood-thinning drugs, tetracyclines	Difference in effectiveness of drugs
ULCER MEDICATIONS cimetidine (Tagamet), famotidine (Pepcid), ranitidine (Zantac)	Poor diet	Increased stomach irritation, damage to stomach lining (Follow diet prescribed by your doctor)

Sources: National Consumers League, Food and Drug Administration, American Pharmaceutical Association

HEALTH DANGER SIGNALS

These symptoms may indicate a more serious illness and the need for medical attention.

1. Loss of appetite.
2. Excessive thirst.
3. Rapid weight loss (10 pounds in 10 weeks) or gain — without a change in eating habits.
4. A sore or bruise that does not heal within three weeks.
5. A mole or other skin growth that changes in color, shape or size or that starts to itch or bleed.
6. Bluish tinge to lips, fingernails or inside of eye lids.
7. Chronic swelling of ankles.
8. Severe headaches, for no apparent reason.
9. Unmotivated episodes of dizziness or fainting.
10. Disturbances in sight, smell or balance.
11. Persistent tremors or shaking in one part of body.
12. Persistent joint pain.
13. Shortness of breath — for no obvious reason.
14. Chest pain.
15. Unusual numbness, tingling or pain in arms or hands.
16. Hoarseness that lasts for more than a week.
17. Persistent cough.
18. Coughing up bloody phlegm.
19. Difficulty swallowing.
20. Sudden vomiting, not preceded by nausea.
21. Vomiting blood or a black or dark brown substance.
22. Persistent abdominal pain or indigestion.
23. Attacks of constipation or diarrhea, or other change in your normal bowel habits.
24. Black, tarry stools.
25. Bleeding from the rectum.
26. Bloody or cloudy urination.
27. Painful or difficult urination.
28. Unusual discharge or bleeding from tip of the penis in men; from the nipples in women.
29. For women, change in breast shape or skin (puckering or bulging) or a lump or thickening in breast.
30. For women, "spotting" or vaginal bleeding between period or after menopause.

Sources: American Cancer Society, American Diabetes Association, American Heart Association

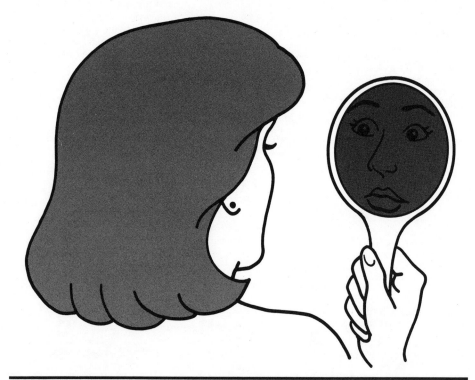

GUIDE TO GENERIC DRUGS

A drug sold under its generic (descriptive) name is less expensive than, and just as effective as, one with the manufacturer's brand name. Before buying any over-the-counter medication, look for its generic equivalent, as given below. For prescription drugs, ask your doctor to prescribe a generic.

Brand name	Generic name	Drug type	Class
Achromycin	Tetracycline	Tetracycline	Antibiotic
Adapin	Doxepin	Tricyclic anti-depressant	Antidepressant
Advil	Ibuprofen	Analgesic	Painkiller (over the counter)
Amcill	Ampicillin	Penicillin	Antibiotic
Amoxil	Amoxicillin	Penicillin	Antibiotic
Anacin	Aspirin and caffeine	Salicylate	Painkiller (over the counter)
Anacin 3 with codeine	Acetaminophen and codeine	Narcotic analgesic	Painkiller
Anhydron	Cyclothiazide	Thiazide diuretic	Blood pressure drug
Aquatensen	Methyclothiazide	Thiazide diuretic	Blood pressure drug
Ascriptin	Buffered aspirin	Salicylate	Painkiller (over the counter)
Asendin	Amoxapine	Tricyclic anti-depressant	Antidepressant
Barbita	Phenobarbital	Narcotic analgesic	Barbiturate
Bayer	Aspirin	Salicylate	Painkiller (over the counter)
Bromo Seltzer	Buffered acetaminophen	Analgesic	Painkiller (over the counter)
Bufferin	Buffered aspirin	Salicylate	Painkiller (over the counter)
Coufarin	Warfarin sodium	Estrogen	Blood-thinning drug
Coumadin	Warfarin sodium	Estrogen	Blood-thinning drug
Darvon	Propoxyphene	Narcotic analgesic	Painkiller
Datril	Acetaminophen	Analgesic	Painkiller (over the counter)
Declomycin	Demeclocycline doxycycline	Tetracycline	Antibiotic
Demerol	Meperidine	Narcotic analgesic	Painkiller
Diabinese	Chlorpropamide	Insulin	Antidiabetic
Digifortis	Digitalis	Digitalis glycoside	Heart drug
Digiglusin	Digitalis	Digitalis glycoside	Heart drug
Dilantin	Phenytoin	Benzodiazepine	Antiseizure drug
Dolacet	Propoxyphene and acetaminophen	Narcotic analgesic	Painkiller
Dolene	Propoxyphene	Narcotic analgesic	Painkiller
Duretic	Methyclothiazide	Thiazide diuretic	Blood pressure drug
E-Mycin	Erythromycin	Erythromycin	Antibiotic
Elavil	Amitriptyline	Tricyclic antidepressant	Antidepressant
Empirin	Aspirin	Salicylate	Painkiller (over the counter)

Brand name	Generic name	Drug type	Class
Empracet with Codeine	Acetaminophen and codeine	Narcotic analgesic	Painkiller
Endep	Amitriptyline	Tricyclic antidepressant	Antidepressant
Enduron	Methyclothiazide	Thiazide diuretic	Blood pressure drug
Enovid	Norethynodrel and mestranol	Estrogen	Birth control drug
Erythrocin	Erythromycin lactobionate	Erythromycin	Antibiotic
Iletin	Isophane insulin suspension	Insulin	Antidiabetic
Inderal	Propranolol	Beta-adrenergic blocking agent	Heart drug
Insulatard	Isophane insulin suspension	Insulin	Antidiabetic
Lanoxin	Digoxin	Digitalis glycoside	Heart drug
Lasix	Furosemide	Thiazide diuretic	Blood pressure drug
Librium	Chlordiazepoxide	Benzodiazepine	Antiseizure drug
Liquaemin	Heparin	Estrogen	Blood-thinning drug
Liquiprin	Acetaminophen	Analgesic	Painkiller (over the counter)
Lithane	Lithium carbonate	Tricyclic antidepressant	Antidepressant
Lithonate	Lithium carbonate	Tricyclic antidepressant	Antidepressant
Lithotabs	Lithium carbonate	Tricyclic antidepressant	Antidepressant
Loestrin	Norethindrone and ethinyl	Estrogen	Birth control drug
Lopressor	Metoprolol	Beta-adrenergic blocking agent	Heart drug
Luminal	Phenobarbital	Narcotic analgesic	Barbiturate
Maalox	Alumina and magnesia	Antacid	Antacid (over the counter)
Marplan	Isocarboxazid	Tricyclic anti-depressant	MAO inhibitor
Measurin	Aspirin	Salicylate	Painkiller (over the counter)
Motrin	Ibuprofen	Analgesic	Painkiller (over the counter)
Nardil	Phenelzine	Tricyclic anti-depressant	MAO inhibitor
Nembutal	Pentobarbital	Narcotic analgesic	Barbiturate
Nuprin	Ibuprofen	Analgesic	Painkiller (over the counter)
Ortho-Novum	Norethindrone and mestranol	Estrogen	Birth control drug
Panmycin	Tetracycline	Tetracycline	Antibiotic
Pargesic 65	Propoxyphene	Narcotic analgesic	Painkiller
Parnate	Tranylcypromine	Tricyclic anti-depressant	MAO inhibitor
Pavadon	Acetaminophen and codeine	Narcotic analgesic	Painkiller
Pethadol	Meperidine	Narcotic analgesic	Painkiller

Brand name	Generic name	Drug type	Class
Pheno-Squar	Phenobarbital	Narcotic analgesic	Barbiturate
Phillips Milk of Magnesia	Magnesia	Antacid	Antacid (over the counter)
Proxagesic	Propoxyphene	Narcotic analgesic	Painkiller
Proxene	Propoxyphene	Narcotic analgesic	Painkiller
Rau-Sed	Reserpine	Rauwolfia alkaloid	Blood pressure drug
Robimycin	Erythromycin	Erythromycin	Antibiotic
Rolaids	Dihydroxaluminum sodium carbonate	Antacid	Antacid (over the counter)
Sandril	Reserpine	Rauwolfia alkaloid	Blood pressure drug
Seconal	Secobarbital	Narcotic analgesic	Barbiturate
Serpasil	Reserpine	Rauwolfia alkaloid	Blood pressure drug
Sinequan	Doxepin	Trycyclic anti-depressant	Antidepressant
St. Joseph	Aspirin	Salicylate	Painkiller (over the counter)
Tegretol	Carbamazepine	Benzodiazepine	Antiseizure drug
Tempra	Acetaminophen	Analgesic	Painkiller (over the counter)
Tetracyn	Tetracycline	Tetracycline	Antibiotic
Tolinase	Tolazamide	Insulin	Antidiabetic
Tuinal	Secobarbital and amobarbital	Narcotic analgesic	Barbiturate
Tylenol	Acetaminophen	Analgesic	Painkiller (over the counter)
Tylenol with codeine	Acetaminophen and codeine	Narcotic analgesic	Painkiller
Valadol	Acetaminophen	Analgesic	Painkiller (over the counter)
Valium	Diazepam	Benzodiazepine	Antiseizure drug
Valrelease	Diazepam	Benzodiazepine	Antiseizure drug
Vibramycin	Demeclocyline doxycycline	Tetracycline	Antibiotic

Source: Food and Drug Administration

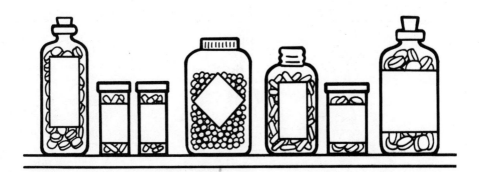

THE HUMAN SKELETON

Here's an inside look at what keeps your body together.

BONES (Front view)

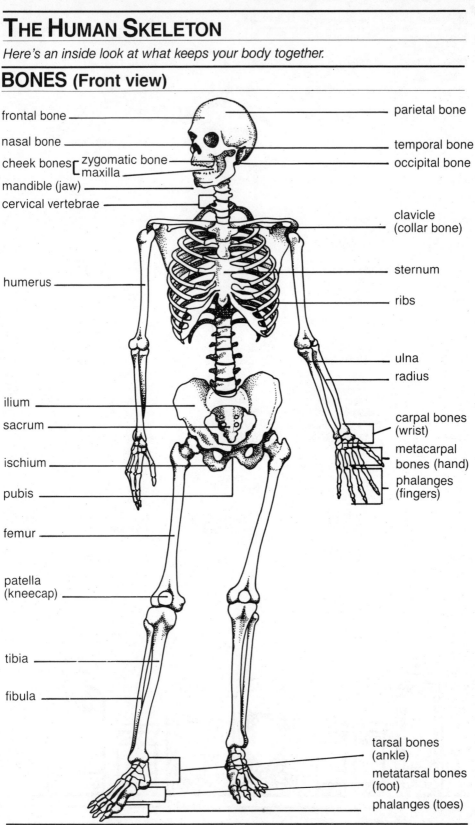

frontal bone

nasal bone

cheek bones ⎧ zygomatic bone
            ⎩ maxilla

mandible (jaw)

cervical vertebrae

humerus

ilium

sacrum

ischium

pubis

femur

patella
(kneecap)

tibia

fibula

parietal bone

temporal bone

occipital bone

clavicle
(collar bone)

sternum

ribs

ulna

radius

carpal bones
(wrist)

metacarpal
bones (hand)

phalanges
(fingers)

tarsal bones
(ankle)

metatarsal bones
(foot)

phalanges (toes)

BONES (Back view)

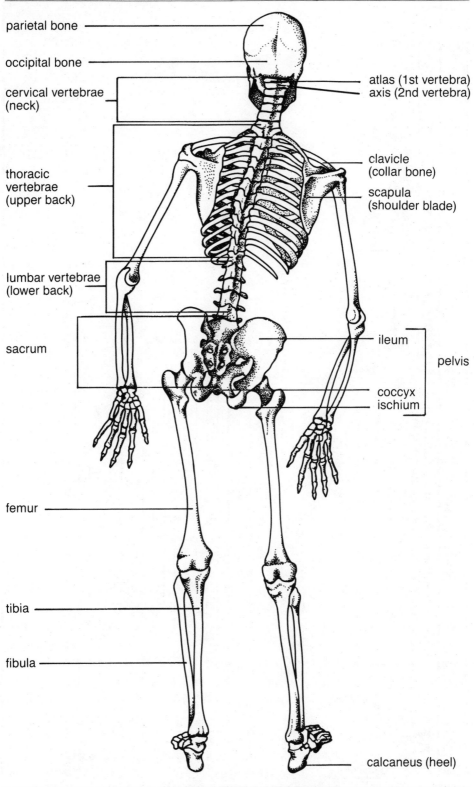

parietal bone

occipital bone

cervical vertebrae
(neck)

thoracic
vertebrae
(upper back)

lumbar vertebrae
(lower back)

sacrum

femur

tibia

fibula

atlas (1st vertebra)
axis (2nd vertebra)

clavicle
(collar bone)

scapula
(shoulder blade)

ileum

pelvis

coccyx
ischium

calcaneus (heel)

WEEKLY WEIGHT LOSS CHART

Weighing more than the suggested weight ranges below can be hazardous to your health. Try to reduce weight gradually by increasing physical activity; eating less fat and fatty foods, sugar and sweets; and avoiding alcohol. Always weigh yourself only once a week, on the same day, to allow for the body's natural weight fluctuations.

Initial Weight: _____

	WEIGHT	– / + LBS.
Week 1:	_____	_____
Week 2:	_____	_____
Week 3:	_____	_____
Week 4:	_____	_____
Week 5:	_____	_____
Week 6:	_____	_____
Week 7:	_____	_____
Week 8:	_____	_____
Week 9:	_____	_____
Week 10:	_____	_____
Week 11:	_____	_____
Week 12:	_____	_____
Week 13:	_____	_____
Week 14:	_____	_____
Week 15:	_____	_____
Week 16:	_____	_____
Week 17:	_____	_____
Week 18:	_____	_____
Week 19:	_____	_____
Week 20:	_____	_____
Week 21:	_____	_____
Week 22:	_____	_____
Week 23:	_____	_____
Week 24:	_____	_____

Source: U.S. Dept. of Agriculture (HEW conference on obesity, 1973)

DESIRABLE WEIGHTS

These ranges are based on statistics that relate weight to longevity. Heights given are without shoes; weight, without clothes.

HEIGHT	WOMEN	MEN
4'10"	92-119	—
4'11"	94-122	—
5'	96-125	—
5'1"	99-128	—
5'2"	102-131	112-141
5'3"	105-134	115-144
5'4'	108-138	118-148
5'5"	111-142	121-152
5'6"	114-146	124-156
5'7"	118-150	128-161
5'8"	122-154	132-166
5'9"	126-158	136-170
5'10"	130-163	140-174
5'11"	134-168	144-179
6'	138-173	148-184
6'1"	—	152-189
6'2"	—	156-194
6'3"	—	160-199
6'4"	—	164-204

Breast Self-Examination (BSE)

Breast self-examination should be done once a month so you become familiar with the usual appearance and feel of your breasts. Familiarity makes it easier to notice any changes in the breast from one month to another. Early discovery of a change from what is "normal" is the main idea behind BSE.

If you menstruate, the best time to do BSE is 2 or 3 days after your period ends, when your breasts are least likely to be tender or swollen. If you no longer menstruate, pick a day, such as the first day of the month, to remind yourself it is time to do BSE.

Here is how to do BSE:

1. Stand before a mirror. Inspect both breasts for anything unusual, such as any discharge from the nipples, puckering, dimpling, or scaling of the skin.

The next two steps are designed to emphasize any change in the shape or contour of your breasts. As you do them you should be able to feel your chest muscles tighten.

2. Watching closely in the mirror, clasp hands behind your head and press hands forward.

3. Next, press hands firmly on hips and bow slightly toward your mirror as you pull your shoulders and elbows forward.

Some women do the next part of the exam in the shower. Fingers slide over soapy skin, making it easy to concentrate on the texture underneath.

4. Raise your left arm. Use three or four fingers of your right hand to explore your left breast firmly, carefully, and thoroughly. Beginning at the outer edge,

press the flat part of your fingers in small circles, moving the circles slowly around the breast. Gradually work toward the nipple. Be sure to cover the entire breast. Pay special attention to the area between the breast and the armpit, including the armpit itself. Feel for any unusual lump or mass under the skin.

5. Gently squeeze the nipple and look for a discharge. Repeat the exam on your right breast.

6. Steps 4 and 5 should be repeated lying down. Lie flat on your back, left arm over your head and a pillow or folded towel under your left shoulder. This position flattens the breast and makes it easier to examine. Use the same circular motion described earlier.

Repeat on your right breast.

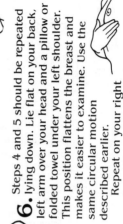

Source: U.S. Dept. of Health and Human Services; National Cancer Institute

CHILDHOOD ILLNESSES

These are the most common diseases of childhood. An infected child should be kept home, given a variety of liquids and encouraged to rest, but not be forced to stay in bed or eat solid food. Always consult your physician first before administering any treatment.

ILLNESSES	SYMPTOMS	TREATMENT
Chickenpox	Small red spots filled with fluid, which burst or dry out after a few days and crust over; mild fever.	Itching may be relieved with a lotion or wet compresses. Do not give aspirin unless directed by doctor.
Diphtheria*	Fever; swollen neck glands; sometimes, a grayish membrane in nose or throat that may cause swallowing or breathing difficulty.	Treated with antitoxin and antibiotics and prolonged bed rest.
Middle-ear infection	Earache, feeling of fullness in ear; fever; impaired hearing; sometimes, discharge from ear.	To relieve pain: acetaminophen; heating pad on low setting, against ear. Antibiotics and ear drops are often prescribed.
Measles*	Fever, runny nose, hacking cough, red eyes; by day 3, tiny white spots appear inside mouth, sore throat develops; by day 4 or 5, red, raised spots appear around ears, then spread over body.	Fluids, medication (gamma globulin), confinement. Relieve itching with calamine lotion.
Mumps*	Chills, moderate fever, loss of appetite, swelling of one or both glands between ears and jaw, pain in chewing or swallowing (in boys, testes may become inflamed).	Fluids, soft diet, medication and confinement. Apply warm compresses to swollen area.
Pinworms	Itching around anal area (tiny white worms can sometimes be seen in bowel movement or around child's anus at night).	Medication for entire family. Relieve inflammation with ointment. Wash all bedding and underwear in very hot water.
Poliomyelitis*	Headache, sore throat, fever pain and stiffness in back and neck muscles; in severe cases, weakness or paralysis of arms or legs; or difficulty in swallowing, speaking or breathing.	For mild cases, bed rest. For severe cases, moist heat, physical therapy, medication; or mechanical respiration. Must be under a doctor's care.
Roseola	High fever for 3 or 4 days; after fever falls, reddish pink rash appears on chest and abdomen.	Bed rest, fluids. May reduce fever with sponge baths.
Rubella (German measles)	Swollen lymph nodes at back of ears and neck, slight fever; by day 3, reddish, nonitchy spots appear on face, then spread.	Rest, fluids. Little risk to children, but dangerous to fetus if contracted in early pregnancy.
Scarlet fever	Very high fever, sore throat, vomiting, furred tongue; by day 2, bright red rash appears on face, then spreads; bright red tongue.	Bed rest, fluids, prescribed antibiotic. The danger is that it could develop into rheumatic fever if left untreated.
Strep throat	Severe sore throat, tonsillitis, fever (may take the form of scarlet fever, as described above).	Bed rest; antibiotic may be prescribed. The danger is that it could develop into rheumatic fever if left untreated.
Whooping* cough	Runny nose, sneezing, thick mucus, hacking cough that becomes more severe, leaving child gasping; vomiting may follow bouts of coughing.	May require hospitalization. At home, bed rest, antibiotics, smaller but more frequent meals (to lessen vomiting).

*Preventive vaccine is available (see page 65 for immunization schedule).

Source: Richard L. Saphir, M.D., Clinical Professor of Pediatrics, Mount Sinai Hospital, New York, N.Y.

YOUR CHILDREN'S IMMUNIZATION RECORDS

Most pediatricians recommend the following schedule of vaccinations for healthy infants and children.

CHILD'S NAME:			
AT AGE	**VACCINE**	**POSSIBLE SIDE EFFECTS**	**DATES**
2 mos.	DTP[1]	Irritability, mild fever, soreness and swelling at injection site. Less common (report to doctor): inconsolable crying for more than 3 hours, excessive sleepiness, limpness or paleness, fever of 105 or higher, convulsion	_____ _____
	OPV[2]	Avoid giving when child has stomach or intestinal infection; could affect effectiveness of vaccine	_____ _____
4 mos.	DTP		_____ _____
	OPV		_____ _____
6 mos.	DTP		_____ _____
1 yr.	TB Test[3]		_____ _____
15 mos.	Measles	Low-grade fever; mild rash	_____ _____
	Mumps		_____ _____
	Rubella[4]	Joint pain	_____ _____
18 mos.	DTP		_____ _____
	OPV		_____ _____
	Hib conjugate[5]		_____ _____
4-6 yrs. (school entry)	DTP Booster		_____ _____
	OPV Booster		_____ _____
14-16 yrs.	Td[6]		_____ _____
Every 10 years for life	Td		_____ _____

1. DTP: Diphtheria, tetanus (lockjaw), pertussis (whooping cough)
2. OPV: Oral polio vaccine, for poliomyelitis
3. TB Test: for tuberculosis
4. Rubella: German measles. These three can be given in one combination shot.
5. Hib: Hemophilus influenza
6. Td: Tetanus-diphtheria booster

Source: American Academy of Pediatrics

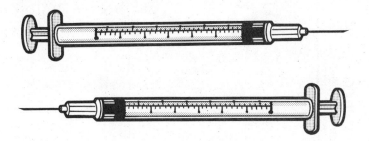

INFANT DEVELOPMENT CHART

This chart gives you general guidelines for your baby's physical, mental, and social development, based on observations by pediatricians and child-development experts. However, this is not a rigid schedule. Your baby is unique and will develop at his own pace.

AGE	BOYS		GIRLS		LANGUAGE DEVELOPMENT	MOTOR DEVELOPMENT
	HT	WT	HT	WT		
1-2 mos.	21 in.	11 lbs.	21 in.	10 lbs.	Mewing; responds and attends to speaking voice.	Raises self with arms while lying down.
3-4 mos.	23 in.	15 lbs.	24 in.	13 lbs.	Cooing; babbling.	Sits with support.
4-5 mos.	25 in.	17 lbs.	26 in.	16 lbs.	Single syllable.	Sits alone momentarily.
6 mos.	26 in.	18 lbs.	27 in.	17 lbs.	Vocalizes to social stimulation.	Rolls from back to stomach.
7 mos.	26½ in.	19 lbs.	28 in.	18 lbs.	Squealing.	Sits alone quite steadily for long periods of time.
8 mos.	27 in.	20 lbs.	28 in.	19 lbs.	Clear vocalization; responds to bye-bye.	Stands up holding onto furniture.
9 mos.	28 in.	22 lbs.	28½ in.	20 lbs.	Two syllables: na-ma, da-da.	Walks while adult holds onto hands.
10-11 mos.	29 in.	23 lbs.	29 in.	21 lbs.	Responds to simple commands; first words.	Stands alone, sits down after standing.
12-14 mos.	30 in.	25 lbs.	30 in.	23 lbs.	Five-word or more vocabulary.	Walks alone.
15-16 mos.	31 in.	26 lbs.	31 in.	24 lbs.	Understands a prohibition.	Walks sideways.
17-18 mos.	31½ in.	27 lbs.	32 in.	25 lbs.	Understands a simple question.	Walks backwards.
19 mos.	32 in.	28 lbs.	32 in.	26 lbs.	Two words in combination.	Walks up stairs with help.
20-23 mos.	33 in.	28 lbs.	33 in.	27 lbs.	Names a picture in book.	Stands on left foot alone.
24 mos.	34 in.	29 lbs.	34 in.	27 lbs.	Repeats things said; understands two prepositions "in" and "under".	Jumps off floor with both feet; jumps from last stair step to floor.

FIRST AID
& SAFETY

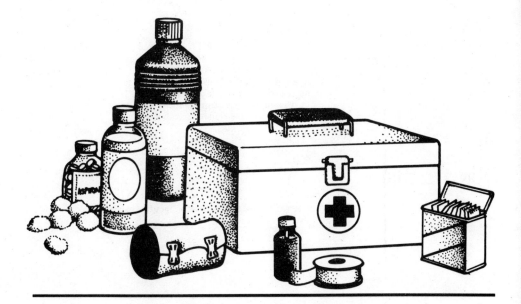

FIRST AID

Follow these procedures in emergencies, but contact your physician if in doubt or if injury is severe. (Severely injured patients should not be given any food or drink.) A tetanus shot may be needed in the case of burns and whenever skin is broken.

INJURY	WHAT YOU CAN DO
SKIN WOUNDS	
Bruises	Rest injured part. Apply cold compresses (do not let ice touch skin) for half hour. If skin is broken, treat as a cut. For wringer injuries and bicycle-spoke injuries, consult doctor immediately.
Scrapes	Sponge off gently with clean water and soap, using wet gauze or cotton. Apply sterile dressing, preferably nonadhesive or "film" type.
Cuts	*Small:* Wash with clean water and soap. Hold under running water. Apply sterile gauze dressing. *Large:* Apply dressing. Press firmly and elevate to stop bleeding. (Use tourniquet only if necessary to control bleeding.) Bandage. Get medical help. Do not use iodine or other antiseptics without medical advice.
Punctures	Consult doctor.
Slivers	Wash with clean water and soap. Remove with tweezers or forceps. Wash again. If not easily removed, consult doctor.
BURNS AND SCALDS	
Limited extent, caused by heat	Any burns of any size on face, hands, feet or genitals should be seen immediately by doctor. Immerse extremity burns in cold water or apply cool (50°-60°) compresses to torso or face for pain relief.
Extensive	Keep victim lying down. Remove nonadhered clothing from burn area if possible. Apply cool wet compresses to injured area, but not over more than 25% of the body at one time. Keep victim warm and take to hospital or doctor. Do not use ointments, etc.
Electrical	Disconnect power source if possible or pull victim away from source using wood or cloth — do not use bare hands. Victim may require CPR. Burn should be evaluated by a doctor.
Sunburn	Children under 1 year old may suffer serious injury and should be examined by a doctor.
FRACTURES	
Signs: Any deformity of an injured part usually means a fracture	Do not move victim until fracture has been splinted. (Use firm material as splint. Secure with bandage or cloth below joint below break, above joint above break and at level of break.) If skin is broken, apply pressure to control bleeding and secure bandage, then apply splint. If a neck or back injury is suspected, victim should be moved only with medical assistance, to avoid causing paralysis.
SPRAINS	
	Elevate injured part. Apply only cold compresses. If severe pain or swelling present, seek medical advice.
CONVULSIONS	
	Seek medical advice. Lay victim on his side with head lower than hips. Put nothing in mouth. Sponge with cool water if fever present.

CHOKING

Victim less than 1 year old	Place infant face-down along your arm, his head lower than his trunk (Rest your forearm on your thigh.) Rapidly deliver 4 measured blows between the infant's shoulder blades, with the heel of your hand. If breathing does not start, roll infant over and rapidly compress chest 4 times, as for CPR, below.
Child over 1 years old	Place child on his back; kneel at his feet. Place heel of one hand on child's abdomen, in the midline between navel and ribcage; place your other hand on top of your first. Apply 6 to 10 rapid inward and upward thrusts (Heimlich manuever) until foreign object is expelled.
Older children and adults	Can be treated with abdominal thrusts as above in a sitting, standing or recumbent position. Reach around victim from behind to position hands on abdomen.

If breathing does not start, open victim's mouth with your thumb over his tongue and fingers wrapped around his lower jaw. If you see the foreign object, sweep it out with your finger. If first aid fails, transport victim to a medical facility immediately.

SHOCK

Signs: Pale, cold, clammy skin; chills; weak, rapid pulse; nausea or vomiting	Keep victim's airway open. If vomiting, turn head so that vomit drains from mouth. If not vomiting, lay victim down and elevate his legs (if bones are not broken) to keep head lower than trunk. Loosen victim's clothing; keep him comfortable and warm. Give water only, only if victim is conscious and able to swallow. Reassure victim of help. Call physician or emergency squad.

CARDIOPULMONARY RESUSCITATION (CPR)*

To use in case of breathing emergency, drowning, electric shock and smoke inhalation.

Pulmonary support	Place victim on back. Straighten neck (unless a neck injury is suspected) and lift jaw. Give slow steady breaths into victim's mouth with nostrils pinched closed (or into infant's nose and mouth). Breathe at least 15 breaths a minute (or 20 breaths a minute for infants) using only enough air to move victim's chest up and down.
Cardiac support (if no pulse or heart beat)	Place victim on firm surface. *For infants,* use 2 fingers to depress breastbone 1/2″ to 1″ at a level that's one finger's-breadth below nipples; compress 100 times a minute. *For children,* depress lower third of breastbone with heel of your hand at 80 compressions a minute. *For older child or adult,* depress lower breastbone 1-1/2″ to 2″, 60 times a minute. *For all victims,* give 1 new breath (pulmonary respiration technique above) for every 5 compressions.

Take a certified CPR course to learn these techniques properly.   *Source: American Academy of Pediatrics*

FIRST AID FOR POISONING

Instructions on product labels for specific treatment of poisoning may be wrong; always contact your doctor or poison control center for instructions.

SWALLOWED POISONS

Signs:
- Unconsciousness, confusion, sudden illness or pain, or convulsions
- Presence of poison container
- Burns around lips or mouth
- Pupils contracted or dilated
- Chemical odor on breath

Conscious Victim:
- Dilute the poison with a glass or two of water or milk if the victim is not having convulsions.
- Have someone call your local poison control center or doctor or emergency rescue squad for advice, while you administer first aid.
- Save poison container and sample of vomit for analysis.
- Do not neutralize with counteragents. Do not give oils.

Unconscious Victim:
- Keep victim's airway open.
- Call emergency rescue squad.
- Give mouth-to-mouth resuscitation or cardiopulmonary resuscitation (CPR) if necessary.
- Do not give fluids. Do not induce vomiting. If victim vomits, turn head to side so vomit drains from his mouth.
- Save poison container and sample of vomit for analysis.

Convulsions:
- Call emergency squad as soon as possible.
- Do not attempt to restrain victim; try to position him so that he will not injure himself.
- Loosen tight clothing.
- Watch for obstruction of victim's airway and correct it by tilting his head. Give mouth-to-mouth resuscitation or CPR if necessary.
- Do not force a hard object or finger between victim's teeth.
- Do not give any fluids.

- Do not induce vomiting.
- After convulsion, turn victim on his side or in prone position, with his head turned to allow fluid to drain from his mouth.

Have On Hand:
You may need to use these products on the advice of your physician or poison control center.
- Syrup of ipecac (to induce vomiting)
- Activated charcoal (to bind, or deactive, poison)
- Epsom salts (a laxative)

If poisoning occurs where medical help is unavailable and the victim has taken an overdose of drugs or medication, you may induce vomiting. DO NOT induce vomiting if a strong acid, alkali or petroleum product (drain cleaner, oven cleaner, toilet bowl cleaner, furniture polish, gasoline or kerosene, etc.) has been swallowed. Get the victim to a hospital as quickly as possible.

Source: American National Red Cross

INHALED POISONS

Fuel gases, auto exhaust, dense smoke from fires or fumes from poisonous chemicals.

- Get victim into fresh air. (Be careful not to inhale the poison yourself.)
- Loosen victim's clothing.
- If victim is not breathing, start rescue breathing promptly. Do not stop until patient is breathing or help arrives.
- Have someone call a physician, poison control center or rescue unit.
- Transport victim to a medical facility promptly.

Source: American Academy of Pediatrics

POISONOUS PLANTS

Many common household and garden plants can be toxic — most often to pets and young children, who will put anything in their mouths. Symptoms may vary from a mild stomachache, a skin rash or swelling of the mouth and throat, to reactions that can affect the heart, kidneys and other organs. Therefore, it is important that you know the names of all plants, weeds, shrubs and trees in and around your home.

Angel trumpet tree	Holly berries	Peyote (mescal)
Apricot kernels	Horsetail reed	Philodendron
Arrowhead	Ivy (Boston, English and others)	Poison hemlock
Avocado leaves	Jequirity bean or pea	Poison ivy
Betel nut palm	Jerusalem cherry	Poison oak
Bittersweet	Jimson weed (thorn apple)	Pokeweed
Buckeye	Lantana camara (red sage)	Potato sprouts
Caladium	Laurels	Ranunculus
Castor bean	Marijuana	Rhododenron
Cherries — wild and cultivated	Mayapple	Rhubarb blade
Daphne	Mistletoe	Rosary pea
Devil's ivy	Moonseed	Tobacco
Dieffenbachia (dumb cane)	Mother-in-law plant	Tomato vine
Elderberry	Mushrooms (unless store-bought)	Water hemlock
Elephant ear	Nightshade	Wisteria
English ivy	Oleander	Yew
Foxglove		

Source: New York City Poison Control Center, Dept. of Health

POISONOUS FLOWERS

Beware of ingesting any parts of these plants, not just the flowers. For specific information on any plant or flower, contact your local Poison Control Center.

Azalea	Jack-in-the-pulpit	Poinsettia
Buttercups	Jessamine (Jasmine)	Poppy (except California poppy)
Calla lily	Jonquil	Primrose
Crocus, autumn	Larkspur	Star-of-Bethlehem
Daffodil	Lily of the valley	Sweet pea
Delphinium	Lobelia	Tulip
Four-o'clock	Monkshood	Wisteria
Hyacinth	Morning glory	
Hydrangea	Narcissus	
Iris	Periwinkle	

Source: New York City Poison Control Center, Dept. of Health

FIRST AID FOR PETS

These emergency procedures are not substitutes for veterinary care; after rendering first aid, have your pet examined by a professional.

For your own safety, always muzzle an injured or frightened animal before administering treatment; use a 2- to 3-foot strip of gauze, a necktie or other soft material.

HEMORRHAGE

Symptoms:
Blood loss through open wounds; if possibility of internal hemorrhaging, take to veterinarian immediately — animal may go into shock.

Treatment:
1. Place clean, sterile piece of gauze or other material directly over wound and apply pressure. (Check first for fracture or foreign materials in wound before using this method.)
2. If this does not seem to stop the bleeding, apply pressure to artery nearest the wound, on the side between the wound and the heart. These pressure points are:
   Brachial artery: on inside of foreleg, just above the elbow joint.
   Femoral artery: on inside of hindleg, near where leg joints body
   Coccygeal artery: on underside of tail.
3. A tourniquet, on limbs or tail only, can be applied as a last resort. Fasten a 1″-wide strip of cloth or rubber between wound and the body, preferably above a joint. Tighten just enough to reduce, but not stop, blood flow. Replace with a pressure bandage as soon as possible.
4. Small wounds can be cleansed with hydrogen peroxide and left uncovered.

RESPIRATORY DIFFICULTY

Symptom:
Heart stops beating.

Treatment:
For medium-size to large dogs —
1. Place dog on its right side on a firm surface.
2. Depending on size of animal, place one or both your palms on its chest wall directly behind its elbow.
3. Press firmly and release, about 70 times per minute. If your technique is correct, you will be able to feel a pulse with each compression.

For cats and small dogs —
1. Place animal on its right side of a firm surface.
2. Place on hand (use your fingers) under the body and the other hand above it, so the entire cardiac area is enclosed.
3. Using both hands, compress this region, then release your grip. Repeat this procedure about 70 times per minute. (With very small animals, you may be able to use one hand.)

FRACTURES

Symptoms:
Pain around injured area; loss of function, unnatural movement and deformity of the limb or other area involved.

Treatment:
1. Handle injured part as little as possible. Do not attempt to place broken bones in proper position. If you suspect a spinal injury, do not move animal yourself.
2. Be sure to apply emergency muzzle before attempting any first aid.
3. Immobilize injured part with splint or bandage. Before splinting, cover area with soft material to provide extra support and prevent undue friction. A piece of stiff cardboard, shaped like the injured area, will do as a splint.
4. Take pet to veterinarian.

BURNS

Symptoms:
Blistering of tissues; singed fur.

Treatment:
1. Never touch a burn unless you have thoroughly scrubbed your hands first. Use only clean, preferably sterile, materials.
2. If burns are NOT severe or extensive, cover with a commercial burn preparation. If not available, soak a clean piece of linen in a strong infusion of tea and apply to burn.
3. Severe burns should be treated only by a veterinarian. Cover burned area with a material that will not stick to the wounds and bring pet to a vet.

4. Fluid loss is a serious effect of burns, so try to get your pet to drink.

POISONING

Call local Poison Control Center for reference. Bring sample of poison or of animal's vomit to veterinarian for analysis.

At-home treatment may involve a demulcent (such as milk and raw egg white or olive oil) to soothe irritation or an emetic (1 teaspoon 3% hydrogen peroxide per 5 lbs. of dog's weight; just 1 teaspoonful for cats) to induce vomiting.

Symptoms for Corrosive Poisoning:
Corrosives are defined as poisons, either alkali or acid, that burn on contact with body tissue. Examples of alkalis: ammonia, bleach, drain cleaners. Examples of acids: lye, battery fluid, rust removers. Signs: Blisters or burns around mouth.

Treatment:
1. Alkali poisoning (ammonia or sodium hydroxide; found in drain cleaners): Give large quantities of a dilute acid, such as 5% acetic acid, citric acid or vinegar. Acid poisoning (substances in car batteries or etching fluids): Give dilute alkali such as baking soda in water, limewater or chalk.
2. Flush burns with water, then also treat with the dilute alkali or acid solution.
3. Give liberal amounts of demulcents. Do NOT give emetics.

Symptoms for Irritant Poisoning:
Irritants are poisons that inflame or otherwise irritate tissues. Examples: Decaying plant and animal matter or poisonous plants. Signs: Vomiting.

Treatment:
1. Vomiting usually follows consumption of an irritant such as decaying vegetable or animal matter or a poisonous plant, even some houseplants.
2. Give pet a demulcent after it has vomited.
3. Take to a veterinarian.

Symptoms for Narcotic Poisoning:
Breathing difficulties or unconsciousness caused by ingesting sedatives or barbituates

Treatment:
1. If animal has breathing difficulties, artificial respiration must be started.
2. ONLY if animal is fully conscious, administer an emetic.
3. Seek veterinary help immediately.

Symptoms for Convulsant Poisoning:
Animal will become restless and twitch at first, then become stiff. Loud noises will cause it to convulse. These poisons are found in many small animal pest control poisons. Strychnine is commonly used in cases of malicious poisoning.

Treatment:
1. Seek veterinary help immediately.

Symptoms for Rat Poisons:
Most rat poisons are extremely toxic, causing death by internal hemorrhaging. Poison may have been ingested directly or by eating poisoned dropping or parts of a poisoned rat.
1. Veterinary aid is required immediately.

HEATSTROKE
Symptoms:
High temperature, hot and dry skin, dizziness, unconsciousness, convulsion. Animals left in cars even on mildly warm days can succumb in a short time.

Treatment:
1. Remove animal from heated area immediately.
2. Immerse pet in cold water, hose water over it or reduce its temperature by some other means.
3. Massage its body.
4. Check rectal temperature. Do not stop cooling measures until body temperature returns to normal. (100.9 − 101.7 for a dog; 100.4 − 101.6 for a cat.)
5. Have pet examined by veterinarian immediately.

SHOCK
Symptoms:
Glassy-eyed appearance, rapid and shallow breathing, rapid but weak pulse, subnormal temperature, and slow capillary refill time (to check this, press finger firmly against pet's gums until they whiten beneath your finger; quickly remove finger and note time it takes for color to return — normally, 1 or 2 seconds)

Treatment:
1. Keep animal warm, but not hot.
2. Keep animal's head lower than its body.
3. Take pet to veterinarian as soon as possible.

CARDIAC ARREST
Symptoms:
Breathing may stop or be impaired.

Treatment:
1. Open animal's mouth and extend tongue to see far back into the pharynx,
2. Check carefully for obstructions. Clear away all mucus and blood.
3. Close animal's mouth.
4. Inhale and cover front part of animal's nose with your mouth to completely seal nose area. (You may wish to cover pet's muzzle with a handkerchief first.)
5. Exhale, gently forcing air into animal's lungs. Watch for expansion of chest so you do not overinflate. But you must introduce enough air to make the chest wall clearly expand. After it has expanded, allow it to return to normal, then repeat at a rate of about 10 to 12 breaths per minute.

Source: The Animal Protection Institute of America

H ere's what to do to prepare for and survive hurricanes, tornadoes, winter storms and other vagaries of nature. Most important, keep tuned to local disaster reports and follow the instructions outlined by authorities.

Earthquakes

DURING:
● Stay calm and stay where you are: If indoors, stay indoors; if outdoors, stay outdoors. (Most injuries occur as people are entering or leaving buildings.)

● If indoors, take cover under a desk, table, bench or against inside walls or doorways. Stay away from glass, windows and outside doors. If outdoors, move away from buildings and utility wires. Stay in the open until the shaking stops.

● Don't run through or near buildings. The greatest danger from falling debris is just outside of doorways and close to outer walls.

● If in a moving car, stop as quickly as safety permits, but stay in vehicle until shaking stops. When you drive on, watch for hazards created by earthquake — fallen objects, downed electric wires, or broken or undermined roadways.

AFTER:
● Check for injuries. Do not attempt to move seriously injured persons unless they are in immediate danger of further injury.

● Check utility lines and appliances for damage. If you smell gas, open windows and shut off main gas valve. Then leave building and report gas leakage to authorities. Don't re-enter building until a utility official says it is safe.

● If water pipes are damaged, shut off the supply at the main valve. Emergency water may be obtained from hot water tanks, toilet tanks and melted ice cubes.

● Check to see that sewage lines are intact before flushing toilets.

● If electrical wiring is shorting out, shut off current at main meter box.

● Check chimney for cracks and damage. Unnoticed damage can lead to a fire. Approach chimneys with great caution; the initial check should be made from a distance.

● Stay out of severely damaged buildings. Aftershocks can shake them down.

● Stay off telephone, except to report an emergency.

● Be prepared for additional earthquake shocks.

Floods

BEFORE:
● Listen to local radio or TV for flood warnings and instructions. Find out how many feet your property is above or below possible flood levels, so when predicted flood levels are broadcast, you can determine if you may be flooded.

● Stock up on food that requires no cooking or refrigeration, and store drinking water in closed, clean containers, in case electrical or water services are interrupted.

● Be sure portable radio, emergency cooking equipment and flashlights are in working order.

● Keep first-aid supplies and family's medications handy.

● Keep car's fuel tank full.

● Keep plastic sheeting, lumber, sandbags handy for emergency waterproofing.

● If flooding is likely and time permits, move essential items and furniture to upper floors of house. Disconnect any electric appliances that can't be moved — but don't touch them if you are wet or standing in water.

● If told to evacuate, do so PROMPTLY. Follow instructions of your local government. Shut off water, gas or electric service before leaving. Lock doors and windows; secure outdoor movable objects. Travel with care.

AFTER:

● Do not eat food touched by flood waters.

● Wells should be pumped out and water tested before drinking.

● Electrical equipment should be checked and dried before returning it to service.

● Keep tuned to local radio or TV stations for instructions.

● Stay away from disaster areas.

HURRICANES

BEFORE:

● When your area receives a hurricane warning, keep listening to your local radio or TV station for official bulletins.

● Leave low-lying areas that might be swept by high tides or storm waves. Leave mobile homes, which may overturn in high winds.

● Moor boats securely or move them to secure area.

● Shutter, tape or board up windows.

● Secure outdoor objects; anchor them or store inside.

● Store drinking water in clean bathtubs, jugs, bottles, pots. Turn refrigerator to maximum cold and don't open door unless necessary.

● Check your battery-powered equipment: emergency cooking facilities, radio, flashlights.

● Fill up your car's gas tank.

● Stay in a safe place — indoors, at home if it is sturdy and on high ground — until hurricane passes completely.

● If told to evacuate, do so PROMPTLY. Shut off water, gas or electric service. Travel with care.

AFTER:

● Remain in shelter until informed by authorities that it is safe to leave.

● Keep tuned to local radio or TV station for instructions.

● Drive carefully along debris-filled streets. Stay out of disaster areas.

● Avoid loose or dangling wires. Report broken or damaged sewer, water or electrical lines.

● Be cautious before re-entering your home. Check for gas leaks and check water and refrigerated food for spoilage.

INDOORS:

● Stay away from doors, windows, fireplaces, radiators, stoves, sinks, pipes, electrical appliances — or anything near water or that might carry an electric charge.

● Do not use telephone (except in an emergency) or electrical appliances. Disconnect TV.

OUTDOORS:

● Do not stand beneath a natural lightning rod, such as a tall, isolated tree or a telephone pole. Keep yourself lower than the nearest conductive object — and stay a safe distance from it (about twice its height).

● Stay away from tractors and other metal farm equipment; wire fences, clotheslines, metal pipes, rails and other metallic "paths"; bicycles, motorcycles, scooters, golf carts and clubs.

● Get out of, and away from, open water.

● Avoid standing in small isolated sheds or other small structures in open areas.

● Avoid hilltops, high ground, open spaces. Seek shelter in a low area under a thick growth of small trees. In open areas, find a low place such as a ravine or valley.

● If your skin tingles or hair stands on end (indicating that lightning is about to strike), drop to your knees, bend forward and put hands on knees — but do not lie flat on the ground.

● Persons struck by lightning carry no electrical charge and should be given first aid immediately — treatment for burns or mouth-to-mouth resuscitation, CPR, artificial respiration, whatever is necessary.

TORNADOES

● If a tornado watch has been announced, keep tuned to your local radio or TV station. Also keep watching the sky, especially to the south or southwest (a tornado's typical travel pattern). If you see revolving funnel-shaped clouds, call the local police or weather-service office immediately.

● If a tornado warning has been issued, take shelter immediately to protect yourself from being blown away, struck by falling objects or injured by flying debris. Your best protection is an underground shelter or cave or a substantial steel-framed or reinforced concrete building. But if none is available and you're:

AT HOME:
● Go to an underground storm cellar or basement fallout shelter, if you have one. If not, go to a corner of your basement and take cover under a sturdy workbench or table (not in location that might be under heavy appliances on the floor above). If home has no basement, take cover in the center part of the house, on the lowest floor, in a small room such as a closet or bathroom, or under sturdy furniture. Open some windows on the side away from the tornado's approach, but stay away from windows. If you live in a mobile home or trailer, find other shelter.

AT WORK:
● Go to a designated shelter area or an interior hallway on the lowest floor.

AT SCHOOL:
● Follow school authorities' instructions, such as taking shelter in interior hallways on the lowest floor and staying out of

structures with wide, free-span roofs (auditoriums, gymnasiums).

IN THE OPEN:
● Take cover and lie flat in the nearest depression, such as a ditch, culvert, excavation or ravine; cover your head with your arms.

WINTER STORMS

BEFORE:
● Use heating fuel sparingly. Have emergency heating equipment (campstove or wood for fireplace) and candles on hand.

● Stock up on food that requires no cooking or refrigeration, and store drinking water in closed, clean containers, in case electrical or water services are interrupted.

● Be sure portable radio, emergency cooking equipment and flashlights are in working order. Have ready snow removal equipment and rock salt or calcium chloride for melting ice on walkways.

● If you must go outside, dress warmly, in several loose-fitting lightweight layers, and keep all parts of your body covered.

Do not overexert yourself shoveling snow, pushing cars or walking in the snow.

● Travel only if necessary. Make sure tank is full and car is equipped with snow tires or chains; keep container of sand, shovel, scrapers and other winter storm supplies in the trunk. Travel by daylight.

● If stranded with no source of help in sight, do not leave your car. If you occasionally run the engine to keep warm, keep window partially open for ventilation. If car runs out of gas, keep windows closed. Do not fall asleep; exercise to keep awake and keep warm.

Sources: Federal Emergency Management Agency; National Weather Service

BABYSITTER'S CHECKLIST

Parents: Don't forget to fill in this vital information for your children's sake as well as your babysitter's. **Babysitter:** If you have any other questions, add them to this list and don't let parents leave until they've answered them!

CHILD'S NAME: _____   _____

Bedtimes: _____   _____
✔ TV Programs Allowed   _____   _____
✔ Foods Not Allowed   _____   _____
✔ Food Allergies   _____   _____
✔ Other Allergies   _____   _____
✔ Special Health
  Concerns   _____   _____
✔ Medications   _____   _____
  (But don't give any medicine unless you've been given detailed, written
  instructions from parents!)
✔ Special Reminders   _____   _____

LOCATIONS OF:

✔ First Aid Supplies _____
✔ Dangerous Items (medicines, cleaning supplies and
  other potential poisons) _____
✔ Emergency Exits _____
✔ Important Telephone Numbers _____

IMPORTANT TELEPHONE NUMBERS

PARENT(s): Number(s) where parent(s) can be reached away from home

_____

ALTERNATIVES: Numbers of friends, relatives, neighbors when parent(s) cannot be reached

_____
_____
_____

FIRE DEPARTMENT _____
POLICE DEPARTMENT _____
POISON CONTROL CENTER _____
AMBULANCE _____
DOCTOR _____
DENTIST _____
GAS COMPANY _____
ELECTRIC COMPANY _____
TELEPHONE COMPANY _____
TAXI SERVICE* _____
OTHER IMPORTANT NUMBERS _____
_____
_____

TELEPHONE EMERGENCY HOT LINE (if available) _____

*Leave money for cabfare, in case of emergency.

Sources: Consumer Product Safety Commission; Rutgers University Cooperative Extension

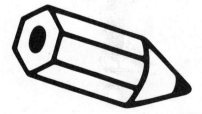

HOME & CAR MAINTENANCE

ENERGY-SAVING (AND MONEY-SAVING) TIPS

Here are some easy ways to cut down on your energy needs and costs.

HEATING

1. Check filters in your warm air heating system monthly and replace or clean them when they become dirty.

2. Storm windows and doors can cut heating costs by as much as 15%. Double-glazed and thermopane windows, or even plastic across windows can also minimize heat escape.

3. Properly insulate walls, ceiling and floors. Caulk and weatherstrip cracks.

4. Moist air feels warmer than dry air at the same temperature, so raise humidity levels with a room humidifier or set shallow pans of water on top of radiators or near heating vents.

5. Keep thermostat at the lowest comfortable temperature (you use 3% more heating fuel for every degree over 70). During the day, keep curtains open to let sun help heat your home. At night, close drapes to keep warmth indoors.

COOLING

1. Air conditioner should be the proper size of the area being cooled so it won't overwork or continually turn itself on and off.

2. If you can, locate air conditioner units on the north, east or best-shaded side of your home, where it will be less exposed to sun.

3. Check filter once a month by holding up to the light. If you can't see through it, clean or replace it. Keep condenser coils and fins clean too.

4. Close off rooms that are not occupied. Use timers to turn on unit just before you return home, rather than leave them running all day.

5. Install fan in your attic to exhaust trapped hot air. (Attic temperatures can reach 150°F!)

REFRIGERATOR/FREEZER

1. Check that refrigerator door closes tightly. Clean or replace seals to keep cool air in.

2. Keep unit away from heat-generating appliances (ovens, dishwashers).

3. Keep condenser coils at back and/or bottom of refrigerator clean with a vacuum or brush.

4. Avoid opening refrigerator door more often than is necessary.

5. A freezer's efficiency is increased by keeping its compartment full.

LAUNDRY

1. Only use hot water for heavily soiled laundry, as 90% of washer's energy goes toward heating the water. (Most laundry can be washed in warm water; lightly soiled, in cold.) Use cold water rinses for all loads.

2. Wash only full loads.

3. Dry loads in succession to use the heat left over from the previous cycle.

4. Set timer carefully. Overdrying shortens the life of fabrics as well as uses more energy.

5. Clean lint filter between each load.

HOT WATER

1. Lower setting to 130°-140° if you have a dishwasher; 110°-120° if not.

2. Wrap a blanket of fiberglass around your heater and secure with duct tape to save up to 10% on water-heating costs.

3. Take showers instead of baths, which use up twice as much heated water. Install flow-control device in shower heads and faucets.

4. Use cold water to rinse dishes. Washing dishes by hand usually uses more hot water, but run dishwashers only when you have a full load. (Also, turn off heat during drying cycle and open washer door after rinse cycle to let dishes air-dry.)

COOKING

1. A microwave oven uses about 70%-80% less electricity than a conventional oven.

2. Avoid peeking into the oven too often when baking or roasting. Each peek can lower oven temperature by 25°.

3. It's not really necessary to preheat the oven for foods that will be cooking for more than an hour.

4. For meals, try to prepare foods that can be cooked at about the same temperature so they can be in the oven at the same time.

LIGHTING

1. Though more expensive than incandescent lights, screw-in fluorescent bulbs last 10 times longer and use 75% less electricity.

2. Buy "energy-saving" incandescent bulbs.

3. Match wattage to lighting needs. For instance, a high-wattage reading light is not necessary in an alcove or hallway.

4. Turn off incandescent lights when you leave a room. However, for fluorescent bulbs, turn them off only if you'll be gone more than 15 minutes, because they'll use as much energy to start up again.

Source: Long Island Lighting Co.

DECORATING COLOR GUIDE

Types of color include primary (pure color, such as blue), secondary (a mix of two primary colors, such as green, from yellow and blue) and tertiary (a mix of one primary and one secondary color, such as blue-green) and the range of tints (a color lightened by white) and shades (deepened with black). In deciding on a color scheme, pick hues that you like and that harmonize, as outlined, using the color wheel below. Choose lighter colors for backgrounds; bolder colors for accents.

1.	Red-orange	(tertiary)
2.	Orange	(secondary)
3.	Yellow-orange	(tertiary)
4.	Yellow	(primary)
5.	Yellow-green	(tertiary)
6.	Green	(secondary)
7.	Blue-green	(tertiary)
8.	Blue	(primary)
9.	Blue-violet	(tertiary)
10.	Violet	(tertiary)
11.	Red-violet	(tertiary)
12.	Red	(primary)

Monochromatic	One color + the range of its tints and shades — e.g., blue, powder blue, navy blue. For instance, you might choose light blue walls, deep blue couch, and patterned curtains that contain those colors.
Analagous (related)	Two or more colors near to each other on the color wheel, sharing one color — e.g., yellow, green and blue. Walls might be soft yellow and carpet blue, with upholstery in a floral pattern.
Complementary	Colors directly opposite on the color wheel — e.g., blue and orange. Here blue should be the predominant color for upholstery, perhaps with accents of a deep orange shade, such as rust or terracotta.
Adjacent complementary	Opposite colors + an accent color to the right or left of one — e.g., yellow and violet + blue-violet. Fabric patterns with the darker colors can be brightened by accent pieces in yellow shades such as gold.
Split complementary	One color + the two colors that flank its opposite color — e.g., blue-violet + orange and yellow. Again, the darker color might serve for upholstered pieces; wallpaper or curtains could have a yellow background with a tiny floral print.
Triad	Three colors equidistant on the wheel — e.g., blue, red, yellow. A pattern with all three colors would work with fabrics or wallpaper, against a rug of deep blue.
Neutrals	Black, white and gray can be used as background or accent to most bright or pastel colors. Browns and beiges, which are between red and yellow on the color wheel, work well with tones in that range.

FORMULAS FOR FURNITURE FILLERS

Fillers can be used for repairs or for closing wood cells before finishing. Below are some filler requirements and how to tint neutral-color filler with oil stain, or colors-in-oil, to match different woods.

Proportions for mixing various quantities of filler

HEAVY MIX (16-lb base)			MEDIUM MIX (12-lb base)			THIN MIX (8-lb base)		
Approx. amt. needed*	Paste	Thinner	Approx. amt. needed*	Paste	Thinner	Approx. amt. needed*	Paste	Thinner
2 gal	16 lb	1 gal	1 gal 3 qt	12 lb	1 gal	1½ gal	8 lb	1 gal
5 pt	5 lb	2½ pt	3 qt	5 lb	3 pt 5 oz	1 gal	5 lb	5 pt
2 qt	1 qt	1 qt	2 qt 10 oz	1 qt	2 pt 5 oz	3 qt	1 qt	2 qt
2 pt	1 pt	1 pt	1 at 5 oz	1 pt	1 pt 5 oz	3 pt	1 pt	2 pt
1 pt	1 lb	½ pt	1 pt 20 oz	1 lb	10½ oz	1½ pt	1 lb	1 pt
½ pt	½ lb	4 oz	9 oz	½ lb	5¼ oz	12 oz	½ lb	½ pt

*One pint thinned filler covers approximately 36 square feet.

Density of filler mix required for various woods

No filler needed	Thin filler	Medium filler	Heavy filler
Aspen	Alder	Amaranth	Ash
Basswood	Beech	Avodire	Bubinga
Cedar	Birch	Butternut	Chestnut
Cypress	Cherry	Korina	Elm
Ebony	Gum	Mahogany	Hickory
Fir	Maple	Orientalwood	Kelobra
Gaboon	Sycamore	Primavera	Lacewood
Hemlock	Tupelo	Rosewood	Lauan
Holly		Sapeli	(Philippine
Magnolia		Tigerwood	mahogany)
Pine		Walnut	Locust
Poplar		Zebrawood	Oak
Redwood			Padouk
Spruce			Teakwood

Standard filler colors

Black   Add drop black (a tint of black) to natural filler. Suitable for blackwood or dark mahogany.

White   Color natural base with zinc oxide. Used for limed oak and similar effects on chestnut and ash.

Amber   Tint natural base with yellow or orange oil colors. Suitable for ambered walnut, harvest, wheat mahogany and other bleached finishes.

Light brown   Tint with Vandyke brown to required shade. Can be used on any light-brown wood.

Dark brown   Vandyke brown with a touch of drop black. For walnut, mahogany, etc. Suitable for any medium- to dark-color wood.

Walnut   Half Vandyke brown and half burnt umber.

Light red   Use any red color (Indian red) in oil or japan, toning darker or lighter with drop black or zinc white.

Dark red   Equal parts of burnt umber and rose pink. Add drop black for darker shade. Use for Sheraton mahogany or any other red finish where dark pores are desirable.

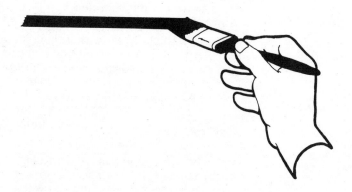

PAINT GLOSSARY

Choosing the right paint for your home-maintenance project depends on your knowing the characteristics of the different types and finishes. Consider, too, their ease of application and cleanup, and the room to be painted and its frequency of use.

TYPES:
(Available as interior or exterior paints with flat or gloss finish)

Alkyd: Solvent-base paint made of synthetic resins. Most durable. Tolerant of surface imperfections; brush marks less visible. Can be applied during cooler temperatures. Nearly odor-free; dries in 4 to 6 hours. Interior use: all surfaces except masonry, plaster or wallboard. Exterior use: all woods and metals.

Enamel: Oil-base paint made with a varnish, or resin, base instead of usual linseed oil. Durable, easy to clean. Generally dries with a gloss finish, but semigloss and flat-finish products are available. Use for trim, window frames, shutters and doors.

Latex: Water-base paint made of plastic resins (such as acrylic or polyvinyl). Easy to apply, very quick-drying and odor-free; good color retention and resistant to peeling and blistering. Tools can be cleaned with soap and water. Least durable; surface can be marred by frequent washings and abrasion. Interior use: all surfaces except wall paper, raw wood or bare steel. Exterior use: wood, stucco, brick, concrete, cement, asphalt, primed metal.

Oil: Solvent-base paint, usually thinned with linseed oil. Long-wearing, highly resistant to staining and damage. Can withstand frequent scrubbings and is often chosen for bathrooms and kitchens. Good one-coat coverage. Strong odor and very long drying period. Tools must be cleaned with turpentine or mineral spirits. Use: most interior and exterior surfaces; however, exterior use has been generally outmoded by latexes and alkyds, because the paint's long-drying time increases possibility of dirt and insects adhering to the surface.

FINISHES:
(Available in both latex and oil bases)

Flat: Paint finish with little (normal flat) or no (dead flat) sheen, therefore reduces glare and minimizes surface imperfections. Becomes dirty easily. Use for siding and larger areas, and for walls in living room, dining room and other nonwork or nonplay areas.

Eggshell: Very low-sheen semigloss, a step above flat finish. Good for walls in moderately used areas.

Satin: Highest level of flat finishes, with sheen similar to that of satin cloth. Has better wearing qualities and more resistant to dirt and damage than dead flats. Good for lightly used, more formal areas.

Semigloss: Has a moderate sheen, almost as easy to clean as gloss. Use for woodwork and for walls of kitchen, bathroom, laundry room, nursery, play room and other moderate- to high-use areas.

Source: Sherwin-Williams Co.; U.S. Dept. of Agriculture

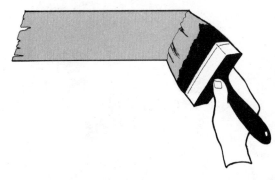

HOUSEPLANT CARE

If you don't have a "green thumb," you can better ensure your indoor garden's longevity by following these specific sun, soil and water requirements for common houseplants.

Plant	Light/Sun	Water	Soil
African Violet (*Saintpaulia ionantha*)	Bright, indirect light for flowering. East or west windows are best	Use "bottom watering" or "wick watering" methods; water only when soil begins to dry out.	Rich.
Aloe	Full, direct sunlight.	Make sure soil is thoroughly dry before watering. Water 1-2 times a week in summer, once every 2-4 weeks in winter.	Regular.
Arrowhead Plant (*Symgonium podophyllum or Nepthytis*)	Medium to dim light.	Keep soil barely moist.	Regular.
Asparagus Fern (*Asparagus sprengeri*)	Bright, indirect sunlight. East or west windows are best.	Soak soil thoroughly with each watering; allow to dry thoroughly between watering.	Regular.
Avocado (*Persea americana*)	Bright, indirect sun; leaves burn easily.	Keep soil moist; use tap water when watering.	Regular.
Baby Tears (*Helxine soleirolii*)	Indirect, filtered, low light from an east or north window.	Keep evenly moist.	Regular.
Boston Fern (*Nephrolepis exaltata*)	Bright, filtered light.	Keep evenly moist without letting roots get soggy or soil dry out.	Rich.
Cactii	Full light.	Water once or twice a week in summer, once every 2-4 weeks in winter.	Regular.
Coleus	Leaves become most colorful when placed in plenty of sunshine.	Keep evenly moist.	Regular.
Croton (*Codiaeum*)	Will grow in shaded areas, but bright sunlight will bring out full color.	Keep evenly moist; never let soil dry out.	Regular.
Dieffenbachia, "Dumb Cane" (*Dieffenbachiamaculata*)	2-3 hrs. of sunlight a day in an east or west window; other times, bright, indirect light.	Keep barely moist; let dry out for a few days before rewatering.	Regular.
Dracaena	Indirect sun or bright light; no direct sunlight.	Keep evenly moist but not soggy. Water when soil feels dry to the touch.	Sandy.
English Ivy (*Hedera helix*)	Bright light, but no direct sun.	Keep barely moist.	Regular.
False Aralia (*Dizygotheca elegantissima*)	Semi-sunny to semi-shady. East or west windows are ideal.	Keep barely moist, damp but not soggy.	Regular.
Grape Ivy (*Cissu rhombifolia*)	Medium to bright light or filtered sun.	Soak soil thoroughly when watering; dry out completely before re-watering.	Regular.

Plant	Light	Watering	Soil
Jade Plant *(Crassula arborescents)*	Full sun with shade at midday.	Allow soil to remain dry for several days between waterings.	Sandy.
Jerusalem Cherry *(Solanun pseudocapsicum)*	Either direct sun or bright light.	Keep moist and allow soil to dry only moderately between waterings.	Regular.
Norfolk Island Pine *(Araucaria excelsa)*	Filtered sunlight from an east or west window.	Provide efficient drainage and allow soil surface to dry before re-watering.	Rich.
Parlor Palm *(Chamaedora elegans)*	Requires low exposure to indirect light.	Keep soil moist but not soggy between March and October; in winter, dry out between waterings.	Regular.
Peperomia	Indirect sunlight or bright, indirect light.	Allow to dry thoroughly between waterings; never allow it to stand in water.	Regular.
Philodendron, Heartleaf *(Philodendron cordatum)*	Any exposure produces growth; does best in well-lighted areas.	Keep moist and never allow to dry out; don't let water remain standing in pot.	Regular.
Philodendron, Split-leaf *(Philodendron pertusum "Monstera deliciosa")*	Bright, indirect lighting.	Soak thoroughly and allow soil surface to remain dry 1-2 days before re-watering.	Regular.
Poinsettia *(Euphorbia pulcherrima)*	Bright, direct sunlight.	Keep constantly moist, but not soggy.	Regular.
Pothos, "Devil's Ivy" *(Scindapsus aureus)*	Bright, indirect sunlight.	Allow soil to dry out moderately between waterings.	Rich.
Prayer Plant *(Macanta leuconeura)*	Indirect sunlight or bright light.	Keep soil moist at all times.	Regular.
Purple Passion Plant, "Velvet Plant" *(Gynura aurantica)*	Direct or partial sunlight for full purple color.	Keep soil evenly moist.	Regular.
Rubber Plant *(Ficus elastica decora)*	Does best in well-lighted windows.	Water only when soil is completely dry; then water thoroughly.	Regular.
Schefflera, "Umbrella Tree" *(Schefflera venulosa)*	Does not like direct sunlight; does best in bright, filtered light.	Soak pot thoroughly; then let soil dry completely before rewatering.	Regular.
Snake Plant *(Sansevieria trifasciata)*	Low light to grow; filtered sunlight to bloom.	Never overwater; plant likes dryness.	Regular.
Spider Plant *(Cholorophytum elatum vittatum)*	Indirect sun or moderately lighted areas.	Keep barely moist.	Regular.
Swedish Ivy *(Plectranthus australis)*	Diffused sun or bright light from a west or south window.	Keep moist but not soggy; allow to dry out slightly between waterings.	Regular.
Wandering Jew *(Zebrina pendula)*	Bright, indirect sunlight.	Water generously, keeping soil most at all times; during winter water less frequently.	Regular.
Weeping Fig *(Ficus benjamina)*	3 hrs. of direct light daily.	Water thoroughly once a week; never let soil dry out.	Regular.
Zebra Plant *(Aphelandra squarrosa)*	Bright, indirect sun.	Water regularly; never let soil dry out.	Rich.

Source: U.S. Dept. of Agriculture, Cornell University Coopeative Extension.

HOUSEHOLD PESTS

U se these control methods to rid your home of indoor pests. When using pesticides, follow caution directions on the label *exactly*. Do not use pesticides for severe pest problems or if there is a possible danger to children, pets or impaired persons. Hiring a professional exterminator is a safer alternative.

Ants

Locate nests (indoors or outdoors) and apply a liquid household insecticide containing diazinon, lindane, malathion or propoxur. Also treat their pathways and entrances.

Bedbugs

Thoroughly wet slats, springs and frames of bed with household surface sprays containing lindane, malathion, ronnel or pyrethrins that are labeled safe for bedding. Spray mattresses completely, including seams and tufts.

Carpet Beetles, Clothes Moths

Clean home often enough to prevent lint, dust and hair from accumulating. Spray fabrics, clothing, blankets, woolens, etc., with stainless household insecticide containing methoxychlor or perthane; treat before storing in airtight container or place moth balls, crystals or flakes in closets or containers. Spray insects' crawling surfaces with spray of 3% to 5% premium-grade melathion or ronnel, or 1/2% lindane or diazinon.

Centipedes

Apply household spray containing lindane directly on pests. Sweep them up with a broom.

Cockroaches

Treat cracks and crevices and infested surfaces with household insecticide of chlorpyrifor, diazinon, malathion, propoxur or ronnel. (For severe infestations, use a spray first, let dry and then use a dust formulation). In cupboards and pantries, remove everything from shelves and drawers before treating. Sprinkle boric acid powder (out of reach of children, pets) in cabinets.

Fleas

Thoroughly vacuum all furnishings in infested rooms. Apply a nonstaining surface spray of methoxychlor, malathion, pyrethins, or ronnel to furnishings, baseboards, floors, carpets. Treat pets with 4% or 5% malathion or 5% methoxychlor dust rubbed into their fur.

Houseflies

Use well-sealed garbage containers. Screen windows and doors. Use fly swatter or a household insecticide labeled for "flying insects."

Mice

Seal any holes in walls, floors, foundations, around pipes. Do not leave food out. Leave mousetraps at right angles to walls, near holes, baited with peanut butter, cake, flour, bacon, nuts, cheese, chocolate or gumdrops.

Mites, Chiggers

Apply household surface spray containing malathion.

Mosquitoes

Be aware of places where water might gather and become a breeding ground: tree holes, rain barrels, outdoor tubs or buckets, cisterns, wells, flower vases, fish bowls. Screen windows and doors.

Pantry Pests (Weevils, Flour Beetles)

Discard infested foods. Empty shelves, thoroughly wash cupboards, then lightly apply a household surface spray containing not more than 2% malathion. When dry, cover shelves with clean paper or foil before replacing food items. Store supplies in glass or metal containers.

Rats

Leave no food or garbage out where rats can get at it. Keep storage areas orderly and clean; stack lumber, cartons, etc., at least a foot above the floor; tightly seal spaces between walls or walls and ceilings. Seal all wall holes, crevices under windows and doors, etc. Use a commercial poison as directed — but not if there may be a danger to children or animals; hire an exterminator.

Spiders

Remove cobwebs with broom or vacuum. Remove loose brick, wood, tile or trash piles in yard or basement. Use household spray containing lindane (but do not spray overhead).

Termites

Use a professional exterminator.

Wasps (Cicada Killers, Hornets, Mud Daubers, Yellow Jackets)

Use a home-approved pesticide. Treat nests after dark, without lights. After treatment of underground nests, cover openings with moist dirt.

Source: U.S. Dept. of Agriculture

CARING FOR YOUR POOL

Follow this checklist to keep your outdoor swimming pool in top condition all summer. Refer to the manufacturer's instructions for operating and maintaining various components.

 Brush and vacuum pool, clean skimmers, and backwash or clean filter as necessary. (Filters should be cleaned if pressure gauge shows 10 to 12 p.s.i. over its original starting pressure.) Use a filter or filter cartridge cleaner at start of season and once a month thereafter.

 Add chlorine stabilizer to previously untreated water, at beginning of season.

Add chlorine once a day (or double dose every other day) at a dosage recommended for your pool's water capacity. It's best to dissolve chemical in bucket of water first, then add to pool.

To ensure proper chlorine level, use a good test kit daily. Maintain chlorine residual level at 1 to 2 ppm (parts per million).

Check pH (acidity/alkalinity) balance daily. Range should be between 7.2 to 7.8, with 7.5 ideal.

Check total alkalinity level. Proper range is between 100 to 150 ppm. Adjustment can be made once, at start of the season.

 Check total hardness level. Maintain between 200 and 500 ppm.

 Every two weeks when outdoor temperature is below 80° and once a week when above 80°, superchlorinate to remove nonfilterable wastes.

 Every 5 to 7 days, use an algaecide to prevent growth of algae.

Have pool water tested and treated for metallic substances, which can discolor water and stain pool walls.

Winterizing:

 During winter, leave water level slightly above bottom of tile and maintain level. Do not put anything, such as logs, in pool to "prevent" freezing.

 Before covering pool, check water's chemical balance and use winterization chemicals.

 Drain all water from piping and skimmers to protect from freezing.

 Winterize pump and heater according to manufacturer's manual.

 Wash filter elements thoroughly and rinse filter tank with fresh water.

Cover pool with solid pool cover before leaves fall, or remove leaves before covering. Use small pump to remove excess water that may accumulate on cover over time.

Before refilling pool in spring, check threads of water pressure relief plug and pipe for tight fit. Check for and clean out clogs. Replace plugs and tighten.

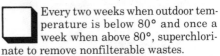

Source: Jayson Pool Service, Sylvan Pools

SPRING CLEANING CHECKLIST

☐ Turn on outdoor water faucets.
☐ Take out hose and check for cracks; replace if necessary.
☐ Take down storm windows.
☐ Wash windows.
☐ Hose off and put up window and door screens.
☐ Have chimney cleaned and furnace serviced (to take advantage of off-season rates).
☐ Launder curtains and washable throw rugs.
☐ Clean blinds and shades.
☐ Turn mattresses and wash mattress covers, dust ruffles, bedspreads and blankets. Have down comforters dry-cleaned.
☐ Wash ceilings, woodwork and ceilings.
☐ Launder or replace shower curtain.
☐ Mend, clean and store winter clothing and outerwear. Discard or take to the thrift shop any clothes that were not worn or were outgrown that season.
☐ Take summer clothes out of storage.
☐ Clean out closets and discard or give away any toys, books, household objects of furniture that are no longer used.
☐ Dust books.
☐ Polish silver, brass or other metal ornaments and fixtures.
☐ Clean out the medicine cabinet.
☐ Organize pantry shelves and discard old spices, condiments and packaged foods (check freshness dates).
☐ Wax fine furniture and wooden floors.
☐ Clean carpets and upholstery.
☐ Install room air-conditioners and clean or replace filters.
☐ Clean out gutters and downspouts.
☐ Check roof for leaks.
☐ Check basement walls for cracks or leaks.
☐ Check exterior siding and paint.
☐ Rake and fertilize lawn and seed bare areas.
☐ Prune and fertilize trees and shrubs.
☐ Plant garden.
☐ Test and, if necessary, repair or replace lawn mower and other outdoor equipment.
☐ Clean out garage, patio and front porch.
☐ Clean and set out outdoor furniture and barbecue grill.
☐ Make a schedule of other major jobs that need to be done (home repairs, refinishing woodwork, painting rooms, etc.).

NEEDLE AND THREAD CHART

Needle sizes run from 1 to 12, with 12 the finest (not used for general sewing). Cotton thread may be indicated by sizes 8 to 100 — the higher the number, the finer the thread. Silk thread, usually used for wool or synthetic fabrics with a high sheen, is classified A (general sewing) or D (buttonholes or topstiching).

FABRIC	THREAD TYPES	NEEDLE SIZES
Filmy: net, organdy, ninon	Extra fine (100 cotton)	10
Very lightweight: batiste, chiffon, nylon tricot, organza, voile and other sheer fabrics	Extra fine (80 to 100 cotton; A silk)	9, 10
Lightweight: challis, chambray, crepe, crepe de chine, cotton knits, eyelet, gauze, georgette, gingham, interlock, jersey, percale, seersucker, silk, taffeta	Extra fine or all-purpose (60 to 80 cotton; A silk)	8,9
Medium-weight: broadcloth, brocade, chino, chintz, corduroy, double knit, flannel, linen, oxford cloth, pique, poplin, satin shantung, suiting, sweatshirt, swimwear, synthetic suedes, terry, velour, velvet, velveteen vinyl, wool crepe	All-purpose (50 to 70 cotton; A silk)	7, 8
Medium- to Heavy-weight: coating, denim, double knit, drapery fabric, fake fur, felt, fleece, gabardine, leather, leatherlike, quilted fabric, sweater knits, ticking, twill, upholstery fabric, woolens	All-purpose (30 to 50 cotton; A silk)	6
Heavyweight: duck, sailcloth	Topstitching (16 to 24 or heavy-duty cotton; D silk)	3 to 5
Very Heavyweight: canvas	Extra strong (8 to 12 or heavy-duty cotton)	1 to 3

Source: Stitch in Time Education Leaflets © Coats & Clark Inc.

STITCHES CHART

STITCH	USE TO	HOW TO
Backstitch	Repair split seams from wrong side and to attach set-in patch	Working from right to left on wrong side, bring needle through to right side and insert $1/8''$ behind. Next, bring needle up $1/8''$ in front of first stitch, then insert where stitch on right side ended.
Basting	Temporarily hold two thicknesses of cloth together and to tack up hem before hemming	Picking up as little fabric as possible (about $1/8''$ between stitches), insert needle for continuous in-and-out stitches, each about $3/4''$ long.
Blindstitch	Repair split seams from wrong side and for hemming heavy fabrics	Working on a slant, take up 1 thread from under fold, then a few from opposite fold. Stitches should not be visible on right side.
Catch stitch	Finish edges of hemmed patch and for hemming medium-weight fabrics	Working from left to right, bring needle up through fabric, then take a tiny stitch with needle pointing left. Cross thread over first stitch to make next stitch.
Fishbone stitch	Pull together torn edges in preparation for darning and to close an unwanted buttonhole	Insert needle about $1/4''$ beyond end of tear; with needle at a slant, alternate stitches on both sides of tear, about $1/8''$ to $1/4''$ apart.
Overcast stitch	Finish raw edges of woven fabrics and in the hemmed and woven-in patch techniques	Make diagonal stitch, taking up fabric above and below edge in one motion.
Rantering stitch	Disguise seamlines of patches	On right side of fabric, insert needle through seam. Pinch fabric on seamline. Stitch back and forth, on a slant, picking up one thread at a time and working as close to seam as possible, stitches about $1/16''$ apart.
Running stitch	Darn	Stitch in a straight line, from left to right, passing needle through fabric at regular intervals. Small stitches, with space between the same size as stitches.

Slip-basting	Baste two layers of fabric together in set-in patch technique	On right side, slip needle along fold of upper layer, draw it through and make small stitch in under layer.
Slipstitch	Hem edges of patches and lightweight garments	Working from right to left, bring needle up through fabric and catch a few threads above fold; bring needle down and take small stitch below fold.
Whipstitch	Stitch armhole seams in linings and repair split seams in gloves	Pass needle through edges at right angles for neat, slanting stitches (similar to overcast stitch, but tighter).

Darning Chart

For repairing tears or small holes or frays by filling in with area with stitches.

1. **Straight Tears:** If darning a tear, first use fishbone stitch to hold torn edges together. Then on wrong side of garment, 1/4" beyond end of hole or tear, make rows of tiny running stitches back and forth, holding the needle against the fabric and weaving through the yarns. When crossing a tear, slip needle between torn edges and fabric edge (1A).

1 **1A**

2. **Diagonal Tears:** Darn as above, but stitch in both lengthwise and crosswise directions, following the grain of the fabric.

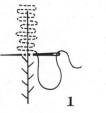

2

3. **L-Shaped Tears:** Darn as above, but overlap stitches at the corner for additional strength.

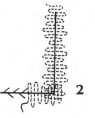

3

4. **Holes:** First fill in lengthwise threads as close together as the original weave. Then fill in crosswise threads by weaving over and under lengthwise threads.

4

Source: Stitch in Time Education Leaflets © Coats & Clark Inc.

STAIN REMOVAL GUIDE FOR FABRICS

T est fabric for color-fastness before using any stain-removing method. Proceed with the steps only as far as needed to remove the stain. Be careful when using cleaning agents as some are poisonous and/or flammable. After treatment, launder or dry-clean item as usual.

SUPPLIES NEEDED

Absorbent materials: Absorbent cotton, white paper towels or facial tissues, soft white cloths (for blotting).

Alcohol, denatured or rubbing: Do not use on acrylic, acetate or triacetate.

Ammonia, household: Do not use on wool or silk.

Amyl acetate (available in drug stores) or nonoily nail polish remover.

Chlorine bleach: Check care label of material to see if safe to use. If not, use an all-fabric bleach.

Detergent, liquid hand-dishwashing.

Drycleaning solvent

Dry-spotter: 1 part coconut oil (available at drug or health-food stores) or mineral oil and 8 parts drycleaning solvent. Store in glass container with tight-fitting lid.

Enzyme product: Enzyme presoak or laundry detergent — check labels.

Eye dropper: For flushing or rinsing stain or applying solutions in small amounts.

Hydrogen peroxide (3% solution): Use, with a drop of ammonia, instead of bleach for final cleaning of blood, chocolate or mustard stains.

Vinegar, white

Wet spotter: 1 part glycerine (available at drug stores), 1 part liquid dishwashing detergent and 8 parts water. Shake well. Store in plastic squeeze bottle.

STAIN   TREATMENT

STAIN	TREATMENT
Alcoholic beverages, cough syrup, coffee, fruit, soda, tea, vegetables, wine	**Washables:** Sponge with cool water. Soak in solution of 1 quart warm water, 1/2 teaspoon detergent and 1 tablespoon vinegar; rinse. (Red wine: Flush with alcohol.) **Nonwashables:** Flush with cool water. Apply wet-spotter with few drops of vinegar; blot. (Red wine: Lukewarm-water rinse. Blot with alcohol.)
Baby food, catsup, cheese sauce, chocolate, egg, gravy, ice cream, milk, sauces, vegetable soups	**Washables:** Sponge with cold water. Cover with absorbent material moistened with dry-spotter until stain is removed; blot occasionally. Flush with drycleaning solvent; let dry. Sponge with water; apply few drops of detergent and few drops of ammonia. Flush with water. Soak in solution of 1 quart warm water to 1 tablespoon enzyme product. Rinse with water. **Nonwashables:** Blot. Cover with absorbent material moistened with solution of 1/2 teaspoon enzyme product and 1/2 cup warm water. Flush with water.
Blood, meat soups, mucus, vomit	**Washables:** Soak in cold water. Soak in solution of 1 quart warm water, 1/2 teaspoon detergent and 1 tablespoon ammonia; blot. If stain persists, soak in solution of 1 quart water with 1 tablespoon enzyme product. **Nonwashables:** Sponge with cold water. Cover with pad moistened with wet-spotter and few drops of ammonia. Moisten with solution of 1/2 teaspoon enzyme product and 1/2 cup warm water for 30 minutes.
Bluing, fabric and hair dyes, food coloring, vegetable colors, watercolor paints	**Washables:** Soak in solution of 1 quart warm water, 1/2 teaspoon detergent and 1 tablespoon vinegar; rinse; let dry. Cover with pad moistened with alcohol; blot; flush with alcohol; let dry. Soak in solution of 1 quart warm water, 1/2 teaspoon detergent and 1 tablespoon ammonia; rinse with water. **Nonwashables:** Sponge with cool water. Apply wet-spotter with few drops of vinegar; blot; flush with water; let dry. Cover with pad moistened with alcohol; blot; flush with alcohol; sponge with water. Apply wet-spotter with few drops of ammonia; flush with water.

STAIN	TREATMENT
Candle wax	Place between paper towels; iron at low temperature; continue changing paper towels and ironing until no more wax melts. Sponge with drycleaning solvent. Apply wet-spotter and few drops of ammonia; flush with water.
Car wax, crayon, grease, lard, makeup, inks (other than ballpoint), margarine, paint (solvent or water base), tar	Sponge with drycleaning solvent. Cover with absorbent material moistened with dry-spotter; blot occasionally. Flush with drycleaning solvent; let dry. Sponge with water. Blot with wet-spotter with few drops of ammonia; flush with water.
Deodorant, perspiration, red dyes, inks or watercolors, urine	**Washables:** Soak in cold water. Soak in solution of 1 quart warm water, 1/2 teaspoon detergent and 1 tablespoon ammonia for 30 minutes; rinse with water; let dry. Cover with alcohol-dampened pad; blot. **Nonwashables:** Sponge with cold water. Cover with pad moistened with wet-spotter and few drops of ammonia; blot; flush with water. Apply wet spotter with few drops of vinegar; blot; flush with water. Apply alcohol; flush with water.
Glues, household cement, lacquer, mucilage, varnish	Sponge with drycleaning solvent. Cover with absorbent material moistened with dry-spotter; blot occasionally. Flush with drycleaning solvent; let dry. Cover with pad dampened with amyl acetate; blot occasionally; flush with drycleaning solvent.
Grass	Sponge with drycleaning solvent; let dry. Rub gently with amyl-acetate-dampened pad; flush with drycleaning solvent; let dry; sponge with water. Add small amount of wet-spotter and several drops of vinegar; flush with water; let dry. Rub gently with alcohol-dampened pad.
Lipstick	Apply drycleaning solvent and dry-spotter and blot immediately. Repeat until no more stain is removed. Let dry; sponge with water. Apply wet-spotter with few drops of ammonia; blot; flush with water. Apply wet-spotter with few drops of vinegar; blot. Flush with water; let dry. Sponge with alcohol; let dry.
Mildew	Gently scrape or brush off excess. Flush with drycleaning solvent. Apply dry-spotter and amyl acetate; blot gently. Flush with drycleaning solvent; let dry. Sponge with water. Pat with wet-spotter and vinegar; flush with water. Pat with alcohol; flush with alcohol; let dry.
Mustard	Gently scrape or brush off excess. Flush with drycleaning solvent; let dry. Sponge with water. Apply wet-spotter and vinegar; flush with water.
Oils (vegetable and fish), butter, chewing gum	Place absorbent material under stain. Cover with pad dampened with drycleaning fluid. Cover with pad moistened with dry-spotter. Flush with drycleaning fluid; let dry. For oils, first sprinkle stain with baby powder to absorb, then brush off before treating. For gum, rub with ice cube or place in freezer to harden; scrape off excess before treating.
Pen ink (ballpoint)	Apply lukewarm glycerine; blot; flush with water. Apply wet-spotter; blot. Add several drops of ammonia; blot; flush with water.
Rust	**Washables:** Use commercial rust remover. Or rub with lemon juice; let dry; wash. NEVER use chlorine bleach. **Nonwashables:** Dry-clean.
Scorch	Wet with hydrogen peroxide and a drop of ammonia. Let stand a few minutes or more. (Keep moist.) Flush with water.
Unknown stains	Sponge with drycleaning solvent. Apply dry-spotter. Flush with drycleaning solvent. Repeat as needed. Apply amyl acetate. Flush with drycleaning solvent; let dry. Sponge with water; add wet-spotter with few drops of vinegar. Apply wet-spotter with few drops of ammonia; let dry. Sponge with alcohol-dampened pad; let dry.

Source: U.S. Dept. of Agriculture

LAUNDRY GUIDE

Proper washing, drying and ironing of fabrics will help to prolong the life of your clothes. But first, always check manufacturers label for specific care instructions.

FABRIC AND CARE

ACETATE, TRIACETATE
Dry-clean. If washable, hand- or machine-wash, gentle cycle, in warm water and all-purpose detergent. Machine-dry at low temperature, or air-dry. Iron on cool setting.

COTTON
Using all-purpose detergent, hand- or machine-wash in warm water (for color-fast items) or cold (for all others); use bleach, if necessary, for whites only. (Dry-cleaning not recommended.) Line-dry, or machine-dry, normal setting; remove while still damp. (For knits, pull into shape; finish drying flat in room air.) Iron, while damp, on hot setting.

LINEN
Dry-clean to keep crisp texture. Or hand- or machine-wash in warm or cool water using all-purpose detergent. Line or machine-dry remove while still damp. Iron while damp.

NYLON, POLYESTER, ACRYLIC
Turn garments inside out during washing and drying to minimize pilling. Using all-purpose detergent, hand- or machine-wash (gentle cycle) in warm water. Drip-dry or dry in machine on permanent-press cycle. If necessary, iron nylon on cool, polyester on warm.

RAYON
Dry-clean. If washable, hand-wash in warm water using mild detergent. Do not wring or twist. Tumble-dry at low setting. Remove while damp and pull into shape. Iron, while damp, at warm setting.

SILK
Dry-clean. If labeled washable, hand-wash in tepid or cold water with mild detergent as soon as possible after wearing, to prevent damage from perspiration. Roll in towel to absorb excess moisture, then air-dry. Iron, while damp, on cool setting.

SPANDEX
Hand- or machine-wash in warm water and all-purpose detergent. Line-dry or machine-dry at moderate temperature. Do not use bleach. Do not overdry.

WOOL
Dry-clean. If washable, hand-wash in cool water and mild detergent. Roll in towel, gently squeeze (do not wring) out excess moisture and pull into shape. Dry flat in room air; do not machine-dry.

Source: Rutgers University Cooperative Extension; International Fabricare Institute

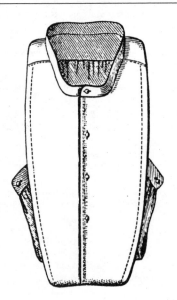

HOME STAIN REMOVAL

For best results, try to clean up spills and stains as soon as they occur. Test stain-removal method on an inconspicuous area first.

SURFACE AND STAIN/TREATMENT

Carpets

Beverages, syrup, inks: Blot up excess. Apply solution of 1 teaspoon detergent to 1 cup cool water. Rinse with clean, cool water; blot excess. Let dry.

Butter, oils, ballpoint inks: Blot or scrape up excess. Apply liquid drycleaning solvent with absorbent material until stain is removed. Let dry; gently brush rug pile. Blood, milk products, egg, sauces: blot or scrape up excess. Apply drycleaning solvent, then clean with solution of 1 teaspoon detergent to 1 cup cool water.

Animal urine: Blot up excess. Rinse several times with clean lukewarm water. Apply solution of half white vinegar, half cool water. Blot up excess, rinse with water, let dry.

Countertop Laminates

Wash with warm, sudsy water. Rub with baking soda and soft, damp cloth or sponge. For tougher stains, wipe with cloth moistened with bleach.

Marble

Food and beverage stains: Make a paste of hydrogen peroxide (hair-bleach strength) and whiting (abrasive powder available at hardware stores). Add a few drops of clear household ammonia. Spread paste on stains, cover with plastic wrap and let stand several hours. Repeat as necessary. Rinse and dry thoroughly.

Butter, oils: Wipe surface with ammonia-dampened cloth. Make paste of equal parts amyl acetate (available at drug stores) and acetone, ammonia and whiting. Spread on stains and cover with plastic wrap and let stand several hours. Repeat as necessary. Rinse and dry thoroughly.

Sinks, tubs

Use baking soda. If badly stained, soak in vinegar or lemon juice. For tough stains, use solution of 1 part oxalic acid to 10 parts water (poisonous; wear protective gloves). Can mix with cornmeal to make a paste. (Do not get any on chrome fixtures.) Rinse off completely.

Upholstery Fabric

Treat as for carpets (above) or as for fabric stains (page 92). Test on inconspicuous area first.

Leather

Briskly rub with solution of warm water and castile or saddle soap. Wipe with clean, damp cloth. Rub with soft, clean cloth to dry.

Vinyl

Sponge with equal parts denatured alcohol and water, or rubbing alcohol alone. Then apply saddle soap. Rinse with clear water. Dry with clean cloth. For grease or oil stains, use a vinyl cleaner.

Painted Walls

Dust. Wash with solution of mild detergent water, washing from bottom up. Crayon marks: Use liquid paint cleaner.

Wallpaper

Test washability in inconspicuous place. Wash with mild detergent and cool water. If nonwashable, rub gently with art gum (available at hardware stores).

Grease stains: Apply paste or rug-cleaning powder moistened with drycleaning solvent; let dry; remove with soft cloth.

Crayon marks: Sponge with drycleaning solvent.

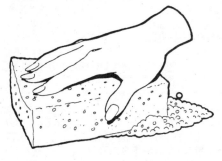

Wood

Spots, rings: Sprinkle cigarette ashes, salt or rottenstone (available at hardware stores) over spot. Gently rub, in direction of gain, with cloth moistened in linseed or mineral oil. Wipe dry with clean cloth. Repolish as usual.

Candlewax: Gently scrape off as much as possible. Wipe remaining spot with cloth moistened with mineral oil or drycleaning solvent. Repolish as usual.

Source: Cooperative Extensive Service of the Northeast States; U.S. Dept. of Agriculture.

KEEPING YOUR CAR IN TUNE

Periodic checkups, inspection and maintenance of your car's ignition, carburetor and emissions systems ensure efficient engine performance. Here's what you should know when your car goes in for a tune-up.

1. INSPECT THE DISTRIBUTOR CAP FOR CRACKS AND FOR EROSION OF THE TERMINALS. CAP AND ROTOR SHOULD BE REPLACED IF NECESSARY.

2. PITTED BREAKER POINTS AND/OR WORN RUBBING BLOCK HINDER PERFORMANCE AND MAY CAUSE STARTING TROUBLE. REPLACE POINTS AND CONDENSER AS PART OF THE TUNE-UP. (NOT APPLICABLE ON CARS WITH ELECTRONIC IGNITION.)

3. LOOSE OR CORRODED CONNECTIONS AT THE COIL CAN CAUSE STARTING TROUBLE.

4. IGNITION WIRES AND BOOTS DETERIORATE WITH AGE, CAUSING THE SPARK TO SHORT CIRCUIT. WIRING USUALLY IS REPLACED WITH EVERY SECOND OR THIRD TUNE-UP.

5. THE SPARK PLUG FIRING TIP GIVES CLUES ON ENGINE CONDITION. LOOK FOR WORN OR BURNED ELECTRODES, SOOTY OR OILY DEPOSITS WHEN INSPECTING SPARK PLUGS. PLUGS SHOULD BE REPLACED AS PART OF A TUNE-UP.

6. INCORRECT TIMING CAN CAUSE "PINGING" OR POOR ENGINE PERFORMANCE. TIMING ADJUSTMENT IS AN ESSENTIAL PART OF TUNE-UP.

7. EVEN MAINTENANCE-FREE BATTERIES CAN ACCUMULATE CORROSION ON TERMINALS. CORRODED CONNECTIONS CUT CURRENT FLOW, CAUSING HARD STARTING AND/OR PREVENT THE BATTERY FROM FULLY CHARGING.

8. ROUGH IDLING OR HARD STARTING MAY BE DUE TO STICKING CHOKE MECHANISM OR BROKEN VACUUM LINES.

9. FUEL FILTERS TRAP DIRT BEFORE GAS REACHES THE CARBURETOR. A CLOGGED FILTER STARVES THE ENGINE OF GAS. THE FUEL FILTER SHOULD BE REPLACED AS PART OF A TUNE-UP.

10. THE AIR FILTER USUALLY IS REPLACED AS PART OF THE TUNE-UP. IF YOU CANNOT SEE LIGHT THROUGH A DIRTY AIR FILTER, CHANGE IT.

11. A TUNE-UP SHOULD INCLUDE IDLE SPEED ADJUSTMENT.

12. THE "STOVE PIPE" PREHEATS AIR TO THE CARBURETOR. IT SHOULD BE CLOSED WHEN COLD, OPEN WHEN ENGINE WARMS UP.

13. THE PCV VALVE IS ANOTHER REPLACEMENT ITEM. WHEN IT STICKS, ENGINE PERFORMANCE IS IMPAIRED.

Source: Car Care Council

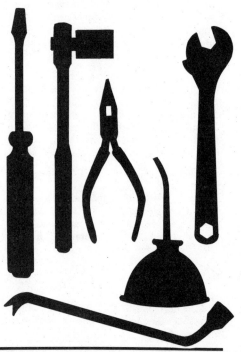

Tire Pressures

Inadequate tire inflation affects tire wear, fuel consumption and car handling. Pressures should be checked in the morning, when the tires are cool.

Recommended inflation pressures:
Check label on glove-compartment or fuel-tank door, passenger-door post or in owner's manual.

Maximum inflation pressures
(usually marked on sidewall):

Load range B	32 psi*
Alpha-numeric	
Standard load	35 psi
P-metric	

For better fuel economy and tire life:
Increase to 2 or 3 more psi over manufacturer's recommended pressure, but do not exceed maximum.

In cold weather:
Increase to 4 psi over manufacturer's recommendation, but do not exceed maximum.

*psi = pounds per square inch

Sources: Goodyear Tire Co.; American Automobile Association

CAR MAINTENANCE CHECKLIST

To ensure your car's best performance, follow the maintenance schedule suggested by the manufacturer. In addition, you can help keep your car in top shape by making the following periodic checks.

WHEN	CHECK
Daily driving	✗ Abnormal vibration ✗ Brake pedal softness/hardness ✗ Brake noise ✗ Steering-wheel pull ✗ Slipping or noise in clutch or automatic transmission ✗ Exhaust-system roar ✗ Horn operation ✗ Windshield wiper operation/efficiency ✗ Dashboard warning lights and gauge readings ✗ Fuel or other unusual odor
Filling the gas tank	✗ Engine oil level ✗ Coolant level ✗ Windshield washer-fluid level
Monthly	✗ Tires and spare for cuts and wear ✗ Tire pressure ✗ Lights operation ✗ Fluid leaks (inspect ground under parked car)
Twice a year (spring and fall)	✗ Power steering fluid level ✗ Brake fluid level ✗ Automatic/manual transmission fluid level ✗ Hydraulically operated clutch fluid level ✗ Rear-axle fluid level ✗ Protection level strength of coolant ✗ Drive belts ✗ Radiator, heater and air-conditioner hoses ✗ Exhaust-system components for signs of rust-through; retighten clamps ✗ Tire-makers' rotation recommendation; rotate tires if enough mileage has been traveled since last rotation (usually at first 7,500 miles, then every 15,000 thereafter) ✗ Four-wheel-drive axle boots for cracks, leaks ✗ Battery and starter motor cable terminals for corrosion
Yearly	✗ Brake lines for cracks, brake pads/linings for wear (Check twice a year if driving is mostly stop-and-go) ✗ Lock cylinders lubrication ✗ Lubrication for door, hood, trunk and fuel door hinges or latches ✗ Lubrication and wear of door weatherstripping ✗ Parking brake and "park" position of automatic transmisson ✗ Underbody of vehicle; flush with water and clean off mud and salt buildup

IN THE GARDEN

PERENNIALS PLANTING GUIDE

Perennials are plants whose roots live from year to year. Though they require attention, they do well in most areas of the country. Below are some of the most common perennials and their planting times.

PLANT	When to plant seed
ACHILLEA (yarrow)	Early spring or late fall
ALLYSSUM (golddust)	Early spring
ANCHUSA (alkanet)	Spring to Sept.
ANEMONE (windflower)	Early spring or late fall
ANTHEMIS (golden daisy)	Spring, after soil has warmed; can be started indoors 8 weeks before
ARABIS (rockcress)	Spring to Sept.
ARMERIA (sea pink)	Spring to Sept.
ARTEMISIA (dusty miller)	Late spring to late summer
ASTER	Early spring
ASTILBE JAPONICA	Early spring
AUBRIETA (rainbow rockcress)	Spring to Sept.
BEGONIA	Summer
CANDYTUFT	Early spring or late fall
CANTERBURY BELLS (campanula)	Spring to Sept.
CARNATION	Late spring
CANTAUREA (cornflower)	Early spring
CERASTIUM (snow-in-summer)	Early spring
CHINESE LANTERNS	Late fall or early winter
COLUMBINE	Spring to Sept.
COREOPSIS	Early spring or late fall
DAISY, (English shasta)	Early spring or late fall. Early spring to Sept.
DELPHINIUM	Spring to Sept.
DIANTHUS	Spring to Sept.
FOXGLOVE	Spring to Sept.
GAILLARDIA	Early spring or late summer
GEUM	Spring or summer
GYPSOPHILIA (baby's breath)	Spring to Sept.
HELIANTHEMUM (sun rose)	Spring to Sept.
HELLEBORUS (Christmas rose)	Late fall or early winter; for spring planting, refrigerate seeds for 2 months before sowing
HEMEROCALLIS (daylily)	Late fall or early spring

PLANT	When to plant seed
HEUCHERA (coral bells)	Early spring or late fall
HIBISCUS (mallow marvels)	Spring or summer
HOLLYHOCK	Spring to Sept.
IRIS	Late fall
LIATRIS (gayfeather)	Early spring or late fall
LINUM (flax)	Spring to Sept.
LUNARIA (money plant)	Early spring
LUPINE	Early spring or late fall
LYTHRUM (blackblood)	Late fall or early spring
MONARDA (horsemint)	Spring or summer
PENSTEMON (beardlip, pagoda flower)	Early spring or late fall
PEONY	Difficult to grow from seed; plant tubers in late fall
PHLOX	Late fall or early winter
PLATYCODON (balloonflower)	Spring and Sept.
POPPY, Iceland and oriental	Early spring
PRIMROSE	Late autumn or early winter; for spring planting, first freeze seed in ice cubes
PYRETHRUM (chrysanthemum, painted daisy)	Spring to Sept.
RUDBECKIA (coneflower)	Spring to Sept.
SALVIA	Spring
SEA LAVENDER (blue statice)	Early spring, while soil is cool
SIBERIAN WALLFLOWER	Early spring, while soil is cool
STOKESIA (Stokes; aster)	Spring to Sept.
SWEETPEA	Early spring
SWEET WILLIAM	Spring to Sept.
TRITOMA (red-hot poker)	Early spring or late fall
TROLLIUS (glove flower)	Late fall
VERONICA (speedwell)	Spring to Sept.
VIOLA CORNUTA (tufted pansy)	Spring to Sept.

Source: U.S. Dept. of Agriculture

ANNUALS PLANTING GUIDE

Annuals play out their life cycle in one year, bringing quick color to your garden. They're easy to grow and do well in most areas of the country.

PLANT	When to plant seed
AGERATUM	After last frost
BABYSBREATH	Early spring or summer
BALSAM	After last frost
CALENDULA	Early spring or late fall
CALLIOPSIS	After last frost
CANDYTUFT	Early spring or late fall
CHINA-ASTER	After last frost
COCKSCOMB	After last frost
COLEUS	Sow indoors anytime; outdoors after last frost
CORNFLOWER	Early spring
COSMOS	After last frost
DAHLIA	After last frost
FORGET-ME-NOT	Spring or summer; shade in summer
FOUR O'CLOCK	After last frost
GAILLARDIA	Early spring through summer; shade in summer
GLOBE-AMARANTH	Early spring
IMPATIENS	Indoors anytime. Set out after last frost
LARKSPUR	Late fall in South, early spring in North
LUPINE	Early spring or late fall
MARIGOLD	After last frost
MORNING-GLORY	After last frost
NASTURTIUM	After last frost
PANSY	Spring or summer; shade in summer

PLANT	When to plant seed
PETUNIA	Late fall (in South)
PHLOX	Early spring
PINK	Early spring, spring or summer; shade in summer
POPPY	Early spring through summer; shade in summer
PORTULACA	After last frost or in late fall
RUDBECKIA	Spring or summer; shade in summer
SALPIGLOSSIS	Early spring
SCABIOSA	Spring or summer; shade in summer
SCARLET SAGE	Spring or summer; shade in summer
SNAPDRAGON	Spring or late fall
SPIDER PLANT	Early spring; spring, or fall
STOCK	
STRAWFLOWER	Early spring
SUMMER-CYPRESS	Early spring
SUNFLOWER	After last frost
SWEET ALYSSUM	Early spring
SWEETPEA	Early spring or late summer through late fall
VERBENA	After last frost
VINCA	After last frost
ZINNIA	After last frost

Source: U.S. Dept. of Agriculture

BULB PLANTING GUIDE

Plants grown from bulbs, corms or tubers bring color in your garden from spring to fall. These varieties are the most common and are easy to cultivate.

FOR SPRING FLOWERING

FLOWER	WHEN TO PLANT
Allium (flowering onion)	Late fall
Amaryllis	Early December in pot; put outside in May
Anemone (windflower)	October
Chinonodoxa (glory-of-the-snow)	Fall
Crocus	Oct. or early Nov.
Daffodil	Sept. and Oct.
Eranthis (winter aconite)	Fall
Fritillaria	Fall
Galanthus (snowdrop)	Sept. or Oct.
Hyacinth	Oct.
Iris, dwarf	Oct. or Nov.
Leucojum (snowflake)	Fall
Lily-of-the-valley	Late summer
Muscari (grape hyacinth)	October
Narcissus	Sept. and Oct.
Ornithogalum (star of Bethlehem)	Sept. to Nov.
Oxalis	In warm climates, Oct. In cold climates, use indoors: Plant in pot in Oct.; keep in cool, dark place until buds appear, then move to bright room
Puschikinia (Lebanon squill)	Fall
Ranunculus	In warm climates: Dec. to mid-April; in cold regions, spring, after danger of freezing has passed
Scilla (squill and bluebells)	Oct. and Nov.
Tulip	Late Oct. or early Nov.

FOR SUMMER FLOWERING

FLOWER	WHEN TO PLANT
Achimenes (nut orchid)	Early spring in pots; plant outdoors after last killing frost
Allium (flowering onion)	Early spring
Amaryllis	May, after soil has warmed
Begonia	Feb. or March, indoors in dark room; when shoots appear, move them to lighted room, then 6 weeks later, plant outdoors
Caladium (including elephant's ears)	Jan. to mid-May in flats; when roots develop, plant outdoors
Calla	Oct., in pots
Canna	March to May, in flats; when shoots appear, replant in pots, then plant outdoors when all danger of frost has passed
Colchicum	August (blooms in autumn)
Dahlia	For dormant roots, plant outdoors in spring after danger of frost has passed
Daylily	Early spring to late summer
Gladiolus	Spring, as soon as soil is dry enough to work, until early July
Gloxinia	Late winter or in spring, in pots; plant outdoors after last killing frost
Iris, tall	Oct.
Ismene (Peruvian daffodil)	Jan. to mid-May, in flats; when roots develop, plant in pots or outdoor
Lilium candidum (Madonna lilly) all other lilium hybrids	Sept. Oct. and Nov.
Lycoris (spider lily)	August
Montbretia	Spring, as soon as soil is dry enough to work, until early July
Peony	Sept. or early Oct.
Tigridia (Mexican shell flower)	Spring, as soon as soil is dry enough to work, until early July
Tuberose	May

Source: U.S. Dept. of Agriculture

PLANTING YOUR VEGETABLE GARDEN

Dates for planting vegetables vary widely from region to region. These common vegetables are grouped according to the approximate times they can be planted and their relative requirements for cool and warm weather. The spring "frost-free date" is usually 2 to 3 weeks earlier than the average date of the last freeze for your area.

Cold-hardy plants for early-spring planting		Cold-tender or heat-hardy plants for later-spring or early-summer planting			Hardy plants for late-summer or fall planting except in the North (plant 6 to 8 weeks before first fall freeze)
Very hardy (plant 4 to 6 weeks before frost-free date)	Hardy (plant 2 to 4 weeks before frost-free date)	Not cold-hardy (plant on frost-free date)	Requiring hot weather (plant 1 week or more after frost-free date)	Medium heat-tolerant (good for summer planting)	
Broccoli Cabbage Lettuce Onions Peas Potato Spinach Turnip	Beets Carrot Chard Mustard Parsnip Radish	Beans, snap Okra New Zealand spinach Tomato	Beans, lima Eggplant Peppers Sweet-potato Cucumber Melons	Beans, all Soybean Squash Sweet corn	Beets Collard Kale Lettuce Mustard Spinach Turnip

Source: U.S. Department of Agriculture

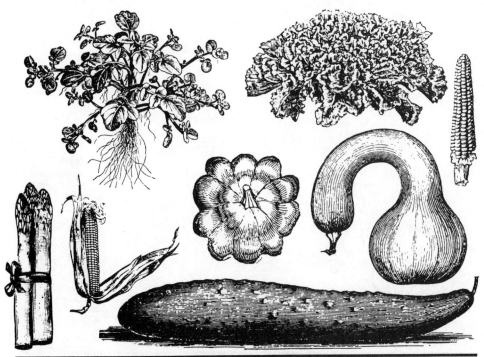

TREE PLANTING GUIDE

The most favorable planting season for shade and fruit trees varies with the region's climate, soil and type of tree, so check with your local agricultural agent before following these general guidelines.

Tree	When To Plant
DECIDUOUS (ash, beech, birch, buckeye, catalpa, elm, hickory, horsechestnut, larch, linden maple, oak, sassafras, weeping willow, etc.)	Bare-rooted, in autumn, after leaves change color and before ground freezes; or in late winter or early spring after the ground has thawed and before buds start to grow.
EVERGREENS Broadleaf (bayberry, eucalyptus, holly, live oak, southern magnolia)	In spring; or autumn, if roots allowed time to grow before the ground freezes.
Needle-leaf (arborvitae, cedar, cypress, fir, hemlock junipere, pine, spruce)	In cold regions: Early fall or in spring after ground has thawed. Balled-and-burlapped or containered trees, anytime the ground is workable; mulch and water after planting. In warm regions: anytime, if watered regularly after planting. Young trees, bare-rooted; larger ones: balled and burlapped.
Palms	During warm, wet months; or anytime if watered regularly after planting.
FRUIT TREES Apple	Anytime when trees are dormant and ground is workable and not waterlogged. Cold regions: early spring; elsewhere: late autumn.
Apricot	Late autumn.
Cherry, nectarine, peach, plum	Fall; spring in cold climates.
Citrus (orange, lemon)	Fall to early spring in frost-free regions only.
Fig	Early spring.
Mulberry	Late spring.
Pear	Between leaf-fall and March.
Persimmon	Late autumn or early spring.

Source: U.S. Dept. of Agriculture

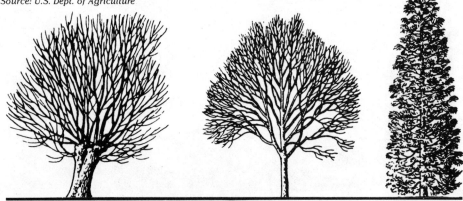

Shrub Planting Guide

In general, deciduous shrubs not grown in containers can be planted in their dormant season, from mid-autumn to early spring; evergreens, from mid- to late autumn or mid-spring. Container-grown shrubs can be planted anytime the soil is not frozen, or very wet or very dry; be careful not to disturb the roots.

SHRUB	WHEN TO PLANT	BUSH, VINE AND CANE FRUITS	WHEN TO PLANT
Azaleas	Fall or early spring	Blackberry, loganberry. raspberry	Autumn; or spring, in very cold regions
Beauty berry	Early spring or fall		
Bluebeard	Spring, as soon as soil is dry enough to work		
Butterflybush	Spring	Blueberry, cranberry	Between autumn and early spring
Buttonbush	Spring	Currant, gooseberry	Autumn, or early spring
Camellias	Fall in the South; spring in the North		
Carolina allspice	Early spring or fall	Grape	Pot-grown vines, anytime; others, late autumn — or early spring in harsh climates
Chaste-tree	Spring		
Crape myrtle	Late fall or early spring	Strawberries	For summer varieties, mid-summer to autumn; spring, where winters are harsh. For autumn varieties (perpetuals), spring.
Devil's walkingstick	Spring, transplant barerooted		
Flowering raspberry	Early spring		
Germander	Early spring or fall	Rhododendron	Fall or early spring
Glory bower	Spring, especially in cold climates	Rose-of-Sharon	Spring
Glossy abelia	Spring	Roses	In colder regions, early spring; other areas, fall or spring
Heath	Spring or fall		
Heather	Spring or fall	Shrubby bushclover	Spring or fall
Hydrangea, house oakleaf peegee snowhill	Early spring or early fall Early spring Spring or fall Early spring or fall	Spirea, Japanese white froebel	Spring or fall Early spring or fall
Leatherwood	Spring or fall	Stewartia	Early spring or fall
Lilacs	Fall, after leaves have dropped and before ground freezes; or spring, before buds unfold	St. John's wort, goldflower Other varieties	Spring only Spring or fall
Nandina	Spring	Summersweet	Fall or spring, carefully
New Jersey tea	Spring; set out very carefully — difficult to transplant	Swamp azalea	In cold climates, spring; in the South, winter
Ocean spray	Early spring or fall		
Potentilla (cinquefoil and golddrop)	Early spring or fall		

Source: U.S. Dept. of Agriculture

FERTILIZER GUIDE

The use and content of commercial fertilizers depend on your locale, soil quality and what specifically will be grown — so consider this just a general guideline. The numbers on fertilizer labels give the percentages of nitrogen (for leaf growth), phosphorus (a bloom, fruit and seed stimulant) and potassium (for roots). For instance, 5-10-5 contains 5% nitrogen, 10% phosphorus and 5% potassium (and 80% inactive ingredients).

PLANT	FERTILIZER	WHEN
Annuals	10-10-10	Every 3 to 4 weeks after planting
Berry bushes, grapes	10-10-10	Early spring; after harvest
Bulbs	10-10-10	At planting; after foliage begins to emerge
Ground covers	5-10-5	Early spring
Houseplants	Fish emulsion	Monthly: Spring and summer — full strength; fall and winter — half strength
Lawns, new established	5-10-5￼ 10-6-4	Early spring; September Early spring; late fall
Perennials	5-10-5	Early spring
Roses	Rose fertilizer	Monthly, until 6 weeks before usual first frost
Shrubs	5-10-5	Early spring; after flowering
	12-6-6	Late spring
Strawberries	10-10-10	At planting, after fruiting
Trees, fruit	12-6-6	Late fall or early spring; after flowering
Trees, shade 　mature	10-6-4 or 12-6-6	After dormancy in fall
young	5-10-5	At planting
	12-6-6	After dormancy in fall
Vegetables 　leafy	High nitrogen	A few days before or at planting
root	High potassium	

GUIDE TO WEEDKILLERS

Below are herbicide formulations to help rid your garden of different types of weeds. Be sure to follow instructions on the product labels exactly.

	Common name(s)	Weeds controlled/Cautions
Foliar contact herbicides	Paraquat; paraquat + diquat	Total kill of foliage and annuals. Repeated treatment needed for perennials; lethal poison to humans and animals; use banned in some areas.
Translocated leaf-acting herbicides for lawns and spot treatment	2,4-D	Daisy, dandelion, docks, buttercup, creeping thistles, plantains, bellbine, convolvulus, annual nettle, ground ivy. Harmful to fish.
	2,4-D + dicamba	Most broad-leaved weeds, such as chickweed, clover, dandelion, ground ivy, henbit, knotweed, oxalis, pigweed, plantains, purslane, thistles, wild onion, etc. Apply at any time during active growth.
	2,4-D + dicamba + silvex	Excellent for control of most lawn weeds. No injury to desirable lawn grasses.
Other translocated leaf-acting herbicides	2,4,5-T	Especially effective against brambles, blackjack oak and Osage orange, and for basal treatment of brush in dormant season; commonly used in combination with 2,4-D as a brushwood killer.
	Dalapon	Perennial grasses such as Bermuda grass, foxtail and cat's-tails; can be used in dormant fruit plantings.
	Glyphosate	Nonselective – controls wide range of weeds. Nonpersistent.
	Prometone	Fast-acting against most annual and perennial broad-leaved weeds and grasses. One application per season is usually enough.
Soil-acting selective herbicides	DCPA	Excellent for control of many broad-leaved weeds in lawns; safe among many vegetables, ornamental shrubs and bedding plants. Very safe.
	Dichlobenil	Selective at low strength; controls wide range of annual and perennial weeds; can be used around evergreens and deciduous plants, but some shrubs harmed. Effectiveness improved by cultivating or mulching after application; does not move in soil; harmful to fish.
	Propachlor	Germinating weeds among some established vegetables, some bedding and herbaceous plants and shrubs. Persists six weeks.
	Simazine	Selective at low strength against germinating annual weeds in rose beds and shrub borders (but some shrubs susceptible, and avoid new growth). Not suitable for light or newly cultivated soils; otherwise, does not move in soil.
	Trifluralin	Annual grasses and broad-leaved weeds among trees, shrubs and herbaceous plants. More effective if soil is cultivated after application.
Soil-acting total herbicides	Ammonium sulphamate (AMS)	Poison ivy, poison oak and weed grasses. Persists 12 weeks.
	Dichlobenil	Total at high strength. Persists several months; does not move in soil; harmful to fish.
	Simazine + amitrole	Persists 12 months; does not move in soil; useful on paths.
	Sodium chlorate	Persists six months or more; moves in soil water; used on derelict land; inflammable when dry, but many brands have fire-depressant.
Lawn moss killers	Ammonium sulphate + ferrous (iron) sulphate	Moss, pearlwort. Ammonium sulphate is a fertilizer that raises soil acidity.
	Mercurous chloride (calomel)	Moss. Poisonous; also a lawn fungicide.
For aquatic weed control	Endothall + fenoprop	Wide range of submerged and emergent species. Wide safety margin for fish.
	Copper sulphate	Algae and aquatic weeds where residual material will not harm fish or animals.
	Diquat	Many aquatic weeds in slow-moving water. Harmless to fish at low doses.

Source: U.S. Dept. of Agriculture

GARDEN PESTS

Here's how to rid your indoor or outdoor garden of common plant pests. When using insecticides, follow directions on product label *exactly;* check suitability for specific plants.

APHIDS

Wash with soapy water (2 teaspoons mild detergent to 1 gallon water), using soft brush or cloth or trigger sprayer. Or swab leaves with rubbing alcohol. Or pick off pests by hand. Or use a commercial spray with malathion or oxydemetonmethyl.

CUTWORMS

Place 3-inch collar of stiff cardboard around plant, pushing 1 inch into soil. Apply diazinon or toxaphene to soil surface.

CASEBEARERS, BAGWORMS

Pick off insects by hand. Or use household insecticide spray containing *Bacillus thuringiensis,* diazinon, malathion or trichlorfon. Remove and completely destroy larvae "bags."

FUNGUS GNATS

To control at maggot stage, avoid overwatering plants. Repot in sterile soil after rinsing off roots. Spray adult gnats with spray containing pyrethrins.

GYPSY MOTH

Band tree trunks 2' to 4' above ground with sticky material, such as tanglefoot. Destroy egg masses before they hatch. Apply *Bacillus thuringiensis,* carbaryl or trichlorfon at caterpillar stage.

JAPANESE BEETLES

Shake trees or shrubs in early morning, catch bugs on plastic sheet and dump them into bucket of water with a little kerosene. Or apply carbaryl, methoxychlor or malathion to foliage or lawn infested with larvae.

MEALY BUGS

Wash with soapy water (2 teaspoons mild detergent to 1 gallon water), using soft brush or cloth or trigger sprayer. Or swab leaves with rubbing alcohol. Or pick off pests by hand. Isolate treated plants to avoid reinfestation. Outdoor plants, apply malathion.

SCALES

Wash with soapy water (2 teaspoons mild detergent to 1 gallon water), using soft brush or cloth or trigger sprayer. Discard heavily infested plants. Outdoors, scrape insects from twigs and crush them; heavy infestation, apply diazinon or malathion.

SLUGS, SNAILS

To trap, put out scraps of board or shingle, or shallow dishes of beer to attract the bugs, then destroy them. Or use commercial traps containing metaldehyde or methiocarb.

SPIDER MITES

Wash with soapy water using trigger sprayer. Dip or spray with malathion or dicofol (be sure to wet undersides of leaves). May need several applications at weekly intervals.

THRIPS

Use commercial pesticide labeled for "houseplants" and "thrips," following product directions.

WHITE FLIES

Spray plants — especially underside of leaves — with malathion, rotenone and pyrethrin combination. May need several applications at weekly intervals.

Source: U.S. Dept. of Agriculture

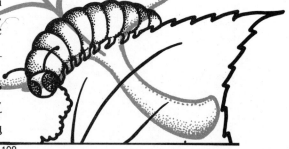

TRAVEL

DISTANCES BETWEEN CITIES

NOTE: These mileages are usually measured city hall-to-city hall.

AIR DISTANCES BETWEEN U.S. CITIES IN MILES

Cities	Birming-ham	Boston	Buffalo	Chicago	Cleveland	Dallas	Denver
Birmingham, Ala.	—	1,052	776	578	618	581	1,095
Boston, Mass.	1,052	—	400	851	551	1,551	1,769
Buffalo, N.Y.	776	400	—	454	173	1,198	1,370
Chicago, Ill	578	851	454	—	308	803	920
Cleveland, Ohio	618	551	173	308	—	1,025	1,227
Dallas, Tex.	581	1,551	1,198	803	1,025	—	663
Denver, Colo.	1,095	1,769	1,370	920	1,227	663	—
Detroit, Mich.	641	613	216	238	90	999	1,156
El Paso, Tex.	1,152	2,072	1,692	1,252	1,525	572	557
Houston, Tex.	567	1,605	1,286	940	1,114	225	879
Indianapolis, Ind.	433	807	435	165	263	763	1,000
Kansas City, Mo.	579	1,251	861	414	700	451	558
Los Angeles, Calif.	1,802	2,596	2,198	1,745	2,049	1,240	831
Louisville, Ky.	331	826	483	269	311	726	1,038
Memphis, Tenn.	217	1,137	803	482	630	420	879
Miami, Fla.	665	1,255	1,181	1,188	1,087	1,111	1,726
Minneapolis, Minn.	862	1,123	731	355	630	862	700
New Orleans, La.	312	1,359	1,086	833	924	443	1,082
New York, N.Y.	864	188	292	713	405	1,374	1,631
Omaha, Neb.	732	1,282	883	432	739	586	488
Philadelphia, Pa.	783	271	279	666	360	1,299	1,579
Phoenix, Ariz.	1,456	2,300	1,906	1,453	1,749	887	586
Pittsburgh, Pa.	608	483	178	410	115	1,070	1,320
St. Louis, Mo.	400	1,038	662	262	492	547	796
Salt Lake City, Utah	1,466	2,099	1,699	1,260	1,568	999	371
San Francisco, Calif.	2,013	2,699	2,300	1,858	2,166	1,483	949
Seattle, Wash.	2,082	2,493	2,117	1,737	2,026	1,681	1,021
Washington, D.C.	661	393	292	597	306	1,185	1,494

Cities	Detroit	El Paso	Houston	Indian-apolis	Kansas City	Los Angeles	Louisville
Birmingham, Ala.	641	1,152	567	433	579	1,802	331
Boston, Mass.	613	2,072	1,605	807	1,251	2,596	826
Buffalo, N.Y.	216	1,692	1,286	435	861	2,198	483
Chicago, Ill	238	1,252	940	165	414	1,745	269
Cleveland, Ohio	90	1,525	1,114	263	700	2,049	311
Dallas, Tex.	999	572	225	763	451	1,240	726
Denver, Colo.	1,156	557	879	1,000	558	831	1,038
Detroit, Mich.	—	1,479	1,105	240	645	1,983	316
El Paso, Tex.	1,479	—	676	1,264	839	701	1,254
Houston, Tex.	1,105	676	—	865	644	1,374	803
Indianapolis, Ind.	240	1,264	865	—	453	1,809	107
Kansas City, Mo.	645	839	644	453	—	1,356	480
Los Angeles, Calif.	1,983	701	1,374	1,809	1,356	—	1,829
Louisville, Ky.	316	1,254	803	107	480	1,829	—
Memphis, Tenn.	623	976	484	384	369	1,603	320
Miami, Fla.	1,152	1,643	968	1,024	1,241	2,339	919
Minneapolis,Minn.	543	1,157	1,056	511	413	1,524	605
New Orleans, La.	939	983	318	712	680	1,673	623
New York, N.Y.	482	1,905	1,420	646	1,097	2,451	652
Omaha, Neb.	669	878	794	525	166	1,315	580
Philadelphia, Pa.	443	1,836	1,341	585	1,038	2,394	582
Phoenix, Ariz.	1,690	346	1,017	1,499	1,049	357	1,508
Pittsburgh, Pa.	205	1,590	1,137	330	781	2,136	344
St. Louis, Mo.	455	1,034	679	231	238	1,589	242
Salt Lake City, Utah	1,492	689	1,200	1,356	925	579	1,402
San Francisco, Calif.	2,091	995	1,645	1,949	1,506	347	1,986
Seattle, Wash.	1,938	1,376	1,891	1,872	1,506	959	1,943
Washington, D.C.	396	1,728	1,220	494	945	2,300	476

Source: National Geodetic Survey

AIR DISTANCES BETWEEN U.S. CITIES IN MILES

Cities	Memphis	Miami	Minne-apolis	New Orleans	New York	Omaha	Phila-delphia
Birmingham, Ala.	217	665	862	312	864	732	783
Boston, Mass.	1,137	1,255	1,123	1,359	188	1,282	271
Buffalo, N.Y.	903	1,181	731	1,085	292	883	279
Chicago, Ill.	482	1,188	355	833	713	432	666
Cleveland, Ohio	630	1,087	630	924	405	739	360
Dallas, Tex	420	1,111	862	443	1,374	586	1,299
Denver, Colo.	879	1,726	700	1,082	1,631	488	1,579
Detroit, Mich.	623	1,152	543	939	482	669	443
El Paso, Tex.	976	1,643	1,157	983	1,905	878	1,836
Houston, Tex.	484	968	1,056	318	1,420	794	1,341
Indianapolis, Ind.	384	1,024	511	712	646	525	585
Kansas City, Mo.	369	1,241	413	680	1,097	166	1,038
Los Angeles, Calif.	1,603	2,339	1,524	1,673	2,451	1,315	2,394
Louisville, Ky.	320	919	605	623	652	580	582
Memphis, Tenn.	—	872	699	358	957	529	881
Miami, Fla.	872	—	1,511	669	1,092	1,397	1,019
Minneapolis, Minn.	699	1,511	—	1,051	1,018	290	985
New Orleans, La.	358	669	1,051	—	1,171	847	1,089
New York, N.Y.	957	1,092	1,018	1,171	—	1,144	83
Omaha, Neb.	529	1,397	290	847	1,144	—	1,094
Philadelphia, Pa.	881	1,019	985	1,089	83	1,094	—
Phoenix, Ariz.	1,263	1,982	1,280	1,316	2,145	1,036	2,083
Pittsburgh, Pa.	660	1,010	743	919	317	836	259
St. Louis, Mo.	240	1,061	466	598	875	354	811
Salt Lake City, Utah	1,250	2,089	987	1,434	1,972	833	1,925
San Francisco, Calif.	1,802	2,594	1,584	1,926	2,571	1,429	2,523
Seattle, Wash.	1,867	2,734	1,395	2,101	2,408	1,369	2,380
Washington, D.C.	765	923	934	966	205	1,014	123

Cities	Phoenix	Pitts-burgh	St. Louis	Salt Lake City	San Francisco	Seattle	Wash-ington
Birmingham, Ala.	1,456	608	400	1,466	2,013	2,082	661
Boston, Mass.	2,300	483	1,038	2,099	2,699	2,493	393
Buffalo, N.Y.	1,906	178	662	1,699	2,300	2,117	292
Chicago, Ill.	1,453	410	262	1,260	1,858	1,737	597
Cleveland, Ohio	1,749	115	492	1,568	2,166	2,026	306
Dallas, Tex.	887	1,070	547	999	1,483	1,681	1,185
Denver, Colo.	586	1,320	796	371	949	1,021	1,494
Detroit, Mich.	1,690	205	455	1,492	2,091	1,938	396
El Paso, Tex.	346	1,590	1,034	689	995	1,376	1,728
Houston, Tex.	1,017	1,137	679	1,200	1,645	1,891	1,220
Indianapolis, Ind.	1,499	330	231	1,356	1,949	1,872	494
Kansas City, Mo.	1,049	781	238	925	1,506	1,506	945
Los Angeles, Calif.	357	2,136	1,589	579	347	959	2,300
Louisville, Ky.	1,508	344	242	1,402	1,986	1,943	476
Memphis, Tenn.	1,263	660	240	1,250	1,802	1,867	765
Miami, Fla.	1,982	1,010	1,061	2,089	2,594	2,734	923
Minneapolis, Minn.	1,280	743	466	987	1,584	1,395	934
New Orleans, La.	1,316	919	598	1,434	1,926	2,101	966
New York, N.Y.	2,145	317	875	1,972	2,571	2,408	205
Omaha, Neb.	1,036	836	354	833	1,429	1,369	1,014
Philadelphia, Pa.	2,083	259	811	1,925	2,523	2,380	123
Phoenix, Ariz.	—	1,828	1,272	504	653	1,114	1,983
Pittsburgh, Pa.	1,828	—	559	1,668	2,264	2,138	192
St. Louis, Mo.	1,272	559	—	1,162	1,744	1,724	712
Salt Lake City, Utah	504	1,668	1,162	—	600	701	1,848
San Francisco, Calif.	653	2,264	1,744	600	—	678	2,442
Seattle, Wash.	1,114	2,138	1,724	701	678	—	2,329
Washington, D.C.	1,983	192	712	1,848	2,442	2,329	—

Source: National Geodetic Survey

AIR DISTANCES BETWEEN WORLD CITIES IN MILES

Cities	Berlin	Buenos Aires	Cairo	Calcutta	Cape Town	Caracas	Chicago
Berlin	—	7,402	1,795	4,368	5,981	5,247	4,405
Buenos Aires	7,402	—	7,345	10,265	4,269	3,168	5,598
Cairo	1,795	7,345	—	3,539	4,500	6,338	6,129
Calcutta	4,368	10,265	3,539	—	6,024	9,605	7,980
Cape Town, South Africa	5,981	4,269	4,500	6,024	—	6,365	8,494
Caracas, Venezuela	5,247	3,168	6,338	9,605	6,365	—	2,501
Chicago	4,405	5,598	6,129	7,980	8,494	2,501	—
Hong Kong	5,440	11,472	5,061	1,648	7,375	10,167	7,793
Honolulu, Hawaii	7,309	7,561	8,838	7,047	11,534	6,013	4,250
Istanbul	1,078	7,611	768	3,638	5,154	6,048	5,477
Lisbon	1,436	5,956	2,363	5,638	5,325	4,041	3,990
London	579	6,916	2,181	4,947	6,012	4,660	3,950
Los Angeles	5,724	6,170	7,520	8,090	9,992	3,632	1,745
Manila	6,132	11,051	5,704	2,203	7,486	10,620	8,143
Mexico City	6,047	4,592	7,688	9,492	8,517	2,232	1,691
Montreal	3,729	5,615	5,414	7,607	7,931	2,449	744
Moscow	1,004	8,376	1,803	3,321	6,300	6,173	4,974
New York	3,965	5,297	5,602	7,918	7,764	2,132	713
Paris	545	6,870	1,995	4,883	5,807	4,736	4,134
Rio de Janeiro	6,220	1,200	6,146	9,377	3,773	2,810	5,296
Rome	734	6,929	1,320	4,482	5,249	5,196	4,808
San Francisco	5,661	6,467	7,364	7,814	10,247	3,904	1,858
Shanghai, China	5,218	12,201	5,183	2,117	8,061	9,501	7,061
Stockholm	504	7,808	2,111	4,195	6,444	5,420	4,278
Sydney, Australia	10,006	7,330	8,952	5,685	6,843	9,513	9,272
Tokyo	5,540	11,408	5,935	3,194	9,156	8,799	6,299
Warsaw	320	7,662	1,630	4,048	5,958	5,517	4,667
Washington, D.C.	4,169	5,218	5,800	8,084	7,901	2,059	597

Cities	Hong Kong	Honolulu	Istanbul	Lisbon	London	Los Angeles	Manila
Berlin	5,440	7,309	1,078	1,436	579	5,724	6,132
Buenos Aires	11,472	7,561	7,611	5,956	6,916	6,170	11,051
Cairo	5,061	8,838	768	2,363	2,181	7,520	5,704
Calcutta	1,648	7,047	3,638	5,638	4,947	8,090	2,203
Cape Town, South Africa	7,375	11,534	5,154	5,325	6,012	9,992	7,486
Caracas, Venezuela	10,167	6,013	6,048	4,041	4,660	3,632	10,620
Chicago	7,793	4,250	5,477	3,990	3,950	1,745	8,143
Hong Kong	—	5,549	4,984	6,853	5,982	7,195	693
Honolulu, Hawaii	5,549	—	8,109	7,820	7,228	2,574	5,299
Istanbul	4,984	8,109	—	2,012	1,552	6,783	5,664
Lisbon	6,853	7,820	2,012	—	985	5,621	7,546
London	5,982	7,228	1,552	985	—	5,382	6,672
Los Angeles, Calif.	7,195	2,574	6,783	5,621	5,382	—	7,261
Manila	693	5,299	5,664	7,546	6,672	7,261	—
Mexico City	8,782	3,779	7,110	5,390	5,550	1,589	8,835
Montreal	7,729	4,910	4,789	3,246	3,282	2,427	8,186
Moscow	4,439	7,037	1,091	2,427	1,555	6,003	5,131
New York	8,054	4,964	4,975	3,364	3,458	2,451	8,498
Paris	5,985	7,438	1,400	904	213	5,588	6,677
Rio de Janeiro	11,021	8,285	6,389	4,796	5,766	6,331	11,259
Rome	5,768	8,022	843	1,161	887	6,732	6,457
San Francisco	6,897	2,393	6,703	5,666	5,357	347	6,967
Shanghai, China	764	4,941	4,962	6,654	5,715	6,438	1,150
Stockholm	5,113	6,862	1,348	1,856	890	5,454	5,797
Sydney, Australia	4,584	4,943	9,294	11,302	10,564	7,530	3,944
Tokyo	1,794	3,853	5,560	6,915	5,940	5,433	1,866
Warsaw	5,144	7,355	863	1,715	899	5,922	5,837
Washington, D.C.	8,147	4,519	5,215	3,562	3,663	2,300	8,562

Source: Encyclopaedia Britannica

AIR DISTANCES BETWEEN WORLD CITIES IN MILES

Cities	Mexico City	Montreal	Moscow	New York	Paris	Rio de Janeiro	Rome
Berlin	6,047	3,729	1,004	3,965	545	6,220	734
Buenos Aires	4,592	5,615	8,376	5,297	6,870	1,200	6,929
Cairo	7,688	5,414	1,803	5,602	1,995	6,146	1,320
Calcutta	9,492	7,607	3,321	7,918	4,883	9,377	4,482
Cape Town, South Africa	8,517	7,931	6,300	7,764	5,807	3,773	5,249
Caracas, Venezuela	2,232	2,449	6,173	2,132	4,736	2,810	5,196
Chicago	1,691	744	4,974	713	4,134	5,296	4,808
Hong Kong	8,782	7,729	4,439	8,054	5,985	11,021	5,768
Honolulu	3,779	4,910	7,037	4,964	7,438	8,285	8,022
Istanbul	7,110	4,789	1,091	4,975	1,400	6,389	843
Lisbon	5,390	3,246	2,427	3,364	904	4,796	1,161
London	5,550	3,282	1,555	3,458	213	5,766	887
Los Angeles	1,589	2,427	6,003	2,451	5,588	6,331	6,732
Manila	8,835	8,186	5,131	8,498	6,677	11,259	6,457
Mexico City	—	2,318	6,663	2,094	5,716	4,771	6,366
Montreal	2,318	—	4,386	320	3,422	5,097	4,080
Moscow	6,663	4,386	—	4,665	1,544	7,175	1,474
New York	2,094	320	4,665	—	3,624	4,817	4,281
Paris	5,716	3,422	1,544	3,624	—	5,699	697
Rio de Janeiro	4,771	5,097	7,175	4,817	5,699	—	5,684
Rome	6,366	4,080	1,474	4,281	697	5,684	—
San Francisco	1,887	2,539	5,871	2,571	5,558	6,621	6,240
Shanghai, China	8,022	7,053	4,235	7,371	5,754	11,336	5,677
Stockholm	5,959	3,667	762	3,924	958	6,651	1,234
Sydney, Australia	8,052	9,954	9,012	9,933	10,544	8,306	10,136
Tokyo	7,021	6,383	4,647	6,740	6,034	11,533	6,135
Warsaw	6,365	4,009	715	4,344	849	6,467	817
Washington, D.C.	1,887	488	4,858	205	3,829	4,796	4,434

Cities	San Francisco	Shanghai	Stockholm	Sydney	Tokyo	Warsaw	Washington
Berlin	5,661	5,218	504	10,006	5,540	320	4,169
Buenos Aires	6,467	12,201	7,808	7,330	11,408	7,662	5,218
Cairo	7,364	5,183	2,111	8,952	5,935	1,630	5,800
Calcutta	7,814	2,117	4,195	5,685	3,194	4,048	8,084
Cape Town, South Africa	10,247	8,061	6,444	6,843	9,156	5,958	7,901
Caracas, Venezuela	3,904	9,501	5,420	9,513	8,799	5,517	2,059
Chicago	1,858	7,061	4,278	9,272	6,299	4,667	597
Hong Kong	6,897	764	5,113	4,584	1,794	5,144	8,147
Honolulu	2,393	4,941	6,862	4,943	3,853	7,355	4,519
Istanbul	6,703	4,962	1,348	9,294	5,560	863	5,215
Lisbon	5,666	6,654	1,856	11,302	6,915	1,715	3,562
London	5,357	5,715	890	10,564	5,940	899	3,663
Los Angeles	347	6,438	5,454	7,530	5,433	5,922	2,300
Manila	6,967	1,150	5,797	3,944	1,866	5,837	8,562
Mexico City	1,887	8,022	5,959	8,052	7,021	6,365	1,887
Montreal	2,539	7,053	3,667	9,954	6,383	4,009	488
Moscow	5,871	4,235	762	9,012	4,647	715	4,858
New York	2,571	7,371	3,924	9,933	6,740	4,344	205
Paris	5,558	5,754	958	10,544	6,034	849	3,829
Rio de Janeiro	6,621	11,336	6,651	8,306	11,533	6,467	4,796
Rome	6,240	5,677	1,234	10,136	6,135	817	4,434
San Francisco	—	6,140	5,361	7,416	5,135	5,841	2,442
Shanghai, China	6,140	—	4,825	4,899	1,097	4,951	7,448
Stockholm	5,361	4,825	—	9,696	5,051	501	4,123
Sydney, Australia	7,416	4,899	9,696	—	4,866	9,696	9,758
Tokyo	5,135	1,097	5,051	4,866	—	5,249	6,772
Warsaw	5,841	4,951	501	9,696	5,249	—	4,457
Washington, D.C.	2,442	7,448	4,123	9,758	6,772	4,457	—

Source: Encyclopaedia Britannica.

BEFORE-VACATION HOME-SECURITY CHECKLIST

Don't leave home without looking over these hints for discouraging would-be burglars and keeping your house safe in your absence.

- [ ] Have the post office hold your mail, or ask a neighbor to take it in for you after each delivery.
- [ ] Ask a neighbor to take in your daily newspaper. Or cancel, rather than suspend, your subscription (thieves have their ways of discovering vacation notices).
- [ ] If you're leaving your car at home, park it in the driveway rather than in the garage. (Remove the distributor cap, though, so it can't be driven away.) Or ask a neighbor to park their car on your property occasionally.
- [ ] Mow the lawn before leaving. If you'll be away for a while, have someone mow weekly.
- [ ] Ask a friend, neighbor or relative to put out trash on pickup days, shovel snow or otherwise give the illusion that someone is home.
- [ ] If you don't have an answering machine, unplug your phone or set the ringing on low so no one can hear that the phone isn't being answered.
- [ ] Leave your keys with a trusted neighbor or nearby relative to check your home every so often.
- [ ] Leave curtains, blinds or draperies open and ask a neighbor to close them at night and open them again in the daylight. If this can't be arranged, just leave them open.
- [ ] Use automatic timers to switch a few lamps and outdoor lights on at staggered times around nightfall and off at what would be your usual bedtime. Also program a radio or TV to go on during the day.
- [ ] Be sure that you've unplugged any other appliances not on timers — especially those that produce heat, such as an iron.
- [ ] If you have an alarm system, test that it is in good working order. Replace batteries more than a year old.
- [ ] Check that all doors and windows are locked — including those of detached garages and shed so no one has access to tools that could be used in a break-in.
- [ ] Let a neighbor know where you can be reached in case of an emergency.
- [ ] Let your local police department know when you'll be away — particularly if it's for a long period of time.

TEMPERATURES AROUND THE WORLD (°F)

Before planning a vacation, consult this chart of average temperatures around the world.

Location	January High	January Low	April High	April Low	July High	July Low	October High	October Low
CANADA								
Ottawa	21	3	51	31	81	58	54	37
Quebec	18	2	45	29	76	57	51	37
Toronto	30	16	50	34	79	59	56	40
Vancouver	41	32	58	40	74	54	57	44
MEXICO								
Acapulco	85	70	87	71	89	75	88	74
Mexico City	66	42	78	52	74	54	70	50
OVERSEAS								
Australia (Sydney)	78	65	71	58	60	46	71	56
Austria (Vienna)	34	26	57	41	75	59	55	44
Bahamas (Nassau)	77	65	81	69	88	75	85	73
Bermuda (Hamilton)	68	58	71	59	85	73	79	69
Brazil (Rio de Janeiro)	84	73	80	69	75	63	77	66
Denmark (Copenhagan)	36	29	50	37	72	55	53	42
Egypt (Cairo)	65	47	83	57	96	70	86	65
France (Paris)	42	32	60	41	76	55	59	44
Germany (Berlin)	35	26	55	38	74	55	55	41
Greece (Athens)	54	42	67	52	90	72	74	60
Hong Kong	64	56	75	67	87	78	81	73
India (Calcutta)	80	55	97	76	90	79	89	74
Italy (Rome)	54	39	68	46	88	64	73	53
Israel (Jerusalem)	55	41	73	50	87	63	81	59
Japan (Tokyo)	47	29	63	46	83	70	69	55
Nigeria (Lagos)	88	74	89	77	83	74	85	74
Netherlands (Amsterdam)	40	34	52	43	69	59	56	48
Puerto Rico (San Juan)	81	67	84	69	87	74	87	73
South Africa (Cape Town)	78	60	72	53	63	45	70	52
Spain (Madrid)	47	33	64	44	87	62	66	48
United Kingdom (London)	44	35	56	40	73	55	58	44
United Kingdom (Edinburgh)	43	35	50	39	65	52	53	44
U.S.S.R. (Moscow)	21	9	47	31	76	55	46	34
Venezuela (Caracas)	75	56	81	60	78	61	79	61
Yugoslavia (Belgrade)	37	27	64	45	84	61	65	47

TEMPERATURES IN THE UNITED STATES

Average Monthly Temperature (°F)[1]

City	Jan.	April	July	Oct.
Albany	21.1	46.6	71.4	50.5
Albuquerque, N.M.	34.8	55.1	78.8	57.4
Anchorage, Alaska	13.0	35.4	58.1	34.6
Asheville, N.C.	36.8	55.7	73.2	56.0
Atlanta, Ga.	41.9	61.8	78.6	62.2
Atlantic City, N.J.	31.8	51.0	74.4	55.5
Austin, Texas	49.1	68.7	84.7	69.8
Baltimore, Md.	32.7	54.0	76.8	56.9
Baton Rouge, La.	50.8	68.4	82.1	68.2
Billings, Mont.	20.9	44.6	72.3	49.3
Birmingham, Ala.	42.9	62.8	80.1	62.6
Bismark, N.D.	6.7	42.5	70.4	46.1
Boise, Idaho	29.9	48.6	74.6	51.9
Boston, Mass.	29.6	48.7	73.5	54.8
Bridgeport, Conn.	29.5	48.6	74.0	56.0

Average Monthly Temperature (°F)[1]

City	Jan.	April	July	Oct.
Buffalo, N.Y.	23.5	45.4	70.7	51.5
Burlington, Vt.	16.6	42.7	69.6	47.9
Caribou, Maine	10.7	37.3	65.1	43.1
Casper, Wyom.	22.2	42.1	70.9	47.1
Charleston, S.C.	47.9	64.3	80.5	65.8
Charleston, W.Va.	32.9	55.3	74.5	55.9
Charlotte, N.C.	40.5	60.3	78.5	60.7
Cheyenne, Wyom.	26.1	41.8	68.9	47.5
Chicago, Ill.	21.4	48.8	73.0	53.5
Cleveland, Ohio	25.5	48.1	71.6	53.2
Columbia, S.C.	44.7	63.8	81.0	63.4
Columbus, Ohio	27.1	51.4	73.8	53.9
Concord, N.H.	19.9	44.1	69.5	48.3
Dallas-Ft. Worth, Texas	44.0	65.9	86.3	67.9
Denver, Colo.	29.5	47.4	73.4	51.9

Source: National Weather Service

Average Monthly Temperature (°F)[1]					Average Monthly Temperature (°F)[1]				
City	Jan.	April	July	Oct.	City	Jan.	April	July	Oct.
Des Moines, Iowa	18.6	50.5	76.3	54.2	Norfolk, Va.	39.9	58.2	78.4	61.3
Detroit, Mich.	23.4	47.3	71.9	51.9	Oklahoma City, Okla.	35.9	60.2	82.1	62.3
Dodge City, Kan.	29.5	54.3	80.0	57.7	Olympia, Wash.	37.2	47.3	63.0	50.1
Duluth, Minn.	6.3	38.3	65.4	44.2	Omaha, Neb.	20.2	52.2	77.7	54.5
El Paso, Texas	44.2	63.6	82.5	63.6	Philadelphia, Pa.	31.2	52.9	76.5	56.5
Fairbanks, Alaska	−12.7	30.2	61.5	25.1	Phoenix, Ariz.	52.3	68.1	92.3	73.4
Fargo, N.D.	4.3	42.1	70.6	46.3	Pittsburgh, Pa.	26.7	50.1	72.0	52.5
Grand Junction, Colo.	25.5	51.7	78.9	54.9	Portland, Maine	21.5	42.8	68.1	48.5
Grand Rapids, Mich.	22.0	46.3	71.4	50.9	Portland, Ore.	38.9	50.4	67.7	54.3
Hartford, Conn.	25.2	48.8	73.4	52.4	Providence, R.I.	28.2	47.9	72.5	53.2
Helena, Mont.	18.1	42.3	67.9	45.1	Raleigh, N.C.	39.6	59.4	77.7	59.7
Honolulu, Hawaii	72.6	75.7	80.1	79.5	Reno, Nev.	32.2	46.4	69.5	50.3
Houston, Texas	51.4	68.7	83.1	69.7	Richmond, Va.	36.6	57.9	77.8	58.6
Indianapolis, Ind.	26.0	52.4	75.1	54.8	Roswell, N.M.	41.4	61.9	81.4	61.7
Jackson, Miss.	45.7	65.1	81.9	65.0	Sacramento, Calif.	45.3	58.2	75.6	63.9
Jacksonville, Fla.	53.2	67.7	81.3	69.5	Salt Lake City, Utah	28.6	49.2	77.5	53.0
Juneau, Alaska	21.8	39.1	55.7	41.8	San Antonio, Texas	50.4	69.6	84.6	70.2
Kansas City, Mo.	28.4	56.9	80.9	59.6	San Diego, Calif.	56.8	61.2	70.3	67.5
Knoxville, Tenn.	38.2	59.6	77.6	59.5	San Francisco, Calif.	48.5	54.8	62.2	60.6
Las Vegas, Nev.	44.5	63.5	90.2	67.5	Savannah, Ga.	49.1	66.0	81.2	66.9
Lexington, Ky.	31.5	55.1	75.9	56.8	Seattle-Tacoma, Wash.	39.1	48.7	64.8	52.4
Little Rock, Ark.	39.9	62.4	82.1	63.1	Sioux Falls, S.D.	12.4	46.4	74.0	49.4
Long Beach, Calif.	55.2	60.9	72.8	67.5	Spokane, Wash.	25.7	45.8	69.7	47.5
Los Angeles, Calif.	56.0	59.5	69.0	66.3	Springfield, Ill.	24.6	53.3	76.5	56.0
Louisville, Ky.	32.5	56.6	77.6	57.7	St. Louis, Mo.	28.8	56.1	78.9	57.9
Madison, Wisc.	15.6	45.8	70.6	49.5	Tampa, Fla.	59.8	71.5	82.1	74.4
Memphis, Tenn.	39.6	62.6	82.1	62.9	Toledo, Ohio	23.1	47.8	71.8	51.7
Miami, Fla.	67.1	75.3	82.5	77.9	Tucson, Ariz.	51.1	64.9	86.2	70.4
Milwaukee, Wisc.	18.7	44.6	70.5	50.9	Tulsa, Okla.	35.2	61.0	83.2	62.6
Minneapolis-St. Paul, Minn.	11.2	46.0	73.1	49.6	Vero Beach, Fla.	61.9	71.7	81.1	75.2
Mobile, Ala.	50.8	68.0	82.2	68.5	Washington, D.C.	35.2	56.7	78.9	59.3
Montgomery, Ala.	46.7	65.2	81.7	65.3	Wilmington, Del.	31.2	52.4	76.0	56.3
Mt. Washington, N.H.	5.1	22.4	48.7	30.5	Wichita, Kan.	29.6	56.3	81.4	59.1
Nashville, Tenn.	37.1	59.7	79.4	60.2					
Newark, N.J.	31.2	52.1	76.8	57.2					
New Orleans, La.	52.4	68.7	82.1	69.2					
New York, N.Y.	31.8	51.9	76.4	57.5					

1. Based on 30 year period 1951-80. Data latest available.

Source: National Oceanic and Atmospheric Administration

PACKING CHECKLIST

This should help simplify your vacation preparation. Make extra copies for future trips.

CLOTHING
- ☐ Accessories
- ☐ Bathrobes
- ☐ Dresses
- ☐ Evening bag
- ☐ Evening shoes
- ☐ Eveningwear
- ☐ Jackets/coats
- ☐ Pajamas
- ☐ Shirts/blouse
- ☐ Skirts
- ☐ Socks
- ☐ Sportswear
- ☐ Stockings
- ☐ Sweaters
- ☐ Travel hangers
- ☐ Trousers
- ☐ Undergarments
- ☐ Walking shoes

TOILETRIES
- ☐ Comb and brush
- ☐ Dual-voltage blow dryer
- ☐ Dual-voltage electric shaver
- ☐ Makeup case
- ☐ Shaving kit
- ☐ Shampoo/conditioner
- ☐ Shower slippers
- ☐ Shower cap
- ☐ Soap
- ☐ Toothbrush and toothpaste

LEISURE TIME
- ☐ Backpack
- ☐ Bathing suits
- ☐ Beach chair/umbrella
- ☐ Beach towels
- ☐ Bicycles
- ☐ Books/magazines
- ☐ Camera and film
- ☐ Fishing poles/tackle box
- ☐ Sunglasses
- ☐ Suntan lotion
- ☐ Tennis rackets
- ☐ Tote bag
- ☐ Travel games for kids
- ☐ Writing home:
  - ☐ Address book
  - ☐ Notepaper/envelopes
  - ☐ Pens/pencils
  - ☐ Stamps

TRAVEL BASICS
- ☐ Currency converter
- ☐ Luggage locks/tags
- ☐ Passports/tickets/itinerary
- ☐ Phrase books/language tapes
- ☐ Tissue paper (for wrinkle-free packing)
- ☐ Travel alarm
- ☐ Travelers' checks
- ☐ Travel guide/maps
- ☐ Dual-voltage travel iron

JUST IN CASE
- ☐ Bug repellent
- ☐ Car tool kit
- ☐ Combination knife/can opener/corkscrew
- ☐ Electrical adapters
- ☐ First-aid kit
- ☐ Flashlight
- ☐ Laundry bag
- ☐ Medications
- ☐ Plastic bags
- ☐ Rain coat/poncho
- ☐ Sewing kit
- ☐ Umbrella

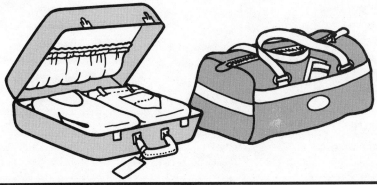

FOREIGN MENU TERMS

Check these translations of common menu items to help you dine out in any language.

FRENCH

Aioli: Garlic mayonnaise sauce

Bacon: Salt pork

Béarnaise: A hollandaise sauce with shallot, tarragon and white wine

Béchamel: Basic white sauce

Belons: Small, plump oysters

Beurre: Butter

Boeuf: Beef

Bourguignon: Braised in wine and onions

Bombe: Fancy dessert of ice cream, ices, fruits and whipped cream

Café: Coffee; **frappé:** iced coffee; **au lait:** with hot milk

Caille: Quail

Canard: Duck

Cardinal: Béchamel sauce made with fish stock and lobster

Cassoulet: Highly seasoned bean-based dish, usually with meat or poultry added

Cerises: Cherries

Champignons: Mushrooms

Chasseur: Highly seasoned wine sauce with mushrooms, shallots, tomatoes

Choufleur: Cauliflower

Citron: Lemon

Coq au Vin: Chicken cooked in wine sauce with onions, ham, mushrooms

Coquilles St. Jacques: Scallop dish

Croûte: Pastry or bread crust

Diablé: Deviled; highly seasoned sauce of herbs vinegar, white wine and shallots

Dinde, dindon: Turkey

Echalote: Shallot

Entrecôte: Rib steak

Escargots: Snails, usually served in garlic sauce

Estouffade: Steamed, braised or stewed

Farci: Stuffed

Foie gras: Goose or duck liver

Fraises: Strawberries

Framboises: Raspberries

Frit, frite: Fried

Fromage: Cheese

Fruits de mer: Seafood

Gateaux: Cakes

Gigot: Leg of lamb

Grenouilles: Frogs' legs

Grillé: Grilled

Haricots: Beans; **verts:** green beans

Hollandaise: Basic sauce of egg yolks, lemon juice, butter

Homard: Lobster

Huile: Oil

Huitres: Oysters

Jambon: Ham

Jardinière: Made with finely chopped vegetables

Lait: Milk

Laitue: Lettuce

Langouste: Crayfish; langoustines: prawns

Lapin: Rabbit

Lard: Bacon

Legumes: Vegetables

Limon: Lime

Madeleines: Shell-shaped tea cakes

Meunière: Sauce of browned butter flavored with lemon juice and parsley

Mijote: Simmered

Mornay: Rich cheese sauce

Moules: Mussels

Moutarde: Mustard

Mouton: Mutton (lamb)

Noisettes: Nuts

Noix: Walnuts

Oeufs: Eggs; **brouillés:** scrambled; **durs;** hard-cooked; **poeles:** sunny-side up

Oie: Goose

Oignon: Onion

Pain: Bread

Palourde: Clams

Pane: Breaded

Pâté: Food finely ground to a paste

Pâte: Pastry

Persillade: Parsley sauce

Petits pois: Small green peas

Pétoncles: Scallops

Poché: Poached

Poire: Pear

Poisson: Fish

Poivre: Pepper

Pomme: Apple

Pommes de terre: Potatoes

Porc: Pork

Potage: Soup

Pot-au-feu: Classic beef-vegetable soup

Poulet: Chicken

Quenelles: Dumplings of finely minced meat or poultry

Ragout: Stew

Raisin: Grape

Raisin sec: Raisin

Riz: Rice

Rôti: Roasted

Sucre: Sugar

Talmouse: Cheesecake

Truite: Trout

Vapeur, à la: Steamed

Veau: Veal

Velouté: Velvety cream sauce

Vol-au-vent: Pastry shell, filled with meat or poultry, or sometimes fruit, in a rich sauce

ITALIAN

Abbracchio: Young lamb

Abbrustolito: Toasted

Aceto: Vinegar

Affogato: Poached or steamed

Affumicato: Smoked

Aglio: Garlic

Agnello: Lamb

Agro dolce: Sweet-and-sour

All'olio: In oil

Alici: Anchovies

Amaretti: Macaroons

Anguille: Eels

Anitra: Duck

Antipasto: Appetizer servings of cold cuts, sausages, olives, marinated vegetables and more

Aragosta: Lobster

Arancia: Orange

Arrabbiata, all': Tomato sauce enlivened with chili peppers, bacon, black pepper

Arrostito: Roasted

Arselle: Mussels

Baccala: Dried, salted codfish

Basilico: Basil

Bollito: Boiled

Bolognese: Tomato sauce with chopped meat, bacon, onion, carrots

Braciolette ripiene: Stuffed beef or veal rolls

Brasto: Braised

Brodettato: Stewed

Brodo: Broth

Bue: Beef

Burro: Butter

Cacciatora: "Hunter-style" — cooked in wine with garlic, herbs, onions, tomatoes, olives

Caffé: Coffee; **espresso:** strong black coffee

Calamari: Squid

Capocollo: Peppery smoked pork

Carbonara: Uncooked pasta sauce of olive oil, grated cheese, smoked ham, eggs, black pepper

Carciofo: Artichoke

Carne: Meat

Cavoflore: Cauliflower

Ceci: Chick-peas

Ciliege: Cherries

Cipolla: Onion

Ciuppin: Fish stew

Coniglio: Rabbit

Costa: Rib or chop

Costaletta: Cutlet or chop

Cozze: Mussels

Fagliolini: Green beans; **fagiolo:** bean

Farcito: Stuffed

Fegato: Liver

Ferri, ai: Grilled

Fichi: Figs

Florentina: Made with spinach

Formaggio: Cheese

Forno, al: Roasted or baked

Fragole: Strawberries

Frittata: Omelet

Fritto: Fried

Frutta: Fruit

Frutta di mare: Seafood

Funghi: Mushrooms

Gamberi: Shrimp

Granchio: Crab

Granturco: Corn

Griglia: Broiled or grilled

Imbottito: Stuffed

Impanati: Breaded

Lardo: Bacon

Latte: Milk

Lattuga: Lettuce

Legumi: Vegetables

Lesso: Boiled

Limone: Lemon

Lumache: Snails

Maiale: Pork

Manzo: Beef

Marinara: Spicy, meatless tomato sauce

Marinato: Pickled, marinated

Mela: Apple

Melanzane: Eggplant

Minestrone: Thick vegetable soup

Mozzarella in carrozza: "Sandwiches" of mozzarella cheese between bread slices, dipped in flour and beaten egg and fried

Oca: Goose

Olio: Oil

Osso buco: Braised shin of veal, cooked with chopped vegetables, garlic and herbs

Ostriche: Oysters

Pancetta: Bacon (belly bacon)

Pane: Bread

Panettone: Fruit cake

Panino: Sandwich, roll

Panna: Cream

Pasta: General term for all noodles, macaroni, spaghetti, etc.

Patate: Potatoes

Peoci: Mussels

Pepe: Ground black pepper

Peperoncini: Hot dried red peppers

Pera: Pear

Pesca: Peach

Pesche: Fish

Pesto: Sauce of basil, olive oil, garlic, grated cheese and pine nuts (pignoli)

Piccata: Thin slice of meat cooked with lemon

Piselli: Peas

Pizza de ricotta: Cheesecake

Polenta: Cornmeal or cornmeal mush (like hominy grits), often topped with a tomato or butter sauce

Pollo: Chicken

Polpette: Meatballs

Pomodoro: Tomato

Prosciutto: Dried, salted, spiced, pressed Italian ham

Ragù: Chopped-beef sauce with bacon, tomato, butter, onion, cream

Riso: Rice

Risi e bisi: Pea-and-rice dish

Risotto: Boiled rice with a savory sauce

Salsiccia: Dry pork sausage

Saltimbocca: Veal and ham or pork covered in butter and wine

Sarde: Sardines

Scaloppine: Thin slices of meat, usually veal, with various sauces

Scampi: Prawns

Scungili: Conch

Senape: Mustard

Sfingi: Cream puffs, cookies, doughnuts

Sfolgie: Very flaky pastry

Sformato: Pie, pudding

Sogliola: Fillet of sole

Stracciatella: Broth with beaten egg yolks and grated cheese

Stufato: Stew

Sugo: Gravy or sauce

Sul carbone: Charcoal-grilled

Tacchino: Turkey

Tartufi: Truffles; ball of ice cream covered with hardened chocolate

Tonno: Tuna

Torta: Tart, pie, cake

Tortoni: Rich frozen custard

Trota: Trout

Umido, in: Stew

Uova: Egg; **alla coque:** soft-cooked; **al tegame** or **strapazzate:** scrambled; **sode:** hard-cooked

Uva: Grapes

Uva secca: Raisin

Vitello: Veal

Vongole: Clams

Zabaglione, Zabaione: Frothy egg-and-wine dessert

Zeppole: Fried dough

Zucca: Squash

Zucchero: Sugar

Zuppa: Soup

SPANISH

Aceite: Oil

Acetunas: Olives

Aji: Chili pepper

Ajo: Garlic

Almendras: Almonds

Anguilas: Eels

Arroz: Rice

Asado: Roasted

Atún: Tuna

Azúcar: Sugar

Bacalao: Salted cod

Berenjena: Eggplant

Boniatos: Sweet potatoes

Buñuelos: Buns, fitters, doughnuts

Café: Coffee; **cargado:** strong; **débil:** weak

Calabaza: Squash or pumpkin

Calamares: Squid

Caldereta: Stew

Caldo: Broth, bouillon

Camarón: Shrimp

Cangrejo: Crabmeat

Caracoles: Snails

Carne: Meat

Cazuela: Casserole

Cebolla: Onion

Centollos: Crabs

Cerdo: Pork

Cerezas: Cherries

Chorizos: Hot, hard pork sausages

Chuletas: Cutlets or chops

Churros: Deep-fried dough

Cocido: Hearty stew

Coliflor: Cauliflower

Conejo: Rabbit

Cordero: Lamb

Empanada: Meat-filled tarts

Empanizado: Breaded

Esquexada: Fish salad

Estofado: Stew or casserole dish

Fideos: Spaghetti, noodles

Flan: Caramel custard

Frambuesas: Raspberries

Presas: Tiny, sweet strawberries

Frijoles: Beans

Frito: Fried

Fruta: Fruit

Gallina: Hen

Garbanzos: Chick-peas

Gazpacho: Classic cold soup/salad of tomatoes, onion, cucumber, garlic

Guisado: Fricasse, stew

Guisantes: Green peas

Helados: Ice cream

Higos: Figs

Hongos: Mushrooms

Horno: Baked

Huevos: Eggs; **duros:** hard-cooked; **revueltos:** scrambled; **pasados por agua:** soft-cooked

Jamón: Ham

Judías: Beans

Langosta: Lobster; langostinos: large shrimp

Leche: Milk

Lechuga: Lettuce

Legumbres: Vegetables

Lenguardo: Sole

Limón: Lemon

Maiz: Corn

Mantecado: Butter cake; ice cream

Mariscos: Shellfish

Mejillones: Mussels

Naranja: Orange

Olla gitana: All-vegetable stew

Olla odrida: Stew with ham and garbanzos

Ostras: Oysters

Paella: National dish or rice, saffron and seafood, meat and/or poultry

Pan: Bread

Pasa: Raisin

Pasteles: Pastries

Patatas: Potatoes

Pato: Duck

Pescado: Fish

Pollo: Chicken

Queso: Cheese

Rellena: Stuffed meat

Relleno: Minced meat

Salado: Salted

Salchicha: Sausage

Salsa: Sauce

Sanchocho: Chowder

Setas: Mushrooms

Sopa: Soup

Ternera: Veal

Tortilla: Omelet

Trucha: Trout

Uvas: Grapes

Vaca: Beef

Verduras: Vegetables

CHINESE

Unless you can read Chinese character writing, restaurant dishes are more easily identified by the region where they originated. But descriptions of some standard dishes also follow.

Cantonese: Southern cooking, as is offered in the majority of Chinese restaurants in America. Favored ingredients: Black beans, crabs, oyster and hoisin sauces, water chestnuts, roast pork, salted fish, shrimp paste. Relies on fresh food and therefore uses less soy sauce and fewer seasonings. Foods are usually stir-fried or steamed, blanched or poached.

Peking/Mandarin: Northern Chinese style. Favored ingredients: Garlic, scallion, soy sauce, duck, mutton (lamb). Bread, noodles and very thin "pancakes" are used instead of rice. Foods are substantial, strongly flavored. "Sizzling" platters, Peking Duck, Moo Shu Pork, Hot and Sour Soup and the hot pot (a type of fondue made with boiling stock) are typical dishes from this region.

Shanghai: Eastern cooking flavoring fish and rice, hairy crabs, braised or gravy-laden dishes, soy sauce, sugar and vinegar, steaming and stir-frying in sesame oil and soy sauce — a heavier, richer cuisine than Cantonese. Typical dish: Lion's Head — a fist-size seasoned meatball.

Szechuan/Hunan: From western China, this is the most pungent cooking style, often combining a variety of flavors — hot, sour, salty, sweet. Favored ingredients: red hot peppers and peppercorns, snow mushrooms, onions, ginger, garlic. Typical dish: Gung Bao Ding.

Bao-zi: Steamed buns

Char siu: Cantonese roast pork

Chow: Fried

Chow mein: Fried noodles with mushroom, cabbage, bamboo shoots, shredded meat, onion, soy sauce and sherry

Chun-juan: Spring rolls, or egg rolls; mixture chopped cooked meats and vegetables wrapped in a thin dough and deep-fried

Dim sum: General term for dumplings; also the Chinese "tea" at which different steamed and fried dumplings and buns with a variety of fillings are served.

Ding: "Diced": used for dishes with cubed meat or poultry

Fen: Rice sticks; noodles made of rice

Gun Bao Ding: Diced Chicken with hot peppers, corn and peanuts

Guo-tieh: Dumplings with meat-vegetable filling, panfried on bottom and served-charred side up

Guozha: Deep-fried custard

Lo mein: "Tossed noodles"; noodles cooked with savory brown sauce and tossed with shredded vegetables and meat.

Lichee: Fragrant, sweet fruit (with peelable skin) served for dessert

Mein: Noodles

Moo Shu: Shredded meat, poultry or shrimp and vegetables and mushrooms served with thin pancakes

Moo Goo Gai Pan: Chicken with button mushrooms

Shao mai: Steamed dumplings

Subgum: "many splendored" — special Cantonese topping of vegetables and meat added to a standard dish

Sui-mai: Bun stuffed with sweet lotus-seed paste or roast pork

Wonton: Meat fillings wrapped in thin, pasta-like dough

JAPANESE

Nabemono: Leeks, Chinese cabbage, mushrooms, tofu and fish or chicken boiled in earthenware pot

Udon: Noodles made from white flour

Sashimi: Slices of raw fish eaten with a dip of soy sauce and wasabi (pungent Japanese horseradish)

Shabu-shabu: Sliced beef, cabbage, leeks, etc., cooked at table in pot of boiling water, served with miso (tofu-based) dip.

Soba: Noodles from buckwheat flour

Sukiyaki: Thin slices of beef (sometimes chicken) and vegetables cooked at table in iron pan with sweet, soy-base broth, served with a raw-egg dip

Sushi: General term for dishes, usually raw seafood, served with special vinegar-flavored rice

Ebi: Shrimp

Ikka: Squid

Ikura: Red salmon roe

Maguro: Plain red tuna

Nigiri: Variety of thin, raw pieces of fish

O-toro: High-quality, pink tuna

Take: Octopus

Temaki: Dishes based on a cone of rolled seaweed (nori) and rice

Nigi toro maki: With tuna and scallions

Uni maki: With sea urchin eggs

Tempura: Foods (meat, poultry, seafood, vegetables) deep-fried in light, seasoned batter

Tonkatsu: Deep-fried pork cutlet cut up, served with a Worchestershire sauce-mustard dip.

Yakitori: Chicken and vegetables broiled on skewers.

PHOTOGRAPHY GUIDE

For amateur shutterbugs, these guidelines give light requirements and exposure settings for commonly available film.

ASA 100	Best choice for bright sun (distinct shadows) or electronic flash — plus extremely fine grain that allows for a high degree of enlargement.
ASA 200	Best choice for hazy sun (soft or no shadows), or electronic flash plus fine grain — recommended for automatic 35 mm cameras.
ASA 400	Best choice for natural light indoors and minimum light outdoors — plus stop-action capability.
ASA 1000	Best choice for all low light conditions, etc., and where small lens openings are required.

ASA 100

DAYLIGHT EXPOSURE: Automatic exposure controls — Set film speed at ISO 100. **Manual adjustments** — Set exposure meter for ISO 100 or use the table below.

Bright or Hazy Sun on Light Sand or Snow	1/125	f/16
Bright or Hazy Sun (Distinct Shadows)	1/125	f/11*
Weak Hazy Sun (Soft Shadows)	1/125	f/8
Cloudy Bright (No Shadows)	1/125	f/5.6
Heavy Overcast or Open Shade†	1/125	f/4

*f/5.6 for backlighted close-ups
†Subjects shaded but lighted by sky

Light	Film Speed	Filter
DAYLIGHT	**ISO 100**	**None**
3400 K photolamps	ISO 32	No. 80B
3200 K tungsten	ISO 25	No. 80A

For through-the-lens exposure meters, see camera manual.

FLASH EXPOSURE: Adjustable cameras — Use electronic flash, blue flashbulbs, or flashcubes. Divide flash guide number, from flash manual or flashbulb carton, by the flash-to-subject distance to determine the correct lens opening. **Automatic electronic flash units** or **cameras that determine flash exposure automatically** — Stay within flash range recommended in equipment manual.

ASA 200

DAYLIGHT EXPOSURE: Cameras with automatic exposure controls — Set film speed at ISO 200. Cameras with manual adjustments — Determine exposure setting with an exposure meter set for ISO 200 or use the table below. If camera has DX-encoding, this is automatic.

Bright or Hazy Sun on Light Sand or Snow	1/250	f/16
Bright or Hazy Sun (Distinct Shadows)	1/250	f/11*
Weak Hazy Sun (Soft Shadows)	1/250	f/8
Cloudy Bright (No Shadows)	1/250	f/5.6
Heavy Overcast or Open Shade†	1/250	f/4

*f/5.6 for backlighted close-ups
†Subjects shaded but lighted by sky

Light	Film Speed	Filter
DAYLIGHT	**ISO 200**	**None**
3400 K photolamps	ISO 64	No. 80B
3200 K tungsten	ISO 50	No. 80A

For through-the-lens exposure meters, see camera manual.

FLASH EXPOSURE: Adjustable cameras — Use electronic flash, blue flashbulbs, or flashcubes. Divide flash guide number, from flash manual or flashbulb carton, by the flash-to-subject distance to determine the correct lens opening. **Automatic electronic flash units or cameras that determine flash exposure automatically** — Stay within flash range recommended in equipment manual.

ASA 400

DAYLIGHT AND EXISTING-LIGHT EXPOSURE: Automatic exposure controls — Set film speed at ISO 400. Manual adjustments — Set exposure meter for ISO 400 or use table below.

Home Interiors at Night — Bright Light	1/30	f/2.8
Average Light	1/30	f/2
Fireworks — Shutter on Bulb		f/16*
Interiors with Bright Fluorescent Light	1/60	f/4
Brightly Lighted Street Scenes at Night	1/60	f/2.8
Neon Signs, Other Lighted Signs at Night	1/125	f/4
Floodlighted Buildings, Fountains, Monuments	1/15*	f/2
Night Football, Baseball, Racetracks	1/125	f/2.8
Basketball, Hockey, Bowling	1/125	f/2
Stage Shows — Average Light (Bright 2 stops less)	1/60	f/2.8
Circuses — Floodlighted Acts	1/60	f/2.8
Ice Shows — Floodlighted Acts	1/125	f/2.8
Ice Shows, Circuses — Spotlighted Acts	1/250	f/2.8
School — Stage and Auditorium	1/30	f/2
Bright or Hazy Sun (Distinct Shadows)	1/500	f/11
Cloudy Bright (No Shadows)	1/500	f/5.6

FOR CRITICAL USE

Light	Film Speed	Filter
DAYLIGHT	**ISO 400**	**None**
3400 K photolamps	ISO 125	No. 80B
3200 K tungsten	ISO 100	No. 80A

DAYLIGHT AND EXISTING-LIGHT EXPOSURE:
Cameras with automatic exposure controls — Set film speed at ISO 1000. Cameras with manual adjustments — Determine exposure setting with exposure meter set for ISO 1000 or use table below. If cameras have DX encoding film-speed setting is automatic.

Outdoors in Bright or Hazy Sunlight, Action	1/1000	f/16
Home Interiors at Night — Bright Light	1/30	f/4
Average Light	1/30	f/2.8
Interiors with Bright Fluorescent Light	1/30	f/8
Fireworks — Shutter on Bulb, Camera on Tripod		f/22*
Brightly Lighted Street Scenes at Night	1/60	f/4
Neon Signs, Other Lighted Signs at Night	1/125	f/5.6
Floodlighted Buildings, Fountains, Monuments	1/30	f/2

*Use exposure times longer than 1/60 second with fluorescent light.

Night Football, Baseball, Soccer, Racetracks	1/250	f/2.8
Basketball, Hockey, Bowling	1/125	f/2.8
Stage Shows — Average Light (Bright 2 stops less)	1/125	f/2.8
Circuses — Floodlighted Acts	1/125	f/2.8
Ice Shows — Floodlighted Acts	1/250	f/2.8
Ice Shows, Circuses — Spotlighted Acts	1/250	f/4
School — Stage and Auditorium	1/30	f/2.8

Light	Film Speed	Filter
DAYLIGHT	**ISO 1000**	**None**
3400 K photolamps	ISO 320	No. 80B*
3200 K tungsten	ISO 250	No. 80A*

*For critical use.
For through-the-lens exposure meters, see camera manual.

Source: The Eastman Kodak Company

CAMPING AND HIKING SAFETY

You may not have easy access to medical attention once you're in the Great Outdoors, so it's essential to take precautions.

1 Learn first-aid techniques and carry a first-aid kit.

2 Bring ample supplies of any medication you take regularly.

3 Check with your doctor to see if it's time for a tetanus booster.

4 Never tease or hand-feed a wild animal. Even the smallest mammal can carry rabies or fleas that can infect humans.

5 Never approach a tame- or sick-looking animal. It may be diseased or in pain and may bite.

6 To keep from attracting bears:
• Do not throw aside or bury garbage or food containers. Combustible trash should be burned. Even burn tin cans and other noncombustible containers (except glass) to destroy food odors. Then remove cans from cold ashes, flatten them and take them to trash receptacles at the trail head.

• Store foodstuffs (preferably in air-tight containers) out of reach. Food can be suspended on rope slung between trees some distance from your campsite.

• If previous campers have left the site dirty, clean it up — for your own protection.

• Use dry, packaged food; avoid greasy, odorous foods such as ham and bacon.

• Keep packs and sleeping bags clean and free of food odors. It helps to sleep some distance from your campfire and cooking areas.

7 Scratching insect bits with dirty fingers may cause infection. Wash bites with soap and water, then apply calamine lotion.

8 To avoid stings, wear smooth-finish fabrics — in white, green, tan or khaki, not bright colors. Don't wear perfume or cologne. If allergic to bee stings, have your doctor give you a disensitizing shot and an allergy kit. If stung, scrape out stinger with dull side of knife or with fingernail. Treat with soap, water and antiseptic.

9 Shake out boots and other clothing before putting them on in the morning to rid them of spiders, scorpions and other insects.

10 Stuff bottom of trousers into high socks so ticks won't get underneath while you're hiking. Don't lie in tall grass. At night, check clothing; remove any ticks with tweezers or tissue — avoid contact with bare fingers.

11 Carry a snake bit kit, but to avoid bites:
• Don't stick hands or legs under rocks or logs, or into crevices without first looking to check for snakes.

• Be careful exploring caves.

• Don't walk barefoot.

• Wear high boots or stuff trouser bottoms into socks.

12 Know what poison ivy, oak and sumac look like — and avoid them. If too late, wash blisters with yellow laundry soap, alcohol or just lots of cold water. Wash all clothes that may have come in contact with the plants.

13 To avoid mountain sickness in high altitudes, rest as soon as you feel lightheaded or nauseous. Take your time.

14 To avoid foot blisters:
• Change and wash socks frequently.

• Wear two layers of close-fitting socks that won't slip down into your shoes.

• Cover tender spots with adhesive bandages or tape.

• If a blister forms, wash area, then prick blister with sterilized needle or pin. Let blister dry before covering with adhesive bandage or tape.

15 Don't forget to bring sunscreen to guard against sun and wind burn.

Source: National Parks Service

TIME ZONES

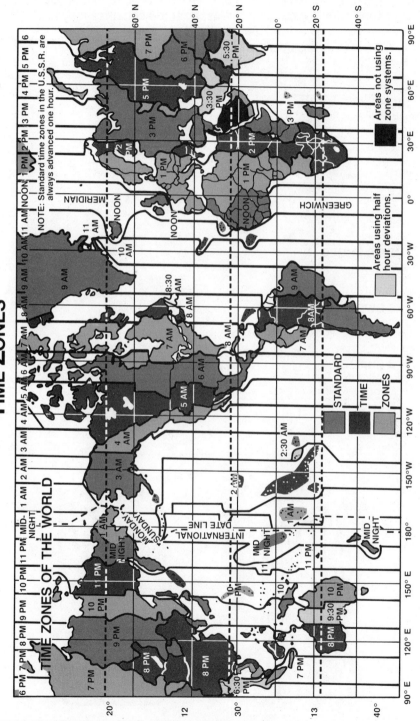

TIME ZONES OF THE WORLD

NOTE: Standard time zones in the U.S.S.R. are always advanced one hour.

Legend:
- STANDARD TIME ZONES
- Areas not using zone systems.
- Areas using half hour deviations.

INTERNATIONAL DATE LINE

GREENWICH MERIDIAN

EUROPEAN CLOTHING SIZES

For the world traveler/shopper, here's how European clothing sizes translate into American. However, sizes can vary slightly from one maker to the next or from one country to the next. Carrying a tape measure is helpful — particularly one that offers conversions to metric measurements, as some countries may also mark their size tags in centimeters.

CHILDREN'S DRESSES/SUITS

American	2	4	6	7	8	9
British	16-18	20-22	24-26	28-30	32-34	36-38
European	40-45	50-55	60-65	70-75	80-85	90-95

JUNIORS' CLOTHING

American	5	7	9	11	13
European	36	38	40	42	44

WOMEN'S CLOTHING

American	6	8	10	12	14	16
British	8	10	12	14	16	18
European						
France	36	38	40	42	44	46
Italy	38	40	42	44	46	48
Rest of Europe	34	36	38	40	42	44

WOMEN'S SHOES

American	4	5	6	7	8	9	10
British	2½	3½	1½	5½	6½	7½	8½
European	35	36	37	38	39	40	41

MEN'S SWEATERS

American	S	M	L	XL
British	34	36-38	40	42-44
European	44	46-48	50	52-54

MEN'S SHIRTS

American/British	14	14½	15	15½	16	16½	17
European	36	37	38	39	41	42	43

MEN'S SHOES

American	6	7	8	9	10	11	12	13
British	5	6	7	8	9	10	11	12
European	39	40	41	42	43	44	45	46

Family Almanac

BIRTHSTONES

Month	Ancient	Modern
January	**Garnet** (precious stone; deep red)	**Garnet**
February	**Amethyst** (clear purple or blue-violet crystallized quartz)	**Amethyst**
March	**Jasper** (opaque, uncrystallized quartz in varying colors)	**Bloodstone** (green chalcedony with red spots) OR **Aquamarine** (blue-green transparent beryl)
April	**Sapphire** (blue corundum precious stone)	**Diamond** (crystallized carbon precious stone)
May	**Agate** (variegated chalcedony)	**Emerald** (green beryl precious stone)
June	**Emerald**	**Pearl** (lustrous concentration formed as abnormal growth within some mollusk shells) OR **Moonstone** (transparent or translucent feldspar) OR **Alexandrite** (grass-green chrysoberyl)
July	**Onyx** (chalcedony in parallel layers of different colors)	**Ruby** (red crystallized corundum precious stone)
August	**Carnelian** (reddish chalcedony)	**Sardonyx** (a variety of onyx) OR **Periodot** (yellow-green chrysolite)
September	**Chrysolite** (olive green magnesium-iron silicate)	**Sapphire**
October	**Aquamarine**	**Opal** (silia; iridescent) OR **Tourmaline** (complex silicate; variable color)
November	**Topaz** (yellow semiprecious stone, fluosilicate of aluminum)	**Topaz**
December	**Ruby**	**Turquoise** (blue hydrous basic phosphate of aluminum) OR **Zircon** (transparent silicate)

Source: Jewelry Industry Council

WEDDING ANNIVERSARY GIFT GUIDE

Year	Traditional	Modern
1	Paper	Clocks
2	Cotton	China
3	Leather	Crystal, glass
4	Linen (silk)	Electrical appliances
5	Wood	Silverware
6	Iron	Wood
7	Wool (copper)	Desk sets
8	Bronze	Linens, lace
9	Pottery (china)	Leather
10	Tin (aluminum)	Diamond jewelry
11	Steel	Fashion jewelry, accessories
12	Silk	Pearls or colored gems
13	Lace	Textiles, furs
14	Ivory	Gold jewelry
15	Crystal	Watches
20	China	Platinum
25	Silver	Sterling silver jubilee
30	Pearl	Diamond
35	Coral (jade)	Jade
40	Ruby	Ruby
45	Sapphire	Sapphire
50	Gold	Gold
55	Emerald	Emerald
60	Diamond	Diamond

Source: Jewelry Industry Council

A Calendar Of Holidays

The dates given for the secular and religious holidays below are the traditional ones, though some may be celebrated on the Mondays or Fridays before or after the official date to create three-day weekends for employees. The Jewish holidays begin on sundown of the previous day.

JANUARY

1	New Year's Day	
6	Epiphany: The Epiphany celebrates the adoration of the magi and Jesus' baptism, twelve days after Christmas.	
15	Martin Luther King's Birthday	

FEBRUARY

2	Groundhog Day: If the groundhog sees his shadow, he returns to his hole and winter lasts another six weeks.	
12	Abraham Lincoln's Birthday	
14	St. Valentine's Day	
22	George Washington's Birthday	
Shrove Tuesday	The day before Ash Wednesday. This marks the end of the carnival season, which once began with the Epiphany. Shrove Tuesday is also known as Mardi Gras or Fat Tuesday.	
Ash Wednesday	Forty weekdays before Easter. This is the first day of Lent, the period of penitence and fasting observed by the Roman Catholic, Eastern and some Protestant churches.	

MARCH

Purim (Feast of Lots)	14th day of Adar, the sixth month of the Jewish calendar. Purim commemorates the deliverance of the Jews from a massacre planned by the Persian minister Haman.	
17	St. Patrick's Day	
Palm Sunday	Seven days before Easter. Palm Sunday celebrates Jesus' triumphant entry into Jerusalem, where palm branches had been strewn along the route.	

APRIL

Good Friday	The Friday before Easter Sunday. Good Friday commemorates Christ's crucifixion.	
Easter	The first Sunday after the first full moon that occurs on or after March 21, or a week later if that full moon falls on a Sunday. Easter Sunday celebrates Christ's resurrection.	
Passover (Pesach)	The first day of Passover falls on the 14th day of Nisan, the seventh month of the Jewish calendar. Passover celebrates the Jews' liberation from slavery in Egypt.	

MAY

Mother's Day	Second Sunday of May	
Ascension Day	The Thursday forty days after Easter. Ascension Day commemorates Christ's ascension into heaven.	
Pentecost (Whitsunday)	The seventh Sunday after Easter. Pentecost commemorates the descent of the Holy Ghost upon the apostles.	
Shabouth (Hebrew Pentecost) 30	Fifty days after Passover. Shabouth celebrates the grain harvest and the giving of the Ten Commandments to Moses on Mt. Sinai. Memorial Day	

JUNE

14	Flag Day. Flag Day commemorates the adoption by the Continental Congress of the Stars and Stripes as the official flag of the United States.	
Father's Day	Third Sunday in June	

JULY

4   Independence Day

SEPTEMBER

Labor Day   The first Monday after the first Sunday in September.

Rosh Hashanah   The first day of Tishri, the first month of the Jewish calendar. Rosh Hashanah marks the Jewish New Year and begins ten days of penitence.

Yom Kippur   Also known as the Day of Atonement. Yom Kippur falls ten days after Rosh Hashanah, and marks the end of the period of penitence.

Sukkoth   Also known as the Feast of Tabernacles. Sukkoth falls on the fifteenth day of Tishri. It celebrates the fruit harvest and commemorates the temporary shelters used by the Jews during their wandering in the wilderness.

OCTOBER

Simchas Torah   The Rejoicing of the Law, as Simchas Torah is also known, falls on the twenty third day of Tishri (the eighth day of Sukkoth). It marks the end of the year's reading of the Torah (Five Books of Moses) and the beginning of the new cycle of readings.

12   Columbus Day

31   Halloween

NOVEMBER

1   All Saint's Day. This day honors all saints, known and unknown, as observed by Roman Catholic and Anglican churches.

Election Day   First Tuesday after the first Monday in November.

11   Veteran's Day. This day honors veterans of America's wars.

Thanksgiving   The fourth Thursday in November.

Advent   The first Sunday of Advent is celebrated four Sundays before Christmas. It is observed by some Christians as a season of prayer and fasting to prepare for the arrival of Christ.

DECEMBER

Hanukkah   Also called the Festival of Lights, Hanukkah occurs on the twenty fifth day of Kislev, the third month of the Jewish Calendar. It begins an eight-day celebration of the purification of the Temple of Jerusalem after its defilement by Antiochus of Syria.

25   Christmas or the Feast of the Nativity. Christmas celebrates the anniversary of the birth of Christ.

31   New Year's Eve

Language Of Flowers

Since ancient times, flowers have signified certain qualities and sentiments. So if you want to get a particularly delicate message across, say it with flowers.

FLOWER	MEANING
Amaryllis	Beautiful but timid
Anemone	Forsaken; illness
Apple Blossom	Preference
Arbor Vitae	Unchanging friendship
Arbutus	Thee only do I love
Bachelor's Button	Hope, single blessedness
Barberry	Petulance, ill temper
Bittersweet, Nightshade	Truth
Bluebell	Constancy
Burdock	Importunity, touch me not
Buttercup	Riches
Cardinal Flower	Distinction; preferment
Carnation	Pure and deep love
Chrysanthemum	A heart left to desolation
White Clover	I promise
Clover, 4-leaved	Be mine
Columbine, Red	Anxious and trembling
Coreopsis	Always cheerful
Crocus	Cheerfulness
Dahlia	Dignity and elegance
Daffodil	Unrequited love
Daisy, Garden	I share your feelings
Daisy, Field	I will think of it
Dandelion	Oracle; coquetry
Fern	Sincerity
Forget-me-not	Do not forget
Foxglove	Insincerity
Fuchsia	Taste; frugality
Geranium	Silliness
Gladiolus	Ready armed
Goldenrod	Encouragement
Hawthorn	Hope
Heliotrope	I adore you
Hibiscus	Delicate beauty
Holly	Am I Forgotten?
Honeysuckle	Devoted love
Hydrangea	Vainglory; heartlessness
Iris	A message for thee
Ivy	Friendship; marriage
Jonquil	Desire; affection returned

FLOWER	MEANING
Larkspur, Pink	Lightness; fickleness
Lavender	Mistrust
Lilac, Purple	First emotions of love
Lilac, White	Youth
Lily of the Valley	Return of happiness
Marigold	Grief; chagrin
Mayflower	Welcome
Mint	Virtue
Milkweed	Hope in misery
Mistletoe	I surmount everything
Morning Glory	Coquetry; affection
Mountain Ash	I watch over you
Narcissus	Egotism; self-love
Nasturtium	Patriotism; splendor
Oleander	Beware
Pansy, Purple	You occupy my thoughts
Peach Blossom	I am your captive
Peony	Ostentation; anger
Phlox	Our hearts are united
Poppy, White	Sleep; oblivion
Primrose	Modest worth; silent love
Rhododendron	Agitation
Rose, Red	I love you
Rose, White	Silence
Rose, Wild	Simplicity
Rose, Yellow	Infidelity
Rosemary	Remembrance
Sage	Domestic virtue
Scotch Thistle	Retaliation
Snapdragon	Presumption
Sweet Pea	A meeting
Sweet William	Gallantry; finesse; dexterity
Tuberose	Dangerous pleasure; voluptuousness
Tulip, Variegated	Beautiful eyes
Tulip, Red	Declaration of love
Violet, Blue	Faithfulness
Violet, White	Purity; candor; modesty
Yarrow	Cure for the heartache
Zinnia	I mourn your absence

Source: Farmer's Almanac

PHRENOLOGY GUIDE

Phrenologists, beginning with 19th-century German physician Franz Joseph Gall and his pupil Johann Caspar Spurzheim, thought it was all in your head. They believed that certain personality traits and mental abilities were located in different areas of the brain and could be detected by feeling for enlargements, or bumps, on that part of the skull. Today, we know that they were only half right, but reading bumps makes for an amusing parlor game.

Source: Encyclopaedia Britannica

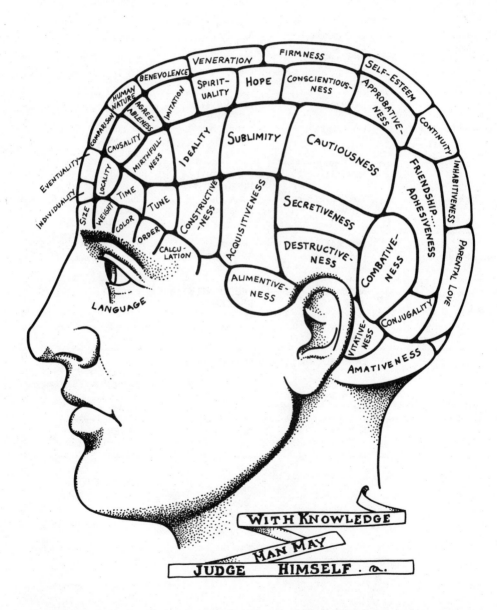

PALMISTRY GUIDE

Your fortune is in your hands, as any palm reader would tell you. The centuries-old art of chiromancy supposes to reveal your character and destiny in the lines, joints and mountains of your hands (particularly the left). Just for fun, here's one key to divining these hand-held secrets.

	NORMAL	EXCESSIVE	ABSENT
A. Mount of Jupiter	Generous ambition	Love of display	Degrading proclivities
B. Mount of Saturn	Prosperous life	Love of solitude	Eventless life
C. Mount of the Sun	Love of fine arts	Notoriety at any price	Material existence
D. Mount of Mercury	Love of science	Thievish tendencies	Useless life
E. Mount of Venus	Love of beauty	Coquettish, excessively frivolous	Cold, selfish
F. Mount of Mars	Courageous, calm	Tyrannical	Cowardly
G. Mount of the Moon	Imagination, chaste aspirations	Disordered brain	Abortive imagination

	NORMAL	FREQUENTLY INTERRUPTED	ABSENT
H. Heart Line	Good heart	Inconstancy	Bad faith, depravity, malice

	NORMAL	FREQUENTLY INTERRUPTED	IN LINKS
I. Head Line	Sound judgment, firm will	Life sickly and short	Lack of steadiness of mind

	NORMAL	SHORT	DOUBLE (JJ)
J. Life Line	Long and happy life	Short life	Success in war

	NORMAL	FREQUENTLY BROKEN	ABSENT
K. Line of Saturn	Good fortune acquired by merit	Varying fortune	Life insignificant

	NORMAL	ENDING IN A V	3 BRANCHES (STRAIGHT AND DEEP)
L. Line of the Sun	Distinction in the arts	Wasted efforts	High reputation

	NORMAL	WAVY	ABSENT
M. Hepatic Line	Harmonious physical development	Bilious temperament	Physical strength

		PRESENT	
N. Venus's Ring		Tendency to debauchery	

O. Armlet		Tranquility, good fortune	

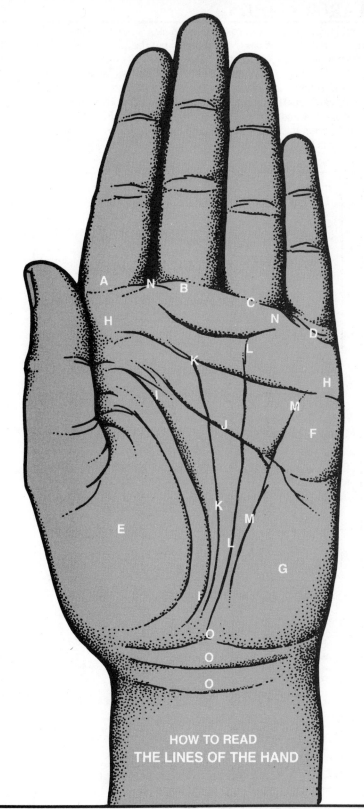

HOW TO READ
THE LINES OF THE HAND

READING TAROT CARDS

S ince the 15th century, these picture cards have been used to look beyond the "facts." One card-reading method has the "Diviner" put the 22 Major Arcana cards in order, from 0 (Joker) to XXI, as the "Questioner" sits opposite, concentrating on his question. Then the Questioner shuffles the deck as he states his question, cuts the deck three times and places it face-down in front of the Diviner. The Diviner places the top card and 9 subsequent cards face-down in front of him, five cards from left to right in one row and another five, left to right, below. Each position and each card itself have different meanings, as outlined below. It's up to the Diviner, who turns each card face-up in turn, to interpret their significance for the Questioner.

MEANING OF POSITION

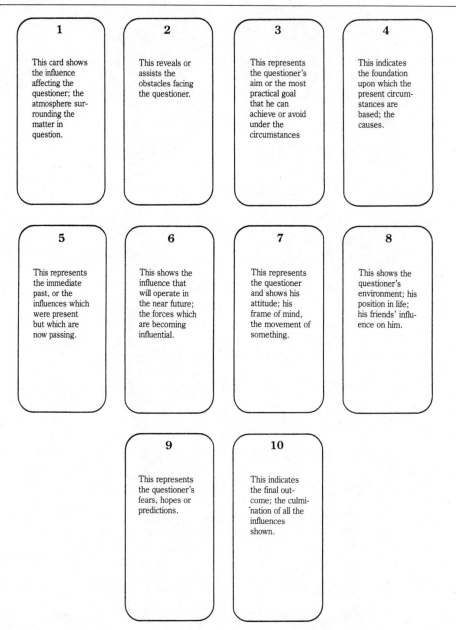

1

This card shows the influence affecting the questioner; the atmosphere surrounding the matter in question.

2

This reveals or assists the obstacles facing the questioner.

3

This represents the questioner's aim or the most practical goal that he can achieve or avoid under the circumstances

4

This indicates the foundation upon which the present circumstances are based; the causes.

5

This represents the immediate past, or the influences which were present but which are now passing.

6

This shows the influence that will operate in the near future; the forces which are becoming influential.

7

This represents the questioner and shows his attitude; his frame of mind, the movement of something.

8

This shows the questioner's environment; his position in life; his friends' influence on him.

9

This represents the questioner's fears, hopes or predictions.

10

This indicates the final outcome; the culmination of all the influences shown.

SUGGESTED INTERPRETATIONS OF GREATER MAJOR ARCANA CARDS

These meanings are all imprinted on the face of each card but this can be used for further study.

Number	Title	Suggested Interpretation
0	The Fool or Joker	Foolishness, Frenzy, Impulsiveness, Heedlessness, Agitation, Blunder.
I	The Magician	Skill, Artistry, Assurance, Determination, Versatility, Competence.
II	The High Priestess	Knowledge, Intelligence, Understanding, Scholarship, Wisdom.
III	The Empress	Activity, Growth, Fertility, Productiveness, Progress.
IV	The Emperor	Nobility, Power, Achievement, Supremacy, Wealth, Dominance.
V	The Hierophant or High Priest	Gentleness, Sacredness, Benevolence, Leniency, Righteousness, Tenderness.
VI	The Lovers	Attraction, Loveliness, Affection, Elegance, Concord.
VII	The Chariot	Domination, Triumph, Discord, Victory, Trouble, Challenge.
VIII	Strength	Fortitude, Firmness, Confidence, Assurance.
IX	The Hermit	Discretion, Tact, Judiciousness, Heed, Circumspection, Preparedness.
X	Wheel of Fortune	Providence, Predestination, Authority, Honor, Principle.
XI	Justice	Morality, Virtue, Fairness, Rectitude.
XII	The Hanged Man	Sacrifice, Transcendence, Glory, Renunciation, Piety.
XIII	Death	Destination, Rebirth, Creation, Renewal.
XIV	Temperance	Harmony, Moderation, Rationality, Friendliness, Forbearance.
XV	The Devil	Evil, Catastrophe, Captivity, Disorder, Violence.
XVI	The Tower	Ruin, Suffering, Affliction, Chastisement, Unexpectedness, Disaster.
XVII	The Star	Truth, Promise, Propitiousness, Fulfillment, Beauty, Immortality.
XVIII	The Moon	Savagery, Peril, Instability, Falsehood, Disillusionment.
XIX	The Sun	Sensitivity, Innocence, Pleasure, Renewal, Restoration, Victory, Perfection.
XX	Judgement	Discovery, Development, Resolution, Conclusion.
XXI	The World	Culmination, Triumph, Self-Awareness, Natural Perfection.

THE LESSER ARCANA CARDS

The Tarot Deck is comprised of two sets: The twenty-two Major Arcana Cards and the fifty-six Lesser Arcana Cards. The Lesser Arcana cards consist of four suits of fourteen cards each. These suits are very much like the suits in an ordinary deck of cards:

The Swords correspond to Spades,
The Cups correspond to Hearts,
The Wands correspond to Clubs,
The Pentacles correspond to Diamonds.

Each suit contains cards from one to ten, plus four cards: a King, a Queen, Knave, and Knight. These cards are generally considered to have the following meanings:

	Wands	Cups	Swords	Pentacles
KING	Favorable	Beware of ill-will	A professional man	A dark man
QUEEN	A good harvest	Women of uncertain character	A widow	Riches

KNIGHT	Alienation	A fortunate visit	Heroic action	A useful man
PAGE	Search for a mate	A good augury	An indiscreet inquiry	A young person
TEN	Difficulties	A good marriage	A friend's reason	A house or dwelling
NINE	Bad news	A good augury for military	A bad omen	Fulfillment of nearby cards
EIGHT	Domestic disputes	Marriage with a fair woman	Scandal for a woman	A young man or a dark girl
SEVEN	A dark child	A fair child; resolution	Good fortune	Improved position
SIX	Betrayal by a friend	Pleasant memories	A good voyage	Caution about the present
FIVE	Financial success	Happiness and success; gifts	Misfortune	Conquest of fortune by reason
FOUR	Unexpected good fortune	Contrary events	Bad news	Pleasant news from a lady
THREE	Very good; useful collaboration	Unexpected advancement	Flight of a lady's lover	Celebrity for a man's oldest son
TWO	Small disappointments	Favorable for business and pleasure	Gifts for a lady; protection for a man	Troubles are imaginary
ACE	Calamities	Inflexible will; unalterable law	Great prosperity or great misery	Most favorable of all cards

Source: Merrimac Publishing

GUIDE TO REFLEXOLOGY

An ancient Chinese technique, reflexology works on the idea that the feet are a "map" of the body: Applying finger pressure to certain points on the feet will relax and release energy from the corresponding body. However, it is considered a holistic health approach and not a substitute for medical treatment.

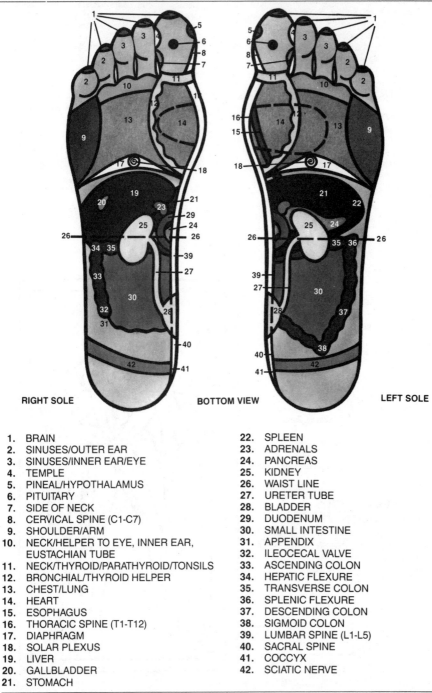

RIGHT SOLE   BOTTOM VIEW   LEFT SOLE

1. BRAIN	22. SPLEEN
2. SINUSES/OUTER EAR	23. ADRENALS
3. SINUSES/INNER EAR/EYE	24. PANCREAS
4. TEMPLE	25. KIDNEY
5. PINEAL/HYPOTHALAMUS	26. WAIST LINE
6. PITUITARY	27. URETER TUBE
7. SIDE OF NECK	28. BLADDER
8. CERVICAL SPINE (C1-C7)	29. DUODENUM
9. SHOULDER/ARM	30. SMALL INTESTINE
10. NECK/HELPER TO EYE, INNER EAR, EUSTACHIAN TUBE	31. APPENDIX
11. NECK/THYROID/PARATHYROID/TONSILS	32. ILEOCECAL VALVE
12. BRONCHIAL/THYROID HELPER	33. ASCENDING COLON
13. CHEST/LUNG	34. HEPATIC FLEXURE
14. HEART	35. TRANSVERSE COLON
15. ESOPHAGUS	36. SPLENIC FLEXURE
16. THORACIC SPINE (T1-T12)	37. DESCENDING COLON
17. DIAPHRAGM	38. SIGMOID COLON
18. SOLAR PLEXUS	39. LUMBAR SPINE (L1-L5)
19. LIVER	40. SACRAL SPINE
20. GALLBLADDER	41. COCCYX
21. STOMACH	42. SCIATIC NERVE

Source: Feet First: A Guide to Reflexology, by Laura Norman (Simon & Schuster, Inc.; 1988), by permission of the author.

SIGNS OF ZODIAC

If you feel your life is ruled by the stars, here is how astrologers define you.

	SIGN	CHARACTERISTICS	COMPATIBLE WITH
♈	**ARIES** The Ram (March 21 to April 20)	Energetic, impulsive, enthusiastic, positive, enterprising, easily angered	Gemini, Leo, Sagittarius, Aquarius
♉	**TAURUS** The Bull (April 21 to May 21)	Stubborn, steadfast, systematic, persevering, kind-hearted, possessive, loves beauty and comfort	Cancer, Virgo, Capricorn, Pisces
♊	**GEMINI** The Twins (May 22 to June 21)	Restless, versatile, clever, exuberant, expressive, fickle, short attention span	Aquarius, Leo, Libra, Aries
♋	**CANCER** The Crab (June 22 to July 23)	Tenacious, patient, loyal, hypersensitive, sympathetic, nurturing, changeable, easily influenced	Taurus, Virgo, Scorpio, Pisces
♌	**LEO** The Lion (July 24 to August 23)	Proud, generous, trusting, energetic, domineering, authoritative, dogmatic	Aries, Gemini, Libra, Sagittarius
♍	**VIRGO** The Virgin (August 24 to September 23)	Exact, methodical, industrious, discriminating, intelligent, chaste, critical, worrier	Taurus, Cancer, Scorpio, Capricorn
♎	**LIBRA** The Balance (September 24 to October 23)	Alert, just, artistic, painstaking, honorable, well-balanced, affectionate, sympathetic, indecisive, procrastinator	Gemini, Leo, Sagittarius, Aquarius
♏	**SCORPIO** The Scorpion (October 24 to November 22)	Energetic, independent, passionate, determined, strong likes and dislikes, ambitious	Cancer, Virgo, Capricorn, Pisces
♐	**SAGITTARIUS** The Archer (November 23 to December 21)	Candid, impulsive, restless, impatient, generous, nature- and sports-loving, curious, tactless	Aries, Leo, Libra, Aquarius
♑	**CAPRICORN** The Goat (December 22 to January 20)	Ambitious, persevering, diplomatic, reserved, miserly	Taurus, Virgo, Scorpio, Pisces
♒	**AQUARIUS** The Water- Bearer (January 21 to February 19)	Honest, probing, broad-minded, amiable, humane, popular, inventive, eccentric	Aries, Gemini, Libra, Sagittarius
♓	**PISCES** The Fish (February 20 to March 20)	Gentle, kind, retiring, sensitive, unlucky, often melancholy, intuitive, secretive	Taurus, Cancer, Scorpio, Capricorn

The stars and constellations shown can be seen in the night sky of the Northern Hemisphere during the seasons indicated.

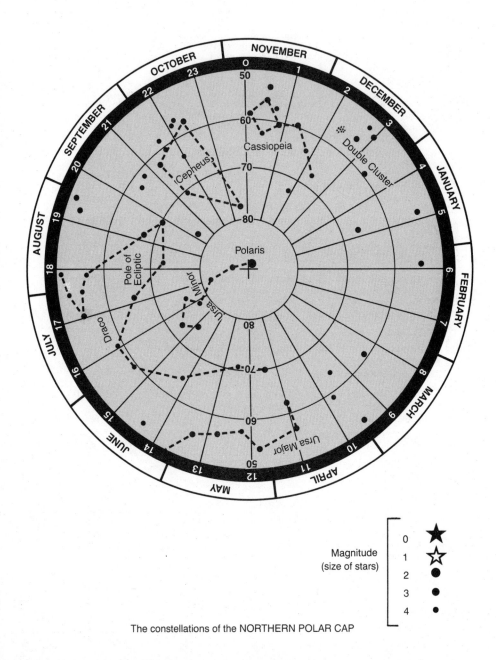

The constellations of the NORTHERN POLAR CAP

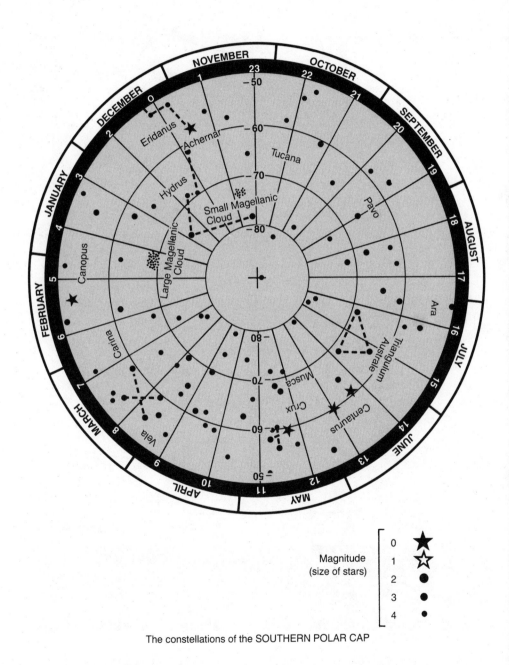

The constellations of the SOUTHERN POLAR CAP

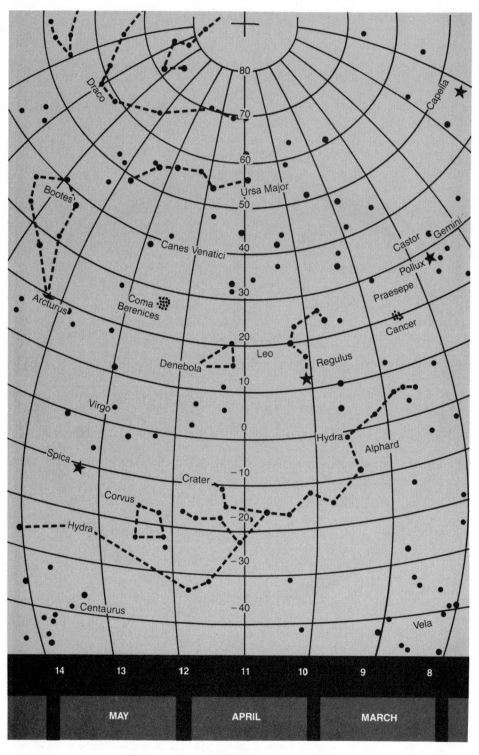

SPRING

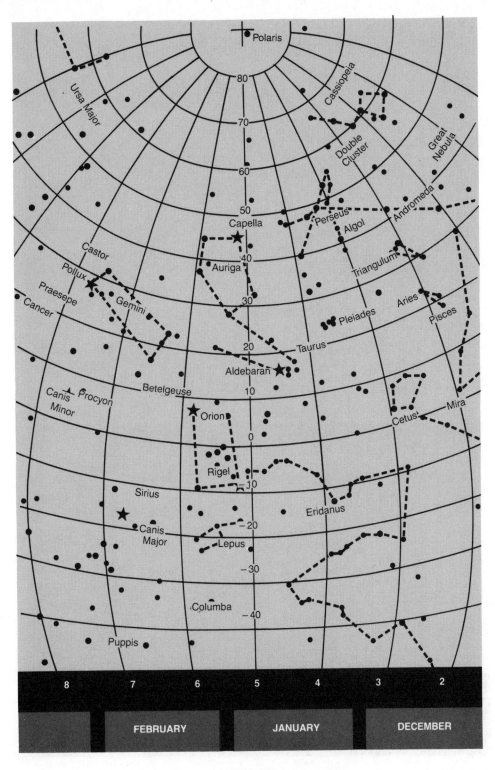

WINTER

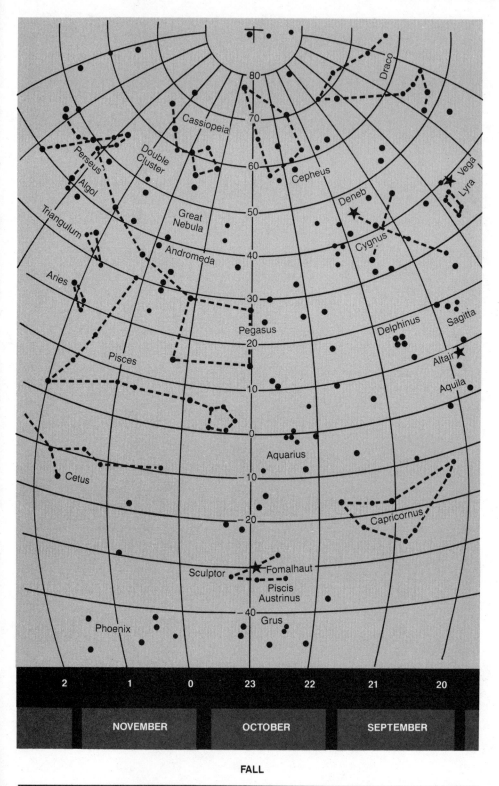

FALL

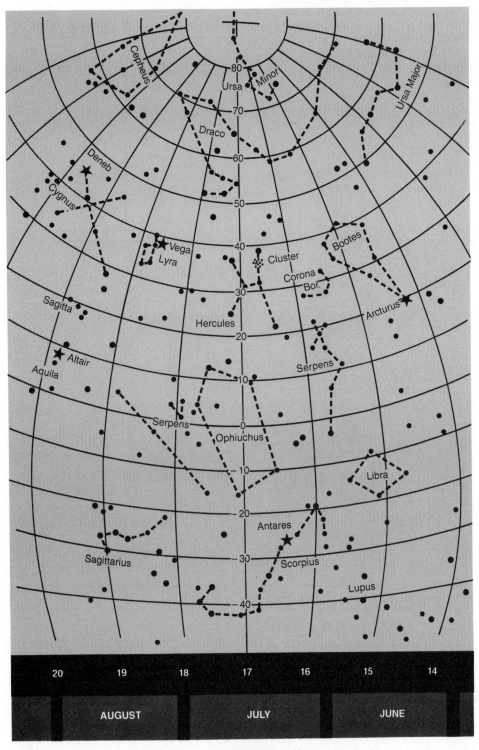

TEMPERATURE CONVERSION CHART

Zero on the Fahrenheit scale represents the temperature produced by the mixing of equal weights of snow and common salt.

	F	C
Boiling point of water	212°	100°
Freezing point of water	32°	0°
Absolute zero	−459.6°	−273.1°

Absolute zero is theoretically the lowest possible temperature, the point at which all molecular motion would cease.

To convert Fahrenheit to Celsius (Centigrade), subtract 32 and multiply by 5/9.

To convert Celsius (Centigrade) to Fahrenheit, multiply by 9/5 and add 32.

°Centigrade	°Fahrenheit	°Centigrade	°Fahrenheit
−273.1	−459.6	30	86
−250	−418	35	95
−200	−328	40	104
−150	−238	45	113
−100	−148	50	122
−50	−58	55	131
−40	−40	60	140
−30	−22	65	149
−20	−4	70	158
−10	14	75	167
0	32	80	176
5	41	85	185
10	50	90	194
15	59	95	203
20	68	100	212
25	77		

Source: National Bureau of Standards

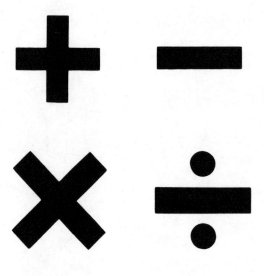

DECIMAL EQUIVALENTS OF COMMON FRACTIONS

1/2	.5000	1/10	.1000	2/7	.2857	3/11	.2727	5/9	.5556	7/11	.6364
1/3	.3333	1/11	.0909	2/9	.2222	4/5	.8000	5/11	.4545	7/12	.5833
1/4	.2500	1/12	.0833	2/11	.1818	4/7	.5714	5/12	.4167	8/9	.8889
1/5	.2000	1/16	.0625	3/4	.7500	4/9	.4444	6/7	.8571	8/11	.7273
1/6	.1667	1/32	.0313	3/5	.6000	4/11	.3636	6/11	.5455	9/10	.9000
1/7	.1429	1/64	.0156	3/7	.4286	5/6	.8333	7/8	.8750	9/11	.8182
1/8	.1250	2/3	.6667	3/8	.3750	5/7	.7143	7/9	.7778	10/11	.9091
1/9	.1111	2/5	.4000	3/10	.3000	5/8	.6250	7/10	.7000	11/12	.9167

Source: National Bureau of Standards

METRIC CONVERSION CHART

To change	To	Multiply by	To change	To	Multiply by
acres	hectares	.4047	liters	pints (dry)	1.8162
acres	square feet	43,560	liters	pints (liquid)	2.1134
acres	square miles	.001562	liters	quarts (dry)	.9081
atmospheres	cms. of mercury	76	liters	quarts (liquid)	1.0567
BTU	horsepower-hour	.0003931	meters	feet	3.2808
BTU	kilowatt-hour	.0002928	meters	miles	.0006214
BTU/hour	watts	.2931	meters	yards	1.0936
bushels	cubic inches	2150.4	metric tons	tons (long)	.9842
bushels (U.S.)	hectoliters	.3524	metric tons	tons (short)	1.1023
centimeters	inches	.3937	miles	kilometers	1.6093
centimeters	feet	.03281	miles	feet	5280
circumference	radians	6.283	miles (nautical)	miles (statute)	1.1516
cubic feet	cubic meters	.0283	miles (statute)	miles (nautical)	.8684
cubic meters	cubic feet	35.3145	miles/hour	feet/minute	88
cubic meters	cubic yards	1.3079	millimeters	inches	.0394
cubic yards	cubic meters	.7646	ounces avdp.	grams	28.3495
degrees	radians	.01745	ounces	pounds	.0625
dynes	grams	.00102	ounces (troy)	ounces (avdp)	1.09714
fathoms	feet	6.0	pecks	liters	8.8096
feet	meters	.3048	pints (dry)	liters	.5506
feet	miles (nautical)	.0001645	pints (liquid)	liters	.4732
feet	miles (statute)	.001894	pounds ap or t	kilograms	.3782
feet/second	miles/hour	.6818	pounds avdp	kilograms	.4536
furlongs	feet	660.0	pounds	ounces	16
furlongs	miles	.125	quarts (dry)	liters	1.1012
gallons (U.S.)	liters	3.7853	quarts (liquid)	liters	.9463
grains	grams	.0648	radians	degrees	57.30
grams	grains	15.4324	rods	meters	5.029
grams	ounces avdp	.0353	rods	feet	16.5
grams	pounds	.002205	square feet	square meters	.0929
hectares	acres	2.4710	square kilometers	square miles	.3861
hectoliters	bushels (U.S.)	2.8378	square meters	square feet	10.7639
horsepower	watts	745.7	square meters	square yards	1.1960
hours	days	.04167	square miles	square kilometers	2.5900
inches	millimeters	25.4000	square yards	square meters	.8361
inches	centimeters	2.5400	tons (long)	metric tons	1.016
kilograms	pounds avdp or t	2.2046	tons (short)	metric tons	.9072
kilometers	miles	.6214	tons (long)	pounds	2240
kilowatts	horsepower	1.341	tons (short)	pounds	2000
knots	nautical miles/hour	1.0	watts	Btu/hour	3.4129
knots	statute miles/hour	1.151	watts	horsepower	.001341
liters	gallons (U.S.)	.2642	yards	meters	.9144
liters	pecks	.1135	yards	miles	.0005682

Source: U.S. Dept. of Weights and Measures

HOW TO READ A BAROMETER

Knowing which way the wind blows and keeping an eye on your barometer can give you a clear idea of what the weather has in store for you.

Barometer (Reduced to Sea Level)	Wind Direction	Character of Weather Indicated
30.00 to 30.20, and steady	westerly	Fair, with slight changes in temperature, for one to two days.
30.00 to 30.20, and rising rapidly	westerly	Fair, followed within two days by warmer and rain.
30.00 to 30.20, and falling rapidly	south to east	Warmer, and rain within 24 hours.
30.20, or above, and falling rapidly	south to east	Warmer, and rain within 36 hours.
30.20, or above, and falling rapidly	west to north	Cold and clear, quickly followed by warmer and rain.
30.20, or above, and steady	variable	No early change
30.00, or below, and falling slowly	south to east	Rain, within 18 hours that will continue a day or two.
30.00, or below, and falling rapidly	southeast to northeast	Rain, with high wind, followed within two days by clearing, colder.
30.00, or below, and rising	south to west	Clearing and colder within 12 hours.
29.80, or below, and falling rapidly	southeast to northeast	Severe storm of wind and rain imminent. In winter, snow or cold wave within 24 hours.
29.80, or below, and falling rapidly	east to north	Severe northeast gales and heavy rain or snow, followed in winter by cold wave.
29.80, or below, and rising rapidly	westerly	Clearing and colder.

Note: A barometer should be adjusted to show equivalent sea-level pressure for the altitude at which it is to be used. A change of 100 feet in elevation will cause a decrease of 1/10th inch in the reading.

Source: National Weather Service

How To Use The Library

Do you know your way around the library? Amherst College librarian Melvil Dewey made the task a little easier in 1876 by cataloging written works according to a decimal numbering system. His system, outlined below, is still in use in most public libraries today.

Dewey Decimal Classification

000 Generalities
010 Bibliography
020 Library and information sciences
030 General encyclopedic works
040
050 General serial publications
060 General organizations and museology
070 Journalism, publishing and newspapers
080 General collections
090 Manuscript and book rarities

100 Philosophy and related disciplines
110 Metaphysics
120 Epistemology, causation, humankind
130 Paranormal phenomena and arts
140 Specific philosophical viewpoints
150 Psychology
160 Logic
170 Ethics (moral philosophy)
180 Ancient, medieval, Oriental
190 Modern Western philosophy

200 Religion
210 Natural religion
220 Bible
230 Christian theology
240 Christian moral and devotional
250 Local church and religious orders
260 Social and ecclesiastical theology
270 History and geography of church
280 Christian denominations and sects
290 Other and comparative religions

300 Social Sciences
310 Statistics
320 Political science
330 Economics
340 Law
350 Public administration
360 Social problems and services
370 Education
380 Commerce (trade)
390 Customs, etiquette, folklore

400 Language
410 Linguistics
420 English and Anglo-Saxon languages
430 Germanic languages/German
440 Romance languages/French
450 Italian, Romanian, Rhaeto-Romanic
460 Spanish and Portuguese languages
470 Italic languages/Latin
480 Hellenic Classical Greek
490 Other languages

500 Pure sciences
510 Mathematics
520 Astronomy and allied sciences
530 Physics
540 Chemistry and allied sciences
550 Sciences of earth and other worlds
560 Paleontology and paleozoology
570 Life sciences
580 Botanical sciences
590 Zoological sciences

600 Technology (Applied sciences)
610 Medical Sciences/Medicine
620 Engineering and allied operations
630 Agriculture and related technologies
640 Home economics and family living
650 Management and auxiliary services
660 Chemical and auxiliary services
670 Manufactures
680 Manufacture for specific uses
690 Buildings

700 The Arts
710 Civic and landscape art
720 Architecture
730 Plastic arts/Sculpture
740 Drawing, decorative and minor arts
750 Painting and paintings
760 Graphic arts/Prints
770 Photography and photographs
780 Music
790 Recreational and performing arts

800 Literature (Belles-lettres)
810 American literature in English
820 English and Anglo-Saxon literatures
830 Literatures of Germanic languages
840 Literatures of Romance languages
850 Italian, Romanian, Rhaeto-Romanic literatures
860 Spanish and Portuguese literatures
870 Italic literatures/Latin
880 Hellenic literatures/Greek
890 Literatures of other languages

900 General geography and history
910 General geography/Travel
920 General biography and genealogy
930 General history of ancient world
940 General history of Europe
950 General history of Asia
960 General history of Africa
970 General history of North America
980 General history of South America
990 General history of other areas

Source: Reproduced from the Abridged Dewey Decimal Classification, Edition 11 (1979) by permission of Forest Press Division, Lake Placid Education Foundation, owner of copyright.

CHOOSING A DOG

Not every dog is right for every family. Before picking your pet, consider the breed's size, personality, exercise and space requirements, coat-care needs and how it will get along with the children in your home.

	SIZE	WITH CHILDREN	CHARACTERISTICS
Akita	Large	Excellent	Good-natured, affectionate; excellent guard dog; easily trained; daily brushing; little exercise.
Airedale	Medium	Very Good	Aggressive, sound temperament; easy to train; occasional brushing; lots of exercise.
Basenji	Medium	Very good	"Barkless," quiet, gentle, clean; regular use of hound glove; regular long runs.
Basset Hound	Medium	Excellent	Docile, friendly; good watch dog; daily brushing, attention to ears and nose; lots of exercise, 3 to 4 walks daily.
Beagle	Medium	Excellent	Hearty, very affectionate; fair watchdog; inclined to wander; little grooming; unlimited, free exercise.
Boxer	Large	Excellent	Clean, affectionate, good guard dog; inclined to fight, needs obedience training; light brushing; lots of supervised exercise.
Bulldog	Medium	Very good	Good-natured, loyal; good watchdog; snores; daily rubdown, avoid overexertion.
Chihauhua	Toy	Excellent	Good guard dog; easily trained; brush daily; lively, though little exercise needed.
Collie	Large	Very good	Loyal, affectionate, good watchdog; responds well to training; extensive grooming; regular, steady exercise.
Dachsund	Small	Excellent	Spunky, playful, willful; good watchdog; daily use of hound glove; regular short walks.
Dalmation	Large	Good	Good-natured, loyal; easily trained; daily brushing, regular bathing; needs lots of exercise.
Doberman Pinscher	Large	Good, with own family	Brave, loyal, willful; superb guard dog; beware of those bred as attack dogs; occasional rubdown; lots of exercise and space.
German Shepherd	Large	Good with older children	Intelligent, powerful; excellent guard dog; trains well; beware of attack-bred dogs; daily brushing; lots of exercise.
Great Dane	Giant	Good	Good-natured, playful; size, though not disposition, may defer intruders; daily grooming; short, regular exercise and lots of space.
Irish Setter	Large	Very good	Very affectionate, lovable, high-strung; poor watchdog; regular grooming; lots of exercise.

	SIZE	WITH CHILDREN	CHARACTERISTICS
Irish Wolfhound	Giant	Good	Well-mannered, loyal; excellent guard dog; regular brushing; long walks on leash, unlimited free exercise.
Lhasa Apso	Small	Good	Demanding, but responsive; easily trained; lots of brushing and combing; lots of exercise.
Pekingese	Toy	Not good	Loyal, brave; good watchdog; daily brushing; should not be overexerted.
Poodles	Toy to Large	Very good	Very intelligent, playful; very trainable; extensive grooming; moderate exercise.
Pug	Toy	Very good	Charming, affectionate; daily brushing; gentle exercise.
Retrievers	Large	Very good	Gentle, calm, reliable; easily trained; poor watchdog; regular brushing; lots of free exercise.
Saint Bernard	Giant	Excellent	Gentle, loyal; easily trained; daily brushing; little exercise, short walks.
Schnauzer	Small	Very good	Intelligent, playful; excellent guard dog; regular grooming; regular, steady exercise.
Sheepdog English	Large	Excellent	Easygoing, loyal; daily brushing; lots of outdoor exercise.
Shih Tzu	Toy	Excellent	Happy, affectionate; train carefully; daily grooming; short, regular walks.
Siberian Husky	Large	Excellent	Kind, gentle, very affectionate, protective; sheds profusely, daily brushing, lots of outdoor exercise.
Spaniels, Cocker	Small	Excellent	Affectionate, adaptable; poor watchdog; very responsive to training; daily brushing and combing; lots of exercise.
Springer	Medium	Good	Intelligent, loyal, calm; poor watchdog; regular grooming; lots of exercise.
TERRIERS: Boston	Small	Good	Affectionate, intelligent; dislikes cold, damp; daily brushing, but rarely sheds; daily walks.
Scottish	Small	Not good with small children	Loyal, feisty, reserved; brave guard dog; occasional grooming; unlimited, confined exercise.
Yorkshire	Toy	Good with gentle children	Affectionate, fearless; good guard dog; regular grooming; long walks, but undemanding.
Whippet	Medium	Very good with gentle children	Clean, affectionate, fast; occasional use of hound glove; lots of fast runs.

Choosing A Cat

lthough most cats make suitable housepets, there are differences in personality that might make one type the best choice for your family.

Longhair Breeds And Characteristics

Angora
Affectionate, friendly, likes to learn and perform tricks.

Balinese
Affectionate, similar to but more even-tempered than the Siamese; sheds little.

Bicolored
Hardy, long-lived easygoing, not high-strung, careful, needs frequent grooming.

Birman
Easygoing, affectionate, intelligent, loving.

Black
Gentle, easy-going, affectionate; needs regular grooming.

Blue Persian
Enjoys, even demands, attention; no special grooming.

Blue-Cream
Attaches to owner, friendly, devoted, demands attention, very active. Usually female; males usually sterile.

Cameo
Gentle, companionable; extra time needed for bathing and combing.

Chinchilla, Red Self, Smoke
Easy to get along with, not temperamental.

Cream
Affectionate, playful, very active, demands attention.

Himalayan
Very devoted, warm, affectionate, likes attention and display of attachment; regular grooming needed.

Maine Coon
Large, robust, likes cooler climates, intelligent, not noisy; easy to groom.

Peke-Face, Tabby
Affectionate, long-lived, enjoys play and attention, not too "independent".

Tortoiseshell
Alert, active, intelligent; careful grooming necessary. Always female.

Turkish
Hardy, active, alert, intelligent, enjoys attention and affection — and water. Big appetite, for its size.

White Blue-eyed strain
Affectionate, though aloof with strangers; very often deaf.

Shorthair Breeds And Characteristics

American Shorthair
Even-tempered, intelligent, affectionate, strong, a hunter — excellent mouser.

Bicolored
Sweet, affectionate; good family pet.

Black
No personality problems; good family pet; regular brushing and combing necessary.

Blue-Cream
Pleasant, no personality problems; ordinary grooming, except during shedding season — comb out with fine-tooth comb.

Bombay
Sturdy, active, fearless, not docile, must be tended and appreciated.

British Blue
Quiet, reflective, not demonstrative, independent; prefers "settled" households.

Cream
Good family pet; easy to maintain.

Siamese
All varieties demand considerable attention and affection. Inquisitive, intelligent, playful and loving, but can be mischievous, greedy and, if neglected, destructive. Highly sexed; piercing cry. Of the various varieties, the Blue-Point is the most even-tempered; the Seal-Point, the most temperamental.

Tabby
Easygoing, gentle, affectionate; excellent family pet.

Tortoiseshell, Calico
Very domestic, affectionate, gentle, companionable. Most are female; males sterile.

White
Companionable, though shy with strangers. Blue-eyed strains usually deaf.

FOREIGN BREEDS AND CHARACTERISTICS

Abyssinian
Friendly, active, playful, intelligent, warm, companionable, not aloof at all; no special grooming.

Burmese Blue, Brown
Hardy, adaptable, very pleasant, active, playful, dauntless.

Egyptian Mau
Playful, active, affectionate. Similar to Siamese, but voice is less piercing.

Exotic Shorthair
Sturdy, even-tempered, affectionate, playful; minimal grooming.

Foreign Lilac
Enjoys attention, gentle but demanding. Similar to Siamese, but voice is softer.

Foreign White
Intelligent, alert, playful, possessive, assertive, usually affectionate. Unlike other whites, blue-eyed varieties not deaf.

Havana
Sweet, companionable, intelligent, playful, mischievous, likes attention, easily trained, enjoys outdoors.

Korat
Excellent family pet: companionable, gentle, affectionate. Warm-weather breed, prone to upper-respiratory problems.

Manx
Tailless. Steady, affectionate, playful, intelligent.

Rex, Cornish
Healthy, pleasant, adaptable, likes people. Big appetite.

Devon
Hardy, likes people and activity. Needs warmth. Prominent ears need regular cleaning.

Russian Blue
Not demonstrative or noisy, hardy; no special grooming.

Sphynx
No visible hair (good pet for those allergic to animal fur). Easy to get along with, accommodating; no special grooming besides regular washing.

U.S. Presidents/Vice Presidents

William Henry Harrison was President only for a month, but you'll find him here, along with the other 40 politicians who have held America's top job, and their Vice Presidents.

No.	Presidents	Term	Vice President(s)	Term
1	George Washington	Apr. 30, 1789-Mar. 3, 1797	John Adams	1789-97
2	John Adams	Mar. 4, 1797-Mar. 3, 1801	Thomas Jefferson	1797-1801
3	Thomas Jefferson	Mar. 4, 1801-Mar. 3, 1809	Aaron Burr / George Clinton	1801-1805 / 1805-1809
4	James Madison	Mar. 4, 1809-Mar. 3, 1817	George Clinton* / Elbridge Gerry	1809-1812 / 1809-1814
5	James Monroe	Mar. 4, 1817-Mar. 3, 1925	Daniel D. Tompkins	1817-1825
6	John Quincy Adams	Mar. 4, 1825-Mar. 3, 1829	John C. Calhoun	1825-1829
7	Andrew Jackson	Mar. 4, 1829-Mar. 3, 1837	John C. Calhoun** / Martin Van Buren	1829-1832 / 1833-1837
8	Martin Van Buren	Mar. 4, 1837-Mar. 3, 1841	Richard M. Johnson	1837-1841
9	William Henry Harrison*	Mar. 4, 1841-Apr. 4, 1841	John Tyler	1841
10	John Tyler	Apr. 6, 1841-Mar. 3, 1845		
11	James K. Polk	Mar. 4, 1845-Mar. 3, 1849	George M. Dallas	1845-1849
12	Zachary Taylor*	Mar. 4, 1849-July 9, 1850	Millard Fillmore	1849-1850
13	Millard Fillmore	July 10, 1850-Mar. 3, 1853		
14	Franklin Pierce	Mar. 4, 1853-Mar. 3, 1857	William R. King*	1853
15	James Buchanan	Mar. 4, 1857-Mar. 3, 1861	John C. Breckinridge	1857-1861
16	Abraham Lincoln*	Mar. 4, 1861-Apr. 15, 1865	Hannibal Hamlin / Andrew Johnson	1861-1865 / 1865
17	Andrew Johnson	Apr. 15, 1865-Mar. 3, 1869		
18	Ulysses S. Grant	Mar. 4, 1869-Mar. 3, 1877	Schuyler Colfax / Henry Wilson*	1869-1873 / 1873-1875
19	Rutherford B. Hayes	Mar. 4, 1877-Mar. 3, 1881	William A. Wheeler	1877-1881
20	James A. Garfield*	Mar. 4, 1881-Sept. 19, 1881	Chester A. Arthur	1881
21	Chester A. Arthur	Sept. 20, 1881-Mar. 3, 1885		
22	Grover Cleveland	Mar. 4, 1885-Mar. 3, 1889	Thomas A. Kendricks*	1885
23	Benjamin Harrison	Mar. 4, 1889-Mar. 3, 1893	Levi P. Morton	1889-1893
24	Grover Cleveland	Mar. 4, 1893-Mar. 3, 1897	Adlai E. Stevenson	1893-1897
25	William McKinley*	Mar. 4, 1897-Sept. 14, 1901	Garret A. Hobart* / Theodore Roosevelt	1897-1899 / 1901
26	Theodore Roosevelt	Sept. 14, 1901-Mar. 3, 1909	Charles W. Fairbanks	1905-1909
27	William H. Taft	Mar. 4, 1909-Mar. 3, 1913	James S. Sherman*	1909-1912
28	Woodrow Wilson	Mar. 4, 1913-Mar. 3, 1921	Thomas R. Marshall	1913-1921

No.	Presidents	Term	Vice President(s)	Term
29	Warren G. Harding*	Mar. 4, 1921-Aug. 3, 1923	Calvin Coolidge	1921-1923
30	Calvin Coolidge	Aug. 3, 1923-Mar. 3, 1929	Charles G. Dawes	1925-1929
31	Herbert C. Hoover	Mar. 4, 1929-Mar. 3, 1933	Charles Curtis	1929-1933
32	Franklin D. Roosevelt*	Mar. 4, 1933-Apr. 12, 1945	John Nance Garner Henry A. Wallace Harry S Truman	1933-1941 1941-1945 1945
33	Harry S Truman	Apr. 12, 1945-Jan. 20, 1953	Alben W. Barkley	1949-1953
34	Dwight D. Eisenhower	Jan. 20, 1953-Jan. 20, 1961	Richard M. Nixon	1953-1961
35	John F. Kennedy*	Jan. 20, 1961-Nov. 22, 1963	Lyndon B. Johnson	1961-1963
36	Lyndon B. Johnson	Nov. 22, 1963-Jan. 20, 1969	Hubert H. Humphrey	1965-1969
37	Richard M. Nixon**	Jan. 20, 1969-Aug. 9, 1974	Spiro T. Agnew** Gerald R. Ford	1969-1973 1973-1974
38	Gerald R. Ford	Aug. 9, 1974-Jan. 20, 1977	Nelson Rockefeller	1974-1977
39	Jimmy (James Earl) Carter	Jan. 20, 1977-Jan. 20, 1981	Walter F. Mondale	1977-1981
40	Ronald Reagan	Jan. 20, 1981-Jan. 20, 1989	George Bush	1981-1989
41	George Bush	Jan. 20, 1989-	J. Danforth Quayle	1989-

*Died in office   **Resigned

THE 50 STATES

If you can never remember what's the capital of North Dakota or which state is the Sooner State, this should help.

STATE	NICKNAME(S)	CAPITAL
Alabama	Heart of Dixie; Cotton State; Yellowhammer State	Montgomery
Alaska	The Last Frontier; Land of the Midnight Sun	Juneau
Arizona	Grand Canyon State	Phoenix
Arkansas	Land of Opportunity	Little Rock
California	Golden State	Sacramento
Colorado	Centennial State	Denver
Connecticut	Nutmeg State; Constitution State	Hartford
Delaware	Diamond State; First State	Dover
Florida	Sunshine State	Tallahassee
Georgia	Peach State; Empire State of the South	Atlanta
Hawaii	Aloha State	Honolulu
Idaho	Gem State; Spud State; Panhandle State	Boise
Illinois	Prairie State	Springfield
Indiana	Hoosier State	Indianapolis
Iowa	Hawkeye State	Des Moines
Kansas	Sunflower State; Jayhawk State	Topeka
Kentucky	Bluegrass State	Frankfort
Louisiana	Pelican State; Creole State; Sportsman's Paradise; Sugar State	Baton Rouge
Maine	Pine Tree State	Augusta
Maryland	Old Line State; Free State	Annapolis
Massachusetts	Bay State; Old Colony	Boston
Michigan	Great Lake State; Wolverine State	Lansing
Minnesota	North Star State; Gopher State; Land of 10,000 Lakes	St. Paul
Mississippi	Magnolia State	Jackson
Missouri	Show-Me State	Jefferson City
Montana	Treasure State	Helena
Nebraska	Cornhusker State; Beef State; Tree Planter's State	Lincoln
Nevada	Sagebrush State; Battle Born State; Silver State	Carson City
New Hampshire	Granite State	Concord
New Jersey	Garden State	Trenton
New Mexico	Land of Enchantment; The Sunshine State	Santa Fe
New York	Empire State	Albany
North Carolina	Tar Heel State; Old North State	Raleigh
North Dakota	Sioux State; Flickertail State	Bismarck
Ohio	Buckeye State	Columbus
Oklahoma	Sooner State	Oklahoma City

State	Nickname	Capital
Oregon	Beaver State	Salem
Pennsylvania	Keystone State	Harrisburg
Rhode Island	Little Rhody; Ocean State	Providence
South Carolina	Palmetto State	Columbia
South Dakota	Coyote State; Sunshine State	Pierre
Tennessee	Volunteer State	Nashville
Texas	Lone Star State	Austin
Utah	Beehive State	Salt Lake City
Vermont	Green Mountain State	Montpelier
Virginia	Old Dominion; Mother of Presidents	Richmond
Washington	Evergreen State; Chinook State	Olympia
West Virginia	Mountain State	Charleston
Wisconsin	Badger State	Madison
Wyoming	Equality State	Cheyenne

157

COUNTRIES AND THEIR CAPITALS

To make it easier for you to find them on a map, the countries have been grouped by continent or region.

AFRICA

Country	Capital
Algeria	Algiers
Angola	Luanda
Benin	Mmabatho
Bophuthatswana	Porto-Novo
Botswana	Gaborone
Burkina Faso	Ouagadougou
Burundi	Bujumbura
Cameroon	Yaounde
Cape Verde	Praia
Central African Republic	Bangui
Chad	N'djamena
Comoros	Moroni
Congo	Brazzaville
Djibouti	Djiouti
Egypt	Cairo
Equatorial Guinea	Malabo
Ethiopia	Addis Ababa
Gabon	Libreville
Gambia	Banjul
Ghana	Accra
Guinea	Conakry
Guinea-Bissau	Bissau
Ivory Coast	Yamoussoukro
Kenya	Nairobi
Lesotho	Maseru
Liberia	Monrovia
Libya	Tripoli
Madagascar	Antananarivo
Malawi	Lilongwe
Mali	Bamako
Mauritania	Nouakchott
Mauritius	Port Louis
Morocco	Rabat
Mozambique	Maputo
Niger	Niamey
Nigeria	Abuja
Rwanda	Kigali
Sao Tome and Principe	Sao Tome
Senegal	Dakar
Seychelles	Victoria
Sierra Leone	Freetown
Somalia	Mogadishu
South Africa, Republic of	Pretoria (administrative); Cape Town (legislative); Bloemfontein (judicial)
Sudan	Khartoum
Swaziland	Mbabane
Tanzania	Dar es Salaam
Togo	Lome
Transkei	Umtala
Tunisia	Tunis
Uganda	Kampala
Venda	Thohoyandou
Zaire	Kinshasa
Zambia	Lusaka
Zimbabwe	Harare (Salisbury)

CARIBBEAN REGION

Antigua and Barbuda	St. John's
Bahamas	Nassau
Barbados	Bridgetown
Cuba	Havana
Dominica	Roseau
Dominican Republic	Santo Domingo
Grenada	St. George's
Haiti	Port-au-Prince
Jamaica	Kingston
St. Lucia	Castries
St. Vincent and the Grenadines	Kingstown
Trinidad and Tobago	Port-of-Spain

CENTRAL AMERICA

Belize	Belmopan
Costa Rica	San Jose
El Salvador	San Salvador
Guatemala	Guatemala City
Honduras	Tegucigalpa
Nicaragua	Managua
Panama	Panama City

EUROPE

Albania	Tirana
Andorra	Andorra la Vella
Austria	Vienna
Belgium	Brussels
Bulgaria	Sofia
Cyprus	Nicosia
Czechoslavakia	Prague
Denmark	Copenhagen
Finland	Helsinki
Germany, East	Berlin
Germany, West	Bonn
Greece	Athens
Greenland	Godthaab
Hungary	Budapest
Iceland	Reykjavik
Ireland	Dublin
Italy	Rome
Liechtenstein	Vaduz
Luxembourg	Luxembourg
Malta	Valetta
Monaco	Monaco-Ville
Netherlands	Amsterdam (The Hague)

Norway	Oslo
Poland	Warsaw
Portugal	Lisbon
Romania	Bucharest
San Marino	San Marino
Spain	Madrid
Sweden	Stockholm
Switzerland	Bern
U.S.S.R.	Moscow
United Kingdom	
England	London
Northern Ireland	Belfast
Scotland	Edinburgh
Wales	Cardiff
Yugoslavia	Belgrade

FAR EAST

China, People's Republic of	Peking
China (Taiwan), Republic of	Taipei
Japan	Tokyo
Korea, North	Pyongyang
Korea, South	Seoul
Mongolia	Ulan Bator
Philippines	Manila

MIDDLE EAST

Bahrain	Manama
Iran	Teheran
Iraq	Baghdad
Israel	Jerusalem
Jordan	Amman
Kuwait	Kuwait
Lebanon	Beirut
Oman	Muscat
Qatar	Doha
Saudi Arabia	Riyadh
Syria	Damascus
Turkey	Ankara
United Arab Emirates	Abu Dhabi
Yemen, People's Democratic Republic of	Aden
Yeman Arab Republic	San'a'

NORTH AMERICA

Canada	Ottawa
Mexico	Mexico City
United States	Washington, D.C.

OCEANIA

Australia	Canberra
Fiji	Suva
Kiribati	Bairiki
Nauru	Yaren
New Zealand	Wellington
Papua New Guinea	Port Moresby
Solomon Islands	Honiara
Tonga	Nuku'alofa
Tuvalu	Funafuti
Vanuatu (New Hebrides)	Port Vila
Western Samoa	Apia

SOUTH AMERICA

Argentina	Buenos Aires
Bolivia	Sucre (judicial); La Paz (administrative)
Brazil	Brasilia
Chile	Santiago
Colombia	Bogota
Ecuador	Quito
Guyana	Georgetown
Paraguay	Asuncion
Peru	Lima
Suriname	Paramaribo
Uruguay	Montevideo
Venezuela	Caracas

SOUTH ASIA

Afghanistan	Kabul
Bangladesh	Dhaka
Bhutan	Thimphu
Burma	Rangoon
India	New Delhi
Maldives	Male
Nepal	Katmandu
Pakistan	Islamabad
Sri Lanka	Sri Jayewardenepura Kotte (Colombo)

SOUTHEAST ASIA

Cambodia	Phnom Penh
Indonesia	Jakarta
Laos	Vientiane
Malaysia	Kuala Lumpur
Singapore	Singapore
Thailand	Bangkok
Vietnam	Hanoi

ABOUT THE AUTHOR

Cheryl Solimini is a freelance writer whose food, fitness and lifestyle articles have appeared in *Country Living, Cosmopolitan's Super Beauty & Fitness Guide, Redbook,* and *Weight Watchers Magazine,* among other national publications. She is also the author of *Great Legs for Short Skirts* (Signet/NAL) and *Baby's First Year* (Galison Books).